THE LAY EVANGELIST'S HANDBOOK

HOW ANY CATHOLIC CAN EVANGELIZE ANYONE

JOE SIXPACK
THE EVERY CATHOLIC GUY

CONTENTS

ACKNOWLEDGMENTS

I would like to thank my best pal Marty Barrack for his love, devotion, advice and input on this book… as well as roughly thirty years of friendship. I would also like to thank the hundreds of souls who helped me hone my skills and learn to follow the Holy Spirit.

It is with an earnest and prayerful heart that I wish to dedicate this book to...

Mary Help of Christians, St. John Bosco's stalwart patroness and, by extension, mine.
St. John Bosco, my friend, helper and patron throughout thirty years of evangelization.
Fr. Killian Mooney (RIP), the priest who started me on the journey of life-long evangelization, and encouraged and loved me when I was at my most unlovable.
Raymond Leo Cardinal Burke, who recognized my zeal for souls and helped kindle the fire of that zeal by being a true spiritual father to me.
Marty Barrack, my partner in crime... the crime of being all-consumed by the love of Christ for souls.
Lyndahl Sale, my most highly favored godson, for smacking me upside the back of my head when I needed it.
Jean, my lovely wife, absolute best friend, and the best half of me.

ONE

WHY THIS BOOK AND HOW TO USE IT

Let Me Tell You a Story

I'm Joe Sixpack—The Every Catholic Guy. Okay, so that's not my real name, but I'm sticking with Joe Sixpack for now. Before I get to the story I want to tell you, I need to mention that I'm a convert and I believe lived Catholicism is the most exciting lived experience ever! I became a Catholic thirty years ago, and I'm still as pumped about the faith today as I was then.

There! I was afraid I'd blow a gasket if I didn't tell you that. I want to tell that to everyone I meet every day, but I know it wouldn't be long before people would see me coming and do an about-face to avoid me. Anyway, now that I've gotten that off my chest, let's get to the story.

Thirty Years Ago

Thirty years ago, I was at the lowest point of my life. I was at rock bottom. I won't bore you with the details about why

I was at the bottom. Just take my word for it that I was. It's as Venerable Archbishop Fulton Sheen said, "Sometimes the only way the good Lord can get into some hearts is to break them."[1] I'd been a Baptist in my youth, but as I grew older and more cynical, I became an agnostic. Consequently, since I felt we humans were on our own and that God didn't really care, I didn't see much value to life... especially mine. That's right: I was contemplating suicide. I didn't see much sense in continuing my miserable life. Because of the underhanded things I'd done, nobody liked me or wanted to be around me anymore... and I didn't much want to be around me, either.

Over the next year, I contemplated how I would end it all. Then I met a man who was a walking Catholic encyclopedia. I'm not 100% certain how he got me to listen to him, but I listened nonetheless. Boy, am I glad I did!

A New Friend

I was perhaps the toughest student my new friend had ever taught. Being the cynical agnostic, I made him *prove* everything he was teaching me. I'd have never believed it if I hadn't experienced it first-hand, but every single teaching of the Catholic faith can be proven from the Bible, ancient extra-biblical writings, history, and logic and right reason.

When my friend proved to me that Jesus was God and that He'd founded the Catholic Church, I made the intellectual decision to become a Catholic—despite the fact that I'd been reared in a vehemently anti-Catholic home. I didn't want to become a Catholic, but once it had been proven to me that Jesus was God and that He'd founded the Catholic Church, I was afraid *not* to join the Church.

It wasn't long, though, before I was at peace with my decision, because it became an emotional decision in short order. No, that's not quite true. It became a ravenous hunger, a longing of the heart, and a passion. Now, thirty years after the fact, I can remember it as if it happened yesterday. What caused me to change my attitude about conversion from dread to eager anticipation was when my friend taught me about (and proved) the Real Presence of Christ in the Holy Eucharist. As I listened to what he told me, it occurred to me that I never had to suffer all my misery alone—that God the Son had been present all along, waiting for me to visit Him in every Catholic Church in the world! I wept and wept and wept—unashamedly, no longer the proud and arrogant tough guy. (For the record, I'm still proud and arrogant. I just wasn't at that particular moment. *But God ain't finished with me yet.*)

Lay Evangelists

Even while yet a catechumen, I began sharing the Catholic faith with anyone who was warm, had a pulse, could at least communicate with grunts, and would stand still long enough to listen.[2] Since that day, I've considered myself a lay evangelist. But I'm not what you typically think of as a lay evangelist. Some who call themselves lay evangelists— the ones you typically think of as lay evangelists—make big-bucks preaching to the choir on the Catholic speakers' circuit. They've never made a convert in their lives (or maybe only a few), but they spend their time and efforts attempting to motivate the lay faithful to share the faith.[3] I'm not saying this sort of "lay evangelist" doesn't have a place. What they do is actually a good thing, but there is little doubt in my mind that they want to all make a full-time living preaching to the choir and have the name recognition of Catholics like Dr. Scott Hahn (who is, incidentally, a very good man and Catholic). If that weren't so, rather than spending all their productive time booking speaking gigs, they'd use that time to actually reach out to souls. I don't have a problem with them speaking to groups of people and making money (many are very good at it!), I just think they shouldn't call themselves lay evangelists. They're not. They're speakers. Period.

The other types of lay evangelists (who are *very* rare) are the ones who draw big crowds with their preaching. That's a tremendously great thing, but they're not able to follow through with the souls they reach and risk losing them altogether. That's the problem with large crowds... unless you've managed to establish a productive system for follow-up. They plant seeds, but most folks don't know what to do or where to go to get those seeds watered and grown. In this case, we could take a few lessons from the late Billy Graham. He *did* manage to set up a system of follow-up. It was easier for him than it would be for us, though. Mission accomplished for Billy Graham was merely getting a person to make an act of faith during an altar call. Mission accomplished would be much more complex for us. Still, I think it could be done; I've just never felt called to do it that way.

Me? I take a little different approach. I've managed to stay under the radar and not attract attention over the years in my work with individuals and small groups. The Holy Spirit has used me to make hundreds of converts and reverts over the last thirty years—eighty-four of whom are my adult godchildren. (Recently, I've begun teaching online in webinars to some good effect—God is blessing the effort.[4] I'm not bragging about the converts. I know I've just been a tool and nothing more. After all, the Holy Spirit could just enlighten every person's soul with Catholic truth and let each one make a decision then and there. I'm not really necessary at all. God has chosen to use human intervention for sharing the Gospel message.

Knowing this, why am I coming onto the radar screen now? Well, I'm getting old, I've had a debilitating stroke, and my time in the field of evangelization is coming to a close. I don't want any attention, but I've learned a lot over the last thirty years; in fact, I could write a three-hundred page book with nothing but anecdotes about my experiences. The key word in that last sentence to explain my voluntary exposure is "experience." I've spent the last thirty years doing something that not one in ten million Catholics do, but that all of us are obligated to do: *evangelize*.[5] My experiences have demonstrated to me that a huge percentage of Catholics want to evangelize, but they don't know how and are afraid to try on their own. I get that. Doing something like this is outside the realm of most people's experience and can be pretty scary; anything outside your comfort zone is scary. So this book is for all those Catholics who want to learn to evangelize and live the true meaning of the Great Commission (Matthew 28:19-20).

Become God's Rock Star!

Before I tell you how I evangelize, let me make one point perfectly clear. This point, this principle, is absolutely vital to your sanity and success as a lay evangelist. In fact, until I learned this principle I was constantly stressed out and had a sense of aggressive urgency that inquirers would always pick up on, and would usually scare them off. So if you learn this simple principle and make it a part of your very being, your efforts as a lay evangelist will make you a rock star among lay evangelists in God's eyes.

Here's the principle: *You **are not** responsible for success.* You're only responsible for doing what God expects of you; making converts is *His* responsibility. Don't try to "go above and beyond the call of duty" to make converts. You can't make converts anyway, and all you can accomplish is getting in God's way. So just relax (breathe deeply), do what you know you're supposed to do (share the faith), and don't worry about anything else. To use a tired old slogan, "Just let go and let God."

Now, let's get back to how I ride in this rodeo.

When I share the faith, I don't do it as you may typically be used to hearing it. Oh, I use the traditional Q&A format of catechesis all right, but I don't do it in the boring old rote method (yawn). In my presentations, I become the storyteller. I include history, Church and papal documents, patristics, apologetics, and anecdotal information from the lives of saints, former students, other people I've known or heard about, and myself—anything I believe might be relevant to the topic and interesting to students. And I only speak in the common language of the average pew-sitting Joe Sixpack Catholic. The result? Well, I'm writing this book, aren't I? And the reason I tell a lot of stories is... that's the way the Boss did it 2,000 years ago.

The key is to make it intriguing, avoiding boredom—to be excited about your Catholic faith (which I am) without being phony about it. You see, excitement is contagious, which is why my students never yawn and always stay engaged. Remember, though, you can't have phony excitement; your students will spot you as a phony in a second and you'll lose all credibility.[6] To get an idea of what I'm saying, read these unsolicited testimonials from attendees of the webinars I've been doing.

> *This was the first full webinar I've sat through. And I was amazed when you said it was time for questions. It just blew me away, as I didn't think an hour had gone by already. So I would've never guessed that an hour would've gone by. It was amazing! I was totally shocked. You have me sucked in! It was a great experience for me. Thank you for everything you do.*
>
> **Randy M**

> *The Gospel letters, though written thousands of years ago, are supposed to draw me closer to God. They, for the most part, don't. You do. YOUR words are more effective in reaching me. I know, for the most part, what the apostles have said. I'm looking for someone who can relate it to today. I have a greater chance of returning back to the flock with what you do.*
>
> **Robert M**

> *I think you are doing a great job! I completed Father John Hardon's Basic Catholic Catechism Course some time ago, but having done it on my own, I feel*

I only had the pieces of the puzzle, and now you are helping me to glue them together.

Silvia P

The weekly catechetical webinars offered by Joe Sixpack are perfectly sound, accurate and engaging. They precisely address the questions troubling the three sadly un-catechized generations who make up most of today's Catholic laity.

Donna S

Your webinars are great. They are short but informative. I have urged a group of friends to give them a try. We all need to improve on our faith. Thanks.

Jim F

Joe Sixpack's style of teaching is down to earth, making it simple for everyone to understand the truths of the Holy Catholic Church. His webinars and catechism lessons are helpful for those new to the Faith, but also for those who need a refresher course. I pray that his Apostolate continues to bear much good fruit!

Maria B

I believe what you are doing is exceptional! I have learned so much about the Catholic faith in the last 2 years.

Mike W

_____

_____

Thanks for sending me the recording of yesterday's "Catholics' Specific Duties." I enjoyed your presentation, which was very informative, and I look forward to the next one on the life of virtue.

It's so comforting to gain knowledge of our Catholic Faith in a different way and be able to have a better understanding of our rich heritage and what it means to believe what and why we believe it, and most of all, what Christ has given to us to lead us back to our Creator. Our road to our salvation! I certainly, want to be a better informed Catholic, and be confident in sharing it with others.

Chuck L

_____

_____

Thank you for this [a recording] and all the information you are sharing with us. You will never know how long I have wanted a program like this. Thank you.

Glenda M

_____

It's important to note that you can't be me or anything like me any more than I can be you or anything like you. We all have gifts God has endowed us with; certain lights, if you will. I didn't put these testimonials in here to boast about what a great lay evangelist I am. My intent is to prove to you that when you share the faith with others, it doesn't have to be boring. Indeed, it can and should be exciting! You actually can become God's rock star.

Every Catholic's Obligations

Now let's talk about you for a moment. Since most of this book is dedicated to the hows and whys of evangelization, we can afford to deviate at this point and talk about you. Presumably, you are a Catholic. I can't imagine a non-Catholic reading this book or even having an interest. But a devout Catholic with all the right intentions? Hey, this is right up your alley.

You're no doubt familiar with the *Catechism of the Catholic Church*, the documents of Vatican II, the Apostles' Creed, the Sacraments, the Ten Commandments, the Code of Canon Law and the seemingly endless obligations they place on a Catholic. Well, all those obligations can be boiled down to two primary obligations. Your two primary obligations are to *become a saint* and to *share the faith*. Every other obligation falls under these two primary obligations. And you can't accomplish one without the other.

On Becoming a Saint

Jesus told us in Mathew 5:48...

"You, therefore, must be perfect, as your heavenly Father is perfect."

You'll notice by the language He used that this is not a suggestion, but a command, because He used the word *must*. He didn't say it's a goal to shoot for. He didn't tell us to give it that old college try. He said we *must* become *perfect*. How perfect? As perfect as God the Father. And how perfect is God the Father? *Infinitely perfect!*

Is it possible to become perfect? You bet! Perfection is the very definition of sainthood. All of the saints were perfect by the time they died. They perhaps didn't achieve absolute perfection until they went through their final passion just prior to death, but they did get there. Indeed, most saints probably had to have recourse to confession right up until their final passion, but because of all their past efforts they were able to persevere at the end and achieve perfection.

Achieving sainthood is more than possible, but we can't do it on our own. While we become true men and women,[7] we simply have to develop a prayer life relationship with God and continually ask Him for the graces to advance in holiness. Will you mess up? Sure you will. You might even commit mortal sin from time to time on your journey to sainthood. The key is to take Christ's example. The Church teaches that all three times He fell under the burden of the cross on the way to Calvary (a metaphorical description of mortal sin), He got right back up again. That's what we have to do every time we fall. In other words, pray an immediate act of contrition and plod forward with a fresh resolve to do as you ought. (It goes without saying that you also need to go to confession at the earliest possible moment.)

Get a Good Spiritual Director

I would strongly recommend you get a good spiritual direc-tor. Be careful about whom you choose to direct your soul. Just because a man's a priest doesn't necessarily mean he'll make a good spiritual director. There are some priests in the world who aren't faithful to the Church's teachings or their sacerdotal vows, but I'm not too worried about you seeking out one like that as a spiritual director, because most priests aren't like that. Indeed, most priests are good, holy men who take seriously the teachings of the Church and their priestly vows. But you still have to be careful. Not because they aren't good priests, but because they might not be equipped for the task.

Not all priests are at all equipped to be spiritual directors. Most aren't trained for it, and among those who are, most haven't been trained in classical spiritual direction. Priests who are not trained, or have been trained in this modern psychologically based mumbo-jumbo, might possibly end up having the opposite of the desired effect and cause grave consequences for your immortal soul. That's not the intention of the priest, though; it's just what it is.

In addition to avoiding the sort of priests mentioned in the previous paragraph, I whole heartedly recommend you avoid asking a nun or lay person to direct you. There may be some very good ones out there, I'm sure, but your best bet is always a priest, because a priest possesses the sacramental graces of Holy Orders. The age of the priest doesn't matter; only the degree of apparent holiness. My spiritual director has only been a priest about eight years, but he's a very holy man who is well-versed in classical spiritual direction.

And under no circumstances let anyone get away with telling you the "old ways" of spiritual direction don't work anymore, that mankind and the Church have advanced beyond those archaic ways. *Baloney!* Times may change, but man is the very same as he was when our First Parents gave us original sin, and the Church is a mere 2,000 years young.

Besides, how many saints do we produce today with the so-called new ways? When classical spirituality and direction were at a peak, hundreds (perhaps thousands) of saints came flowing out of the heart of the Church! If classical spirituality was good enough for the likes of St. Teresa of Avila, St. Anthony of Padua, St. John Bosco, and innumerable others, it should certainly be good enough for you.

On Evangelization

Your other primary obligation is to share the faith. I get a real kick out of watching people's reaction when I tell them that. You'd think I just told them they have to go into a terrorist camp and take out all the camp occupants with a broken, rusty-bladed pocket knife and no back-up. The idea of having to share the Catholic faith with other people is the stuff nightmares are made of for most folks. It's scary and not easy for most people, and I'll admit that. Nothing worth doing, though, is easy. To help make that point, I have a friend who has a phrase in the signature of all her emails: Comfort and Conviction don't live on the same block!

Evangelization is really not that difficult. I realize not everybody can do what I do. I get that. Not every person has what folks call the gift of gab. Even if you're a complete wallflower, though, you can still play a role in evangelization. And I'll get to the various means of evangelization in a moment, but first I want to talk about just who all we have to evangelize.

The very first classification of souls to evangelize is none other than your fellow Catholics. Yup, you read that right; your fellow Catholics. Actually, in this case I'm referring to former Catholics. First of all, we all need to have a genuine conversion of heart every day. You do, I do, even the pope does. But this actually goes much deeper than that, because cradle Catholics are leaving the Church at an alarming rate.

Did you know...?

- one out of every ten Americans is an ex-Catholic
- if they were a separate denomination, they would be the third-largest denomination in the United States, after Catholics and Baptists
- one of three people who were raised Catholic no longer identifies as Catholic
- 6.5 people leave Catholicism for every one that joins
- 50% of young people who were raised Catholic are no longer Catholic today
- and 79% of former Catholics leave the Church before age 23

Do you know why that is? Read what Raymond Leo Cardinal Burke wrote in a letter to me in October 2015.

A gravely defective catechesis which marked the life of the Church in the years following the Second Vatican Ecumenical Council, though not because of the Council, contributed to the loss of faith, the lack of a devotional life and left the subsequent generations devoid of a concrete way to know the Catholic faith and live it.

His Eminence is absolutely correct. Most Catholics—perhaps as many as 95%—suffer from catechetical illiteracy. That's a kind way of saying they are completely, or almost completely, ignorant of what the Catholic Church teaches. If they knew *exactly* what the Church teaches—unvarnished Catholic truth that isn't watered-down milquetoast—almost all of those listed in the statistics above would still be

THE LAY EVANGELIST'S HANDBOOK 15

Catholic. But the simple fact of the matter is that they don't know the faith; they only think they do. Since you're reading this, then you're just the sort of person who can help change that and keep your friends and loved ones from becoming one of these statistics.

This automatically means the next group of people to be evangelized is non-practicing Catholics. You know lots of people in that category; we all do. Perhaps you have close friends or family who are non-practicing Catholics. You're obligated to share the faith with them.

"But, Joe, doing that might soil or ruin my relationship with them."

Tough! Who is your first obligation to: your friends and family, or Jesus? Before you answer that, you might want to stop here and read what Jesus said in Revelation 3:15-16.[8] Besides, by sharing the fullness of the Catholic faith with non-practicing Catholic friends and family, you *are* showing them they're a top priority with you. They'll eventually get that.

The next group is that one made up of almost every Catholic sitting with you at Mass. At this writing, I've lived in this archdiocese for about four years, and the people here know the faith much better than the two dioceses I'd spent the last twenty-six years in. That's not saying much, though. Of all the Catholic laity I've met, I can count on one hand the number of folks who can answer this simple question: *"How many sacraments are there, and name them?"*

Not even five people in four years could tell me how many sacraments there are, much less name them. I've got a hint for those who can't answer this simple question: *You don't know your faith!*

Oddly, though, when I suggest the need for catechesis, I get one of two responses. They either say, "I'll have you know I went to Catholic school" or "I'll have you know I've been a Catholic all my life." They seem to think that these responses mean they know all they're supposed to know, but what they're really telling me is how pitifully, incompetently, and incompletely they were taught. Not too many years ago, it was said of Catholic schools that a child who was educated in them would be Catholic all his life. Obviously, that hasn't been true for many years.

So it is our (*your*) responsibility to find creative ways to defeat the catechetical ignorance our (*your*) fellow parishioners have. With the world changing the way it is (certainly not for the better), this is more imperative than ever!

The final group of people to reach out to are those who make up non-Catholics. Most of the non-Catholics I reach out to are cultivated one-on-one. They're the result of general conversations with people I meet (no one talks to me long before the subject turns to religion), and these are folks God just places in my path.

When I'm actively looking for people to evangelize, I use what I call the *curiosity approach*. The people I use this method on get the totality of Catholic truth just like everybody else. The difference is in the method of presentation.

I learned years ago that the minute you mention the Catholic Church to most people, you can almost hear their minds slam shut. They hate what they believe the Catholic Church to be. If the Church were like most people think it is, I'd hate it, too, but that's because the idea most folks have of the Church is nothing even akin to reality. So I use the curiosity approach, meaning that it's not until about the fifth lesson that they know or realize I'm teaching them Catholicism. By the time they realize what I'm doing, they're hooked! I've made more than a few converts this way. The inspiration for the curiosity approach came right out of the book of Acts, when Paul told the Greeks his notion of who the "unknown god" was (Acts 17:22-31).[9]

Now let's get back to the various means of evangelization. For the faint of heart—those who are terrified of face-to-face evangelization, you really can evangelize and receive all the kudos, admiration and adulation of any professional full-time lay evangelist. Well, actually you won't get that from any human person, but you will get that from the *only* Person who really matters—God. How?

Look, we work for the best Boss in the universe. Can't see yourself doing what I do? Then give temporal and financial support to those who do the sort of evangelization I do!

Here's a little story to demonstrate what I'm talking about:

One day, two men stood outside the parish church after Holy Mass and carried on a conversation. One said to the other, "Why, Bill, you've put on some weight! Don't you work anymore?"

"I work about twenty-four hours a day," replied Bill with all seriousness.

"Impossible!" exclaimed his friend.

"Not with a system," Bill began to explain. "I work twelve hours down at the shop and around the house. Then I support our parish, the diocese, and mission work—that money works even while I'm sleeping."

As is demonstrated in this story, God will give you all of the very same credit (graces) for your participation as He does the lay evangelist or apostolate doing the actual grunt work. For example, there are a few people who are *Joe Sixpack Partners* and contribute a few bucks on the JoeSixpackAnswers.com website every month, and so they get equal credit from God for all the good done through my work because *they make it possible*. After all, since the foundation of Christianity, one factor has been a constant: souls cost money. In other words, it costs money to pay for the activities that allow us to reach people. Even Jesus and His merry band of apostles had a purse for expenses.

(Just in case you're interested in becoming a Joe Sixpack partner, you might want to consider visiting https://www.joesixpackanswers.com/gifts/save_a_soul.html.)

What if you can't make a financial gift? Well, there are two ways you can still contribute and share in the graces. One example is from the webinars I host. It actually takes at least two people to operate the webinar platform efficiently. For about the first six months I did them, I had to try to manage all of it on my own. That was tough too, because I'm a real techno-moron. But then a man volunteered to help me. He manages the chat moderation for when people ask questions while I do the presentations. When the presentation is over, I open the chat moderation to see if there are any questions he couldn't answer. It works out great!

Another example is from one of my godsons. He's a man who is intellectually challenged in the medical sense, what we used to refer to as mildly retarded. In fact, he was so challenged that the bishop where I lived told me he would baptize and confirm the man as long as he could articulate what Baptism is and what it does, what Confirmation is and what it does, and understand the difference between bread and the Holy Eucharist. As you would expect, then, most of his friends are like him. He wanted to share the faith in the worst way. At the time, I was teaching a small group and served them coffee and cookies. Since my godson couldn't competently tell his friends what the Catholic Church teaches, he just invited his friends to come have a cup of coffee and a snack. Then he left the rest up to the Holy Spirit. Several of his friends became Catholics. Now, if my intellectually challenged godson could do it, I know you can!

The second way to evangelize is very closely akin to what my godson did. Find a group where evangelization is done (maybe a St. Paul Street Evangelization chapter), or even an RCIA class.[10] Work-up a little pitch to present to people you know or meet; a little thing designed to get them committed to listening to someone share the faith in all its purity and splendor—but make sure it's unadulterated Catholicism absent of milquetoast, as *watered-down catechesis attracts no one.* Once they commit to listen, make sure you go with them. You be their contact and friend while the lay evangelist does the work.

The third way of evangelizing is really what this book is all about. In fact, it's really what I'm all about. *You can do what I do.* What I do is as simple as falling off a log. Do you have to be as proficient or knowledgeable in catechetics as I am? No, but it helps. Neither was I when I first started. Still, I'll tell you shortly how you can begin doing today—right now—what I do. First, let's talk about how you begin on the road to proficiency and knowledge.

The first thing I'd recommend to anyone is to make a visit online to the Marian Catechist Apostolate. Why this apostolate? Well, let me tell you about it. Actually, I'll quote here from the Marian Catechist Apostolate website to begin.

St. Pope John Paul II was the first to call for a New Evangelization in response to the loss of faith in God in our time. The work of the New Evangelization, he declared, is to proclaim the Good News in such a way as to lead people to faith in Jesus Christ by means of the transformation of their hearts (cf. *Novo Millennio Ineunte*). Servant of God Father John A. Hardon, S.J.[11] was responding to this call for a New Evangelization when he founded the Marian Catechist Apostolate.

In the early 1980s, Pope John Paul II lamented the fact that so many people were living and dying without any knowledge of Jesus Christ. One of the actions he took to reverse this dismal trend was to ask St. Mother Teresa of Calcutta to prepare her Sisters, the Missionaries of Charity, not only to care for the immediate material needs of the poor, but also to evangelize them, to teach them about God's immeasurable love for them and about His desire to be united with them in Heaven for all eternity.

Mother Teresa turned to Father Hardon for the help she needed to prepare her Sisters to evangelize the poorest of the poor. Father Hardon was an eminent theologian and master catechist (one who teaches the Faith), the author of over forty major works of theology, spirituality, and catechesis, and one of the world's most respected authorities on the Catholic Faith. He began to teach the Missionaries of Charity; at the same time, he began to prepare the texts that would eventually become a set of home study courses used to teach the richness of the Catholic Faith and its practice to the lay faithful. Today, the Missionaries of Charity, along with countless lay members of the Church, use Father Hardon's courses to prepare themselves to be effective witnesses of the Faith to all they meet.

In time, Father Hardon established the Marian Catechist Apostolate to form catechists, both spiritually and doctrinally, for the teaching of the Faith. Father Hardon was elated when His Eminence Raymond Leo Cardinal Burke, then-Bishop of La Crosse, Wisconsin, decided to use Father Hardon's home study courses to form catechists in his

Diocese. Several years later, on December 12, 1999, the Feast of Our Lady of Guadalupe, then-Bishop Burke established the Marian Catechist Apostolate as a Public Association of the Faithful. The Apostolate has been placed under the patronage of Our Lady of Guadalupe, Patroness of all America and Star of both the first and the new evangelizations.

Shortly before Father Hardon died on December 30, 2000, he asked Cardinal Burke to assume leadership of the Apostolate. Cardinal Burke accepted and remains today the Episcopal Moderator and International Director of the Marian Catechist Apostolate.

You'll notice in this brief history of the Marian Catechist Apostolate, it talked about courses by Fr. Hardon. These courses, while correspondence courses, are not for the faint of heart. They're actually fairly difficult. But since Jesus deserves the best we can give Him, they're really not all that much to do. I can't recommend these courses highly enough. And since you'll (hopefully) be taking these courses, let me recommend to you that you become a consecrated member of the Marian Catechist Apostolate. If you become a member, and if you're able, you can join Raymond Leo Cardinal Burke every summer for a weekend at the National Shrine of Our Lady of Guadalupe in LaCrosse, Wisconsin for the annual consecration weekend. (Been there, done that, and let me tell you the shrine is gorgeous as well as awe-inspiring, and the event is spiritually invigorating!)

The other thing I'd recommend for you is hooking up with the St. Paul Street Evangelization apostolate. You can find them at streetevangelization.com. They can help support you in all things regarding evangelization. They won't be everybody's cup of tea, but I think they're great.

But you acquired this book because you want to evangelize *now*. Well, I'm going to help you with that.

Guaranteed Success!

From chapter two onward, the rest of this book is a word-for-word presentation of how I present the faith to anyone—practicing Catholics, non-Catholics, and lapsed Catholics—and I include lots of supplementary information in the form of notations telling you what I say and do, as well as why I say and do it. It's unvarnished and blunt. I don't get namby-pamby, I don't water it down, and I don't make apologies for anything said therein. And you can be assured it most certainly isn't politically correct! My approach may disturb some readers who think you have to be all gooey nice, so I'll offer two defenses.

The first defense for the way I do things is this: ***it works!*** My thirty years of successful experience *proves* that it works. I've had a let-the-chips-fall-where-they-may attitude and approach since I first began, and frankly, I don't know of any other lay evangelist who has experienced the level of success God has given me in helping people come home to Rome that doesn't do it this way. My methods certainly work best for me, and they work best for my evangelizing godchildren too, so I suspect they'll work for you too.

Nice Catholicism

My second defense—and clearly the best one—is that I'm merely imitating our Founder. What I present *is **not*** nice Catholicism. Nice Catholicism is namby-pamby milquetoast; a watered-down version of the faith where hard truths are left out or glanced over for fear of offending people. We leave out these hard truths at the risk of costing people their souls! Maybe our own, too.

I don't practice nice Catholicism. Jesus wasn't nice in the things He said either. He was full of love, but love doesn't equate to being nice. He called men broods of vipers (Matthew 3:7, Matthew 12:34, Matthew 23:33, Luke 3:7), white painted sepulchers full of dead men's bones (Matthew 23:27), hypocrites (Matthew 23:13, Luke 12:56, Luke 13:15), liars (John 8:44, 55), and chased them out of the temple by beating them with a whip (John 2:15). Despite that Jesus wasn't nice, He'd already developed quite a following of disciples before He even performed His first public miracle at the wedding feast in Cana. Why? Because truth sells—a lesson Madison Avenue, politicians and (sadly) many Catholics in authority have never learned. People have an inherent need and desire for truth, because the human mind was made for truth. The whole truth, not just partial truth.

Nice Catholicism—worrying about truth being offensive to people and being politically correct—is the biggest reason why Catholics don't know their faith, why so many people leave the Church, and why we aren't making converts these days. Did I mention that 6.5 people leave the Church for every one who joins?

Truth is not controversial and it's not possible for it to be offensive. Truth is truth, plain and simple. Truth may get folks emotionally worked up, but it's not controversial. Is 2+2=4 controversial? Of course not! But someone who doesn't want to face that truth may become emotionally charged. People like those are why there is still a Flat Earth Society today. No kidding! Look it up.

At the end of the day, truth remains truth—it's immutable. The best definition of truth is *when the mind conforms to reality*. It has nothing to do with subjectivism and everything to do with objectivism. Feelings don't come into play when dealing with truth.

You can stand on top of a 40 story building and shout, "I don't believe in gravity!" Then you can leap off the rooftop and repeat that ridiculous phrase all the way to the ground. Does your subjective opinion that gravity doesn't exist in any way alter the objective reality that it does? No! By the way, the person leaping off the roof will at some point between jumping and impact conform his mind to reality. (You'll see this example again later in the book.)

Anyway, to get back to what I was saying, the following presentation from chapter two forward is *exactly* the way I present the faith. I'll add notes here and there, provide all the references I can think of, and even provide for some anticipated questions from students and the proper responses. Remember: all of this stems from 30 years of experience. I've heard every question there is to ask (sane ones, anyway), so it's rare when an inquirer or catechumen can throw me a curve ball. It does happen from time to time, though.

My Guarantee

Can I guarantee you'll make lots of converts using this? No, I can't, because conversion is between the student and the Holy Spirit. **In thirty years of doing this, I've never once asked a single inquirer to become a Catholic.** Whether they convert or not is *none of my business* until the student decides to make it my business. You must always remember that you are merely the sales person, and that the Holy Spirit is the closer. If the sale (conversion) isn't made, it's either because the Holy Spirit has a future plan for the student, or because the student's heart is hardened against the movement of the Holy Spirit (grace). So it's important for you to understand that you haven't failed in your work if there is no "sale."

But here's what I can guarantee: If you will share the faith as I've laid it out in this handbook and follow my instructions, you will earn graces beyond belief and take a *huge* step toward working out your own salvation (Philippians 2:12). Remember that we aren't obligated to be successful, but rather only to perform the tasks God gives us to do. Success as most Catholics see it is not our job. That's a job left to God alone.

Satan Knows the Faith

Before moving on, I want to digress here to mention something I think is important. It's so important, in fact, that you'll probably see it again later in this book.

While you need to know all you can about our holy and ancient faith, there is more to it than knowledge. You actually have to live it. Satan knows the faith better than you or I ever can. The greatest mind the Church ever produced was St. Thomas Aquinas, and Satan knows the faith even better than he did. But what good does Satan's knowledge of Catholicism do him? He's still condemned to hell for all eternity. So in addition to becoming proficient in your knowledge of the faith, *you have to apply it to your own life.*

Recommendations for You

I learned very early in my "career" as a lay evangelist that there are certain things I must do, and several habits I had to acquire in order to perform evangelization well, have credibility with the student, and be taken seriously by everyone —students, potential students, my fellow lay workers, priests & bishops—*everyone*.

The first and most important thing is to stay in a state of grace. Doing this allows you to do the second most important thing, which is to live an outward life that others can respect and admire—not simply a good life, but an *admirable* life. In other words, avoid all appearances of hypocrisy and scandal. (Besides, people will calumniate you enough as it is if you're doing what God wants, so don't give them more ammunition by doing questionable things. I know about being calumniated from experience.) Not only does this give you credibility, but it also motivates others to want to have what you have that makes you so admirable. As a quote often attributed to St. Francis of Assisi says, "Always teach the faith; when necessary, use words."

I recall a married deacon I once met and spent most of the day with. I was fairly impressed with his attitude, knowledge and demeanor. Then I saw him flirting with a young woman, and he lost all credibility with me. He could talk the talk, but apparently didn't know how to walk the walk. You have to be able to do both. I'm not saying he was actually guilty of anything. I don't know. I am saying you have to be mindful of appearances at all times.

Keep in mind that the number one reason cited by non-believers as to why they don't believe is the hypocrisy of Christians. Of course, modern snowflakes also cite things like homophobia, racism and discrimination as reasons not to believe, but we can't worry about that because we have to stand firm on God's teachings, popular or not.

Listen to God Laugh

Our natural tendency is to tell God, "Okay, I'm here. You can go sit down and relax now. I've got this." (Hear that noise? It's God laughing.) That's our natural tendency, but nothing even close to reality. Fact is, you're not even capable of breathing without God. You're not capable of *anything* without God. The sooner you get that through your thick, imperfect human skull (after all these years, I'm still trying to get it), the sooner you'll learn how important it is to develop a daily prayer regimen where you can praise Him, learn to love Him, learn to recognize and respond quickly to His inspirations, and humble yourself enough to realize you need His help to share the faith He gave you and commands you to share. He doesn't need your help, but He does command it. Prayer—*daily prayer*—is as vital as Communion, as vital as breathing.

And that leads to the next important thing. Not everyone can do this, because of jobs and responsibilities, but if possible you need to go to daily Mass. You can go at lunch time if you can't go in the morning; many towns have parishes with midday Mass for folks like you. Take a sandwich along and eat it on the way back to work after Mass (eating less than an hour before Communion means you can't receive the Eucharist). You simply won't believe the benefits of daily Mass! After all, when you participate in the priest's celebration of the Holy Sacrifice of the Mass, you're simultaneously standing in the parish church, in the Upper Room at the Last Supper, at the foot of the cross, in front of the empty tomb, and at the Ascension!

Ever heard of a man named Terry Barber? He's the co-host of the *Terry & Jesse Radio Show* (aka, *Reasons for Faith*), founder of Lighthouse Catholic Media (your parish probably has their kiosk of CDs & DVDs), and president of St. Joseph Communications. Terry's been a friend of mine for over twenty years, and he's within a couple of months of being the same age as me (sixty at this writing). Terry hasn't missed daily Mass since he was sixteen years old—forty-four years—and he is the most productive lay evangelist I've ever known! Although a short man in stature, Terry towers head-and-shoulders over me as a lay evangelist! Ask Terry why he's done so well and he'll tell you he attributes his success to daily Mass.[12]

Along with daily Mass is something else you can and must do. We Catholics are supposed to believe in the Real Presence of Christ in the Holy Eucharist; that He is physically really and truly present in the consecrated Host (Body) and consecrated Wine (Blood) in the chalice. But 70% of Catholics no longer believe in the Real Presence. (Personally, I believe it's not that they no longer believe, but that they never have believed in the first place because they've never been taught. That's neither here nor there right now, though.) Consequently, Jesus sits all alone in millions of tabernacles throughout the world. It shouldn't be that way in your case, though. You should spend at least one hour a week keeping Him company at your local parish church. A daily visit would be better, but you should give Him at least an hour a week.

"But, Joe, I'm too busy to do that! There're the kids' soccer games, I've got my daily workout at the gym, and there's a whole lot of other things on top of my job. I just don't have time!"

You're too busy? For Jesus? Look, there are 128 hours in

a week. In the Old Testament, we were commanded by God to give Him 10% of everything. By all rights, He could demand that we give Him nearly thirteen hours of our time, but all I'm talking about is one. If you're too busy to find one hour out of thirteen to keep Jesus company in the tabernacle, you're just, well, *too* busy. You need to do a little reprioritizing. Turn off the TV, shut down Facebook, stop texting... You get the picture.

Another important thing is frequent confession. The Church recommends confession once a month, but she is especially pleased for you to avail yourself of this sacrament weekly.

"There you go again, Joe. I don't think I need confession that often. I don't have any mortal sin to confess."

I'm genuinely happy you don't have any mortal sins to confess, and I sincerely hope you *never* commit a mortal sin. Believe me, though, you have plenty of sins to confess.

Don't believe me? Have you complained about anything today? Have you been critical of anyone or anything? Have you been impatient or angry with anyone or anything today? Been proud of an accomplishment, but failed to give God as much or more praise for the accomplishment as you did yourself? Have you told a "white lie" lately? Do you still have something you borrowed from someone else you've been meaning to return for quite a while now? Have you suspected someone's motives for something he/she did without evidence supporting your suspicion?

At least one of these probably hit the mark. Everybody commits venial sins, which are what all the above are. Your favorite saint probably committed venial sin right up to the day he or she died... but that doesn't mean it's okay. When we try to excise venial sins (peccadilloes) from our lives, it makes it much easier to avoid mortal sins. Besides, working on getting rid of our pet venial sins helps us to better form our consciences rightly and make advancements in the spiritual life. So get in the habit of going to confession weekly.

Suffering is another thing. All of us suffer; some of our sufferings are big, and some are relatively minor. God permits (but never wills) our suffering for a reason—everything from a simple headache to financial ruin, and from a cold to terminal cancer. He always draws a greater good from any suffering we experience, even if we don't get to see that good. Regardless of what the greater good may be, we can benefit from any suffering He permits to come into our lives today.

You can and should offer back the acceptance of your suffering as a gift to God, in reparation for your own sins and the sins of the whole world. The alternative is to simply waste the suffering and get no benefit from it whatsoever. In fact, by not offering up your suffering you won't be reducing any of the justice you owe God in purgatory. Let me see if I can make it more personal for you with an anecdote.

I'm in a wheelchair now, but it hasn't always been that way. I used to be a furniture maker, specializing in 18th century reproductions. I was also an architectural woodcarver, using the tools and methods of woodcarvers from a thousand years ago. I also enjoyed the outdoors—hiking through the woods and Ozark Mountains, watching the wildlife, fishing, etc. Most of all, I was as busy as a three-legged dog, sharing the faith with anyone I could in one-on-one and small group venues. I loved my life. Then our financial consultant stole everything we had and wiped us out, followed a short time later by my having a major stroke that almost killed me.

A stroke of this magnitude changes everything. Nothing smells, tastes, looks or sounds the same as it did prior to the stroke. I can't write or drive anymore, and I can no longer walk except for short distances; and even then only with the aid of a walker and a brace on my leg to stabilize the ankle. I have memory problems, sometimes forgetting I was even talking. I sometimes can't control my emotions to the point that something that is even the least little bit sad will cause me to cry uncontrollably. It goes without saying, I can't any longer walk in the woods, fish, build a piece of furniture, carve or evangelize the way I used to do.

Did I waste my new suffering? No! Day after day I lay in that hospital, at the time unable to even reposition myself in the bed, and I offered all my suffering to God as a gift in reparation for my sins and the sins of the world. So even while lying there unable to even move in my bed, through the suffering God allowed me to experience, I was able to still be of benefit to many souls I'll never meet... at least, not in this life.

Sometimes, we get the privilege of seeing at least some of the greater good God pulls from our sufferings. Because I refused to wallow in self-pity and was open to learning His will, God moved my evangelistic efforts into the 21st century. Now instead of evangelizing in small groups, I work through webinars. My stroke may very well be someone else's ticket to heaven. If that's the case, give me a thousand strokes![13]

You should offer up your sufferings as they come throughout the day, but there is a way you can start your day and sanctify it in its entirety, offering up your sufferings even when you don't remember to do it as things happen. It's called making a morning offering. The first thing I do every morning before my fifth-point-of-contact plops down in my wheelchair is to pray this prayer:

O my God, in union with the Immaculate Heart of

Mary, I offer Thee the Precious Blood of Jesus from all the altars throughout the world, joining with It the offering of my every thought, word and action of this day.

O my Jesus, I desire today to gain every indulgence and merit I can, and I offer them, together with myself, to Mary Immaculate—that she may apply them to the interests of Thy most Sacred Heart.

Precious Blood of Jesus, save us!

Immaculate Heart of Mary, pray for us!

Sacred Heart of Jesus, have mercy on us!

Here's another one...

O Jesus, through the Immaculate Heart of Mary, I offer you my prayers, works, joys, and sufferings of this day for all the intentions of your Sacred Heart, in union with the Holy Sacrifice of the Mass throughout the world, for the salvation of souls, the reparation of sins, the reunion of all Christians, and in particular for the intentions of the Holy Father this month.

Amen.

By praying one of these morning offerings or another (there are lots of them out there), you will sanctify your whole day, which makes it easier if you forget to offer up some suffering when it comes along.

Another thing I personally believe is vital and spiritually beneficial for both you and your students is for you to make an act of consecration. Well, actually there are four acts of consecration I recommend. I won't talk a whole lot about any of them here, as that's not within the scope of this book. Instead I will recommend a book for each consecration. However, I must tell you this: these four consecrations —each serving a different purpose—will completely revolutionize your life.

The first is an act of consecration to the Sacred Heart of

Jesus, which was popularized by St. Margaret Mary Alacoque in 1673. She had a visitation (an apparition) of Jesus, Who told her:

"My Heart is so full of love for men that It can no longer contain the flames of Its burning love. I must discover to men the treasures of My Heart and save them from perdition."

Therein lies the basis of this consecration. I would recommend *The Enthronement of the Sacred Heart of Jesus*, by Raymond Leo Cardinal Burke.

Another great book is *A Heart on Fire: Rediscovering Devotion to the Sacred Heart of Jesus* by Fr. James Kubick, S.J.

The second consecration I recommend is to the Holy Spirit. For preparation for that consecration I would suggest *The Sanctifier: The Classic Work on the Holy Spirit*, by Bishop Luis M Martinez, a late Bishop of Mexico City (RIP). This work is a classic, written by this holy bishop back in 1957. If someone had told me before I read this that there was enough information on the Third Person of the Blessed Trinity to write an entire book about Him, I wouldn't have believed it.

The Sanctifier isn't about making an act of consecration; it's just about the Holy Spirit. When I first got the book and began reading, I read it straight through without a break. I was simply that captivated by it. After I finished, I started all over again, but this time it took me about a month to read it, despite that I read it daily. I took a lot of time to meditate on what I was reading and to pray. By the time I'd finished, my mind was made up that I had to make an act of consecration to the Holy Spirit. So if you decide to do as I did, you'll have to compose your own prayer of consecration. If I were you, I'd make my consecration in private before a priest—preferably your spiritual director.

The third consecration I'd recommend is to the Immaculate Heart of Mary. Most people would advise you to prepare yourself by reading St. Louis de Montfort's book *True Devotion to Mary*, which is a 33-day preparation for consecration. While that's the one I used, several years after I made my consecration, Fr. Robert J. Fox (RIP) wrote a modern version of de Montfort's classic called *Immaculate Heart of Mary: True Devotion*. The reason I suggest using this book for a preparation is that Fr. Fox had a unique ability to write for modern man's understanding.

The fourth and final consecration I'd recommend is one to St. Michael the Archangel, also known as the warrior angel. A consecration to St. Michael will give you the greatest protection from your most common enemy in evangelization: Satan. St. Michael doesn't take any guff from hell, and if you're consecrated to him, he'll get on the enemy quick, fast, and in a hurry when you need him most.

Here's an example by way of anecdote for you: It's inevitable that when I'm teaching anywhere other than my home or the home of the student there will be disturbances happen out of thin air, threatening to put the kibosh on the lesson. I've actually had a lunatics suddenly come in from off the street to wherever we are and stand right next to us hollering and screaming at the top of their lungs with complete gibberish. I simply ask my student to pause with me to ask St. Michael for help by praying the common prayer to him.[14] And he's never let me down. Always within minutes the lunatic (or whatever disturbance) will suddenly and inexplicably cease. Needless to say, my students are always astonished.[15]

Unlike the other consecrations, this one doesn't require a book to prepare you. All you have to do is pray this novena prayer for nine consecutive days:

Saint Michael the Archangel, loyal champion of God and His Catholic people, I turn to thee with confidence and seek thy powerful intercession. For the love of God, Who hast made thee so glorious in grace and power, and for the love of the Mother of Jesus, the Queen of the Angels, be pleased to hear my prayer.

Thou knowest the value of my soul in the eyes of God. May no stain of evil ever disfigure its beauty. Help me to conquer the evil spirit who tempts me. I desire to imitate thy loyalty to God and Holy Mother Church and thy great love for God and men. And since thou art God's messenger for the care of His people, I entrust to thee this special request: [here mention your request].

Saint Michael, since thou art, by the will of the Creator, the powerful intercessor of Christians, I have great confidence in thy prayers. I earnestly trust that if it is God's holy will, my petition will be granted.

Pray for me, Saint Michael, and also for those I love. Protect us in all dangers of body and soul. Help us in our daily needs. Through thy powerful intercession, may we live a holy life, die a happy death and reach Heaven where we may praise and love God with thee forever. Amen.

Then on the 10th day you simply pray this prayer of consecration:

Saint Michael the Archangel, invincible Prince of the Angelic hosts and glorious protector of the universal Church, I greet thee and praise thee for that splendor with which God has adorned thee so richly. I thank God for the great graces He hast bestowed upon thee, especially to remain faithful when Lucifer and his followers rebelled, and to battle victoriously for the honor of God and the Divinity of the Son of Man.

Saint Michael, I consecrate to thee my soul and body. I

choose thee as my patron and protector and entrust the salvation of my soul to thy care. Be the guardian of my obligation as a child of God and of the Catholic Church as again I renounce Satan, his works and pomps.

Assist me by thy powerful intercession in the fulfillment of these sacred promises, so that imitating thy courage and loyalty to God, and trusting in thy kind help and protection, I may be victorious over the enemies of my soul and be united with God in Heaven forever. Amen.

That's it! Of course, a consecration is more than the utterance of mere words; you need to put your heart and soul into it... then keep it in your heart.

If you want to read a great book on angels, though, I think the greatest one I've ever read on the topic was another by Fr. Fox called *The World and Work of the Holy Angels.*

By the way, the vast majority of the books I recommend are not highbrow, difficult-to-read theological tomes. I'm Joe Sixpack—the Every Catholic Guy, which means I usually read and recommend resources that any common man or woman can easily grasp, so don't fear the books and other resources I recommend. Trust me; if they're not above my head, they certainly won't be above yours. I'm not exactly the brightest light on the Christmas tree.

A Few Tips for Evangelization

Before we get to the actual presentation of the faith the way I do it, let me first give you a few tips about sharing the faith productively.

- **You must always love the student.** I've had a bevy of students I didn't like, but I've

loved them all. Loving them doesn't mean
getting all squishy with your emotions. Loving
them means constantly remembering you hold
in your hand a precious soul created by God,
along with that soul's eternal destiny. No, you
don't make the ultimate decision as to what that
soul does—that's on him (or her), but you are the
conduit from the heart of the Catholic Church
to that person's intellect so the soul can make
the ultimate decision. If you aren't loving them,
they won't complete the studies. That's just the
way it works. That's not to say a student's
failure to complete the studies with you is
always your fault, but a good hard look at
yourself is the best place to start when you
begin to analyze why the student dropped. If
you decide you're at fault, chances are it will be
because you failed in love.

- **You don't have to be an omniscient
  catechist.** In other words, you don't have to
  have all the answers. When I started out, I
  didn't have nearly as much knowledge as I do
  now. I was still a catechumen myself, for crying
  out loud! So you can't be expected to have every
  answer to every question every time. In fact, not
  having all the answers can actually help your
  credibility with many folks. So be honest; when
  you don't know the answer to a question, say so.
  When you don't know an answer, promise the
  student you'll get it as soon as possible. *Then
  keep your promise!* Between the time the
  question is asked and you get the answer, the
  student is likely to forget the question was ever

asked. But if you fail to get the answer to the
question asked, you'd better believe that when
the soul is struggling to make a decision about
conversion, the devil will remind that soul you
didn't keep your promise. In any other situation,
a questioner will simply think you forgot to get
the answer. In this case, the student will think
you and the Church have something to hide.
Remember: you're in a constant battle with the
demonic for the eternal destiny of this soul
(Ephesians 6:12)!

- **Honestly, evangelization is really
  nothing more than sales.** Saying that
  scares most people, but it's true. The great thing
  about this sales job, though, is that all you have
  to do is make the pitch; that is, share the faith—
  in most sales jobs you can get a monkey to make
  the pitch. The Holy Spirit does all the
  important work. He gets the "prospect" for you,
  gets him into a "selling position" and mood, and
  does the "close" after you make the pitch...
  sometimes during the pitch. I've known
  hundreds of sales pros who would give their eye
  teeth for a sales job like that! But along with
  such a great set-up comes an equally great
  responsibility. No matter how tempted you are
  to the contrary, *never ask a student if he/she
  wants to become a Catholic*. That's absolutely
  none of your business until he/she decides to
  make it your business. Asking if the student
  wants to become a Catholic adds pressure to a
  situation where the only one who should be
  applying pressure is the Holy Spirit. Don't try

to do His job for Him. In thirty years of evangelizing souls, I've never once asked someone if he or she wanted to become a Catholic.

- **Practice holy detachment.** When you begin to teach the catechism evangelistically, a bond will develop between you and your student—especially if you are teaching one-on-one. You have to know where the line is in a relationship and strictly observe it. If you get *too* close, it will cloud your judgment and cause the relationship to get too personal. Almost without exception, in one-on-one situations my student begins to rely on me for just about everything. I've heard more confessions than I care to count, despite the fact that I beg students not to tell me certain things.[16] This, among other reasons, is why I recommend that in one-on-one situations you work only with people of your own sex. It's dangerous to the soul—both yours and your student's—to work one-on-one in mixed company. A husband and wife situation is a little different.

- **Limit your sessions.** Never teach more than an hour. When you're coming up on an hour, find a good stopping point and quit there. The only exceptions to this are the first and ninth articles of the Creed and the Holy Eucharist; do them straight through. You can go longer than an hour on other parts of the catechism, but you have to judge this by the attitude and body language of the student. If you can't judge it for yourself, just ask the person if he/she wants to keep going.

- **Prepare well.** I've done this so many times over the last thirty years that I can almost share the faith in my sleep, but you can't do that... yet. So before your appointment to teach a student, go over the planned lesson. Read all the scriptural and document references. Prepare well. Remember: a soul is in your hands. You have an eternal responsibility.

- **Get in the habit of reading the Bible daily.** You don't have to do it for more than 15 minutes a day, but at least do that. Begin with the four Gospels and Acts. Then finish the New Testament. From there you can pick and choose. I've read the Bible through six times, so I can tell you the Gospels and Acts are the best place to start. And for the record, if you begin reading Sacred Scripture every day, you *will* eventually develop a love for it to the point that you are impelled to read it. I recommend the Revised Standard Version—Catholic Edition. When Bible scholars of all faiths need an accurate English version, this is the one they turn to.

- **Read Vatican II.** I'm firmly convinced that every Catholic has an obligation to read the documents of Vatican II—especially someone sharing the faith. You need to know what they say. Unless you're talking to a Marian Catechist, don't take anybody's word for what's in the documents; chances are they are probably

> wrong because they've most likely never read
> them themselves—even sometimes priests.
> You've got to read them for yourself.

Admittedly, the documents are real yawners, because they're written in ecclesiastical language, but the beauty and depth of the content is amazing. Because they're yawners, they're hard to read. It took me two years to read the eight major documents, and another year to read the others. But each paragraph is numbered, so discipline yourself enough to read one numbered paragraph a day. I recommend the Flannery edition of the documents. Start with the eight major documents listed below.

1. *Dogmatic Constitution on Divine Revelation*
2. *Dogmatic Constitution on the Church*
3. *Constitution on the Sacred Liturgy*
4. *Pastoral Constitution on the Church in the Modern World*
5. *Decree on the Apostolate of the Laity*
6. *Decree on Ecumenism*
7. *Decree on the Mission Activity of the Church*
8. *Decree on the Media of Social Communications*

- ***Under no circumstances* do you simply hand a potential student this book or any catechism to read on his/her own!** For starters, it won't get read. That's just human nature. And even if the student reads it, a book won't answer a question. Take this book and ask it a question right now, then wait for an answer. If you hear anything but crickets chirping, you probably need psychotropic medication and don't need to be pursuing this. The book can't give an answer to a question. Besides, when you hand a student a catechism and leave him/her to his/her own devices, the message you're sending is that you have little regard for both the student and our holy and ancient faith. So this is a great big no-no.

- **Finally and most importantly, please consider making acts of consecration to the Holy Spirit, the Sacred Heart of Jesus, the Immaculate Heart of Mary, and St. Michael the Archangel.** Doing this will, believe it or not, make you an invincible foe of the Evil One in all your evangelistic efforts. I could write a book on this topic alone, but it's not the focus of this particular opus. I've covered all this earlier in this chapter.

All right, so now we have the basics down pat, and we're ready to get started... just about. I have two things to tell you first.

You'll find in both the catechetical instruction and my instruction to you that things will be repeated over and over again. This is done because they're important, and repetition is the best teacher. So expect it and get used to it.

The other thing I want to tell you is that if you get stuck in any way—a question you can't answer, a difficulty with a student, you don't understand something in this book, etc.—all you have to do is contact me. As long as God lets me live,

I'll be available to you. (How's that for added value for the price of this book?) You can contact me by going to JoeSix-packAnswers.com and going to the "Ask Joe" page. I'll get back to you as soon as I can; usually within a few hours, but 48 hours at most. We're partners in this together.

Okay, so let's get started!

TWO

HOW I BEGIN WITH EACH STUDENT

This is, word-for-word, how I start teaching each student (except for headings like "Getting Started"). The idea is to let them know exactly what they can expect. What is written here is exactly what I say.

Getting Started

I'm going to try to do this in an organized manner. Here's everything we're going to cover:

- We're going to start with the Apostles' Creed
- Then I'm going to move on to Grace and The Sacraments
- Followed by Christian Morality
- And we'll finish up with the Life of Virtue and the Life of Prayer

Now in the Life of Virtue and the Life of Prayer we're going to talk about the virtuous life and examine the Gospel message by breaking down the Lord's Prayer verse by verse. We'll also do one other thing I believe all Christians should be able to do.

There are two things I think all Christians should be able to do, if they want to claim a belief in God and the Bible. Those two things are to prove the existence of God, which we'll do in a few minutes. The other thing is to prove that the Bible is inspired by God. And that's one of the things we'll do when we study the Life of Virtue and the Life of Prayer.

Before that, we'll study what God says we can and can't do, and why. We'll examine the ten commandments in this order:

- The 1st commandment.
- The 2nd commandment.
- The 3rd commandment—and these three deal with man's relationship with God, then the last seven deal with our relationship to God *and* man. So we'll look at them in this order.
- The 4th commandment.
- The 5th commandment.
- The 6th & 9th commandments together, because they deal with sexual purity.
- The 7th & 10th commandments, because they deal with respect for other people's property.
- Then we'll look at the 8th commandment, as it deals with our respect for one another's good name and reputation.

Prior to that we'll look at the sacraments. There are seven of them, and we'll look at them in this order:

- Baptism
- Confirmation
- Holy Eucharist
- Penance
- Anointing of the Sick
- Holy Orders and
- Holy Matrimony

But we'll start with the Apostles' Creed, which says...

Read or recite it. I recommend reading it, lest you embarrass yourself by not getting it exactly right.

I believe in God, the Father Almighty, Creator of heaven and earth; and in Jesus Christ, His only Son, our Lord; who was conceived by the Holy Spirit, born of the Virgin Mary, suffered under Pontius Pilate, was crucified, died and was buried. He descended into hell; the third day he rose again from the dead; He ascended into heaven, sits at the right hand of God the Father Almighty; from thence He shall come to judge the living and the dead.

I believe in the Holy Spirit, the holy Catholic Church, the communion of saints, the forgiveness of sins, the resurrection of the body, and life everlasting. Amen.

Did you hear anything in that you disagree with?

If they say no (which most will), move on. If they say

yes, identify what it is and promise a complete explanation at the appropriate time until they understand it. Then move on

---

I'm going to use the classical question and answer format. I'll ask a question, then give you a few seconds to think about how you'd answer before giving and explaining the answer. It's simple.

Sometimes I'll be asking questions that might make you feel like I'm insulting your intelligence. That's not the case at all. These sorts of questions are what most people consider really easy questions that anyone ought to know, which is why you're likely to think I'm insulting your intelligence. But it's been my experience that if we have some of these simple questions along the way, we'll always be reading off the same page, never having misunderstandings about how we are defining terms and concepts.

So let's get started with the first article of the Creed, "I believe in God, the Father Almighty, Creator of heaven and earth."

THREE

THE FIRST ARTICLE OF THE CREED

"*I believe in God, the Father Almighty, Creator of heaven and earth.*"

Ask each question as it is written. Just follow what is here. Try to memorize the things said, but any memory work doesn't have to be verbatim. You just have to follow this generally. It's not my ego that insists on this, but rather I've done this innumerable times and tweaked it as I went along. You don't want your parts sounding stiff and unnatural. You'll get the hang of it.

And don't worry if you sound stiff and unsure of yourself the first few times you do it. You're learning, and it takes time to get it down right. Something you'll find very helpful is to be excited. Avoid fake excitement, though. If you're not excited about the Catholic faith, there are only two possible reasons. The first is you don't really know and understand the faith, as it's impossible to know and understand it and not be excited. The second possible reason is you don't really believe it yourself, in which case I beg you to put this book down right now and leave it alone.

The Nature and Existence of God

See, we're even going to start off with one of those simple questions I was talking about...

#1 Who created us?

Wait for the student to answer, then read then more complete answer.

God, who is the all-perfect Supreme Being, the Creator of all things, visible and invisible, and who keeps them in existence, is the One who created us (Genesis 1:27).

When you see scriptural citations in parenthesis, don't hesitate to grab your Bible and show it to the student. I don't always do it, but I do it as often as seems prudent. Not only does it add credibility to what you're teaching, but it promotes getting into the habit of reading the Bible—something we always want to promote.

#2 How do we know God exists?

There are three places in the catechism where non-Catholics will often convert. This is the first place—especially for people in their twenties and early thirties. This age group often has no exposure to religion of any kind. More often than not, if you can prove to them that God exists and that evolution is an unworkable theory, they will often give themselves over to Him completely without reservation. I have honestly met people in this age group who have never heard of Jesus Christ... except as an epithet with the middle initial "H." I'm serious! This age group is taught from the beginning of their exposure to a so-called public education that there is no God and that evolution is a fact rather than a theory.

Although we can't prove God's existence with empirical evidence (yet), we can prove His existence through the use of logic and right reason.

There are actually several ways we can know God exists. The first way is fine for unthinking people—the Bible tells us so—but that won't be intellectually satisfying for you or most others people.

Argument from Design

Let's view God's existence from design. We can see from nature that it could exist only through the design of a

Supreme Architect. Trees "inhale" carbon dioxide and "exhale" oxygen. We inhale oxygen and exhale carbon dioxide. We can't exist without the trees and they can't exist without us. What a logical God!

The food chain teaches us a bit about God's existence. The tiniest microscopic organism is food for the next largest organism, is food for the next largest organism, is food for the next largest organism. And on it goes until it reaches the top of the food chain—humans. We eat, digest the food, our bodies evacuate the waste, then the process starts all over again with the tiniest organism feeding on the waste. What a logical God!

*"Are you crazy? That stuff is all from evolution! Everybody knows about the fact of evolution. It's **science**, man."*

I actually include the above as part of my presentation. It adds a little humor and keeps things lighthearted. Besides, your student might actually be thinking that, but he/she probably won't feel comfortable expressing it out loud.

Whoa! I'm not the one who's crazy. First, evolution isn't a fact; it's a theory. Second, it's a false theory, as it actually violates the very science that is apparently your god.

Evolution contends that order accidentally came from chaos and became the world in nature as we know it—that the chaos gradually became better and more ordered. But the third law of thermodynamics tells us the universe is entropy—that all matter is in a constant state of deterioration from order to chaos. If all matter is in a constant state of deterioration, how in the world could chaos evolve into order? You can't have it both ways. Either evolution is right (a theory) or thermodynamics is right (a proven fact).

Carry on the above explanation with yourself out loud as part of the presentation. You may feel silly doing it, but I assure you it works... well.

Argument from Conscience

We intuitively know the difference between right and wrong. This is called natural law. It's something that used to be taught in every law school, but the political left has managed to banish natural law from our "scholarly" institutions. The reason the political left banished it is because they fear it; it doesn't comport to their agenda. It has been this way since the Supreme Court rulings in 1973 on the Roe-v-Wade and Bolton-v-Doe cases. Since abortion is the unjust taking of a human life, it doesn't conform to natural law.

We intuitively know it is wrong to unjustly take an innocent human life, wrong to disobey legitimate authority, wrong to treat another person unjustly, wrong to steal, wrong to lie, *et cetera*. We know all these things intuitively; that's natural law. The fact that we have natural law implies a lawgiver. Who else could that lawgiver be but God?

"Wait a minute. The conscience is formed from religious teaching in union with the human brain."

What? The thing that debunks your argument that conscience comes from religious teaching and the brain are the sciences of social anthropology and medicine. First, there isn't a neurologist in the world who can tell us what part of the brain the conscience comes from, as the conscience isn't a function of the brain; it's a function of the soul. And, second, anthropologists have discovered tribal communities in remote locations of the world that had a moral code in place that comports to natural law when they were discovered, a moral code without the influence of Judo-Christian religions. So how does your objection hold up to that?

Another self-conversation out loud.

Bad Man, Mad Man Argument

Now let's take a look at what I call the bad man, mad man argument.

The argument I'm about to present is one I thought I had originated, but I later found out it was first developed by an obscure saint in the second or third century. I should have known someone had beaten me to it, as a 2,000 year old Church has already come up with everything that can be thought of.

Oddly, this argument isn't actually intellectually satisfying, but I've found over the years it is the one that is most convincing to most students.

To present this argument, I'll have to ask you to stipulate a couple of things for the sake of brevity.

The first thing I want you to stipulate is that the Old Testament is ancient Hebrew literature. I'm not claiming it is inspired, infallibly true, or anything else; only that it's ancient Hebrew literature.

The second stipulation I'm asking from you is that Jesus of Nazareth was a real historic person. I'm not saying he's the messiah, God, the son of God or anything else; only that he was a real historic person.

"Got to stop you again! You don't have anything to back up that claim other than the Bible."

Another out loud conversation.

Not so! That Jesus was a real historic person is attested to by the writings of men who were contemporaries of Jesus. Specifically, I'm talking about Pliny, Tacitus, Suetonius, and Flavius Josephus. The first three men were pagans and certainly no friends of Jesus. Flavius Josephus was like Paul: he was both a Jew and a Roman citizen, and he was most assuredly not at all sympathetic to Jesus. The writings of these four men, historical scholars tell us, validate the four Gospels, making them historically reliable. So we not only have the testimony of Matthew, Mark, Luke and John, but we also have the writings of Pliny, Tacitus, Suetonius, and Flavius Josephus.

So with these two stipulations made, we can now present our argument.

First, we'll consider the Old Testament prophecies of

the coming messiah. The Old Testament is filled with such prophecies, particularly in the books of Jeremiah, Isaiah, and the Psalms, and there's even the very first promise of a messiah in the early part of Genesis. We're still not claiming these prophecies are true, but rather that they are in the Old Testament.

If we were to take all the messianic prophecies and list them in a column, then read all the accounts of the life of Jesus, we would find that Jesus fulfilled the prophecies perfectly. But does this prove that Jesus was the messiah? No! Applying logic and reason, we can deduce that Jesus of Nazareth could only be one of three types of persons: a bad man, a mad man, or who he says he is.

Could Jesus have been a bad man? Could a bad man—a criminal—wake up one day and decide that he would fulfill all the messianic prophecies? He could reason that if he could convince the people that he was the messiah by fulfilling the prophecies he would be hailed as their king. He could raise an army and rout the Romans out of Israel, become very wealthy and powerful, have lots of women and material wealth, and so on. Could a bad man do that?

No matter the answer given by the student, continue with the next paragraph.

Sure he could, but this sort of reasoning breaks down with one prophecy. One of the prophecies says that the messiah would have to die. Now, would a criminal work so hard to fulfill all the prophecies if he knew he would have to die? I know I wouldn't! One hallmark of a criminal is that they are selfish and think of themselves before they think of anyone else. So Jesus couldn't have been a criminal. Not a chance!

Could Jesus have been a mad man? Could a mad man wake up one day and say, "What's that, God? You say I'm the messiah and I need to start fulfilling prophecy? Okay, God!" Would or could a mad man do that? Again, that is certainly a possibility, especially with a smart lunatic, but reason and experience with the insane tells us this won't work. Why? Consistency. A mad man can't remain consistent long enough to pull this off.

A 20th century example of this is Adolph Hitler. We entered the Second World War in 1941 (Germany declared war against the United States 12-11-41), it was almost three years before we had a significant victory over Germany. Our European enemy had the greatest military and most brilliant war generals the world had ever known, but we defeated them anyway. The reason was Hitler's insanity. As long as Hitler listened to his war generals, the Germans won. It was only when Hitler's insanity kicked in and he began listening to his astrologers instead of his generals that we were able to begin to turn the tide of the war to our favor. That's the nature of insanity.

But Jesus was far from insane. The science of psychology only began in 1879, making it a mere 140 years old. Psychologists agree that if Jesus was nothing else, he was both sane and consistent. While they may not agree with what he taught (or at least the various interpretations of what he taught), they certainly agree he was sane. Therefore, Jesus could not have been a mad man.

If Jesus couldn't have been a bad man, and if he couldn't have been a mad man, then he must have been who he said he was. And who did he say he was?

He said he was God!

Jesus repeatedly claimed to be God (cf. John 10:24-31, et alia), but my personal favorite is found in John 8:58. Here's what took place...

The Jews said to him, "Are we not right in saying you are a Samaritan and have a demon?" Jesus answered, "I have not a demon; but I honor my Father, and you dishonor me. Yet I do not seek my own glory; there is One who seeks it and he will be the judge. Truly, truly, I say to you, if any one keeps my word, he will never see death." The Jews said to him, "Now we know that you have a demon. Abraham died, as did the prophets; and you say, 'If any one keeps my word, he will never taste death.' Are you greater than our father Abraham, who died? And the prophets died! Who do you claim to be?" Jesus answered, "If I glorify myself, my glory is nothing; it is my Father who glorifies me, of whom you say that he is your God. But you have not known him; I know him. If I said, I do not know him, I should be a liar like you; but I do know him and I keep his word. Your father Abraham rejoiced that he was to see my day; he saw it and was glad." The Jews then said to him, "You are not yet fifty years old, and have you seen Abraham?" Jesus said to them, "Truly, truly, I say to you, before Abraham was, I am." So they took up stones to throw at him; but Jesus hid himself, and went out of the temple.[1]

Now Jesus' comment saying "I am" seems pretty innocuous to most of us, and maybe it doesn't even make sense to many of us, but it was enough to make the Jews want to kill him. Why?

To get the answer to that we have to go back to the third chapter of Exodus. It is here that God just gave Moses his marching orders to go to the children of Israel as His messenger and their liberator.

Moses said to God,

If I come to the people of Israel and say to them, "The God of your fathers has sent me to you," and they ask me, "What is his name?" what shall I say to them? God said to Moses, "I AM WHO I AM." And he said, "Say this to the people of Israel, 'I AM has sent me to you.'" [2]

I AM: the statement of the all-eternal. Every Hebrew male in those days was obliged to memorize the entire Pentateuch, or first five books of the Old Testament, so the Jews understood by Jesus' statement exactly who he was claiming to be. He was claiming to be God, so they sought his death for blasphemy.

So, if Jesus couldn't have been a bad man, and He couldn't have been a mad man, and He had to be who He said He is, and He said He is God, **we must conclude that God exists!**

#3 What does "Supreme Being" mean?

This descriptive term for God means He is above all created things, is self-existing, and has all perfections without limit.

#4 What does "self-existing" mean?

By "self-existing" we mean that no other being caused God to exist. He is eternal, which means that He had no beginning, and will have no end (Psalm 90:2).

#5 Does God have a body as we do?

No. God has no body at all. He's pure spirit, with intelligence and free will. When the Bible refers to "the hand of God" or other bodily attributes, this is merely a method of teaching about God so the people could understand. People are better able to understand God's mercy and justice by attributing certain physical characteristics to Him.

#6 Does God ever change?

Because He's perfect, God cannot change. If a thing is perfect, to add or subtract from the thing alters its perfection. This means that it would no longer be perfect. God is all-perfect and can add nothing to His perfection.

Let's say you were a building contractor with 25 years of experience. You decided to use your knowledge and experience to build the perfect house for yourself. After you built the house, you tell yourself it is perfect. No mistakes anywhere, the proportions are just right, you used the latest building technologies; by all appearances, the house is indeed perfect. But a few years later, for whatever reason, you decided to abandon the house, and it remains empty for years. What will happen to that house? It will deteriorate, of course! Deterioration is indicative of imperfection. A perfect thing cannot deteriorate.

God can't deteriorate, age or become imperfect in any way. He *is* perfection.

#7 Is God all-powerful?

Yes, God is all-powerful, which means He can do all things. We call this attribute omnipotence, which means all-powerful. (Omni = all. Potent = powerful. Omni + potent = all-powerful.)

#8 Is God everywhere?

Yes, God is everywhere. There is no place that God is not (Psalm 139:8-10). We call this divine attribute omnipresence. (Omni = all. Presence = being present. Omni + present = present everywhere.)

#9 Does God know everything?

God knows everything: past, present, and future, our most hidden thoughts, desires, words, actions, and (my personal favorite) omissions. We're bound by the restraints of time and space; that is, we can't relive what happened ten minutes ago, nor can we predict what will happen ten minutes from now. God, on the other hand, sees all things, events, and people at the same time. Because He is eternal, and there is no time for Him, everything takes place for Him in the present. This means He sees the creation of the world, the destruction of the world, and everything in between all at the same time. We call this God's omniscience. (Omni = all. Science = knowledge. Omni + science = all-knowing)

#10 Why do we call God the Creator of heaven and earth?

Absolutely nothing existed until God created everything by His almighty power. He created everything by an act of His will. Since He is free in all His actions, nothing compelled God to create the universe. He simply willed it. (Genesis 1:1)

In fact, the reason everything stays in existence is because God keeps everything on His eternal mind. If He were to cease thinking of you for even a nanosecond, you wouldn't cease to exist; you would merely never have existed at all. Think about it.

#11 Did God create only material things?

This question is an excellent opportunity to get your student to begin to think. The most common answer they will give is to say that air is an immaterial creation. They're just not thinking. My general response is to smile and say, "Well, no, not quite. Think about it while I read the answer."

God created both the material and immaterial. What we mean by the immaterial are those things that don't at all affect the five senses of touch, smell, sound, taste and sight.

He created the angels, which are pure spirits. He also created each individual human soul, which is also spiritual. Angels and souls are examples of the immaterial creation of God. (Nehemiah 9:6; Colossians 1:16; I Corinthians 8:6)

#12 Does God care about us?

Yes! We call His love Divine Providence.

#13 Can God ever commit evil?

God is all-perfect. Since evil is an imperfection, God is incapable of doing evil. He permits evil because He respects the free will He gave us, and we often choose evil over good (the tiniest venial sin is still evil). He also permits our evil in order to show us His power and mercy, because He always draws a greater good from any evil—we may not see it right away, but it is there.

The Blessed Trinity

#14 Is there only one God?

Yes, there is only one God. (Isaiah 45:5)

#15 Then what is meant by the Blessed Trinity?

The Blessed Trinity is one and the same God in three divine Persons: God the Father, God the Son, and God the Holy Spirit. God the Father is the first Person of the Blessed Trinity. God the Son is the second Person of the Blessed Trinity. God the Holy Spirit is the third Person of the Blessed Trinity. All three Persons are one God, but each is distinct.

Take me for example (analogously). I'm a father of four sons. I'm also a son; contrary to popular belief, I didn't slide out from under a rock. Who I really am is a spiritual soul, so I'm a spirit. Yet I'm only one person, despite that I can show you I'm a father, son and spirit.

Add your own story, or adjust this one, but keep it personal. Students respond better if it's personal.

Consider your hand. It has five fingers, and the fingers are distinct, not separate. If they were separate you could remove them. But it's still just one hand.

Hard to grasp? Don't feel bad. This is the greatest mystery of our faith. A mystery of faith is a truth we can't fully understand (doesn't violate reason), but we accept it on the authority of the one who revealed it—in this case God. Just try to take a little time to wrap your head around it.

The great St. Augustine (A.D. 354-430) was Bishop of Hippo. One time he was walking along the sea shore trying to think of how he would try to help his congregation understand the Trinity at church the following Sunday. As he walked, he came upon a small boy with a pail. The boy would fill up his pail from the ocean, then run back upon the shore and pour the water into a hole he'd dug. Amused, Augustine asked the boy what he was doing. The little boy told the bishop he was going to empty the entire ocean into that hole.

Augustine said, "Son, don't you realize you can't empty the ocean into that hole? It's impossible."

The little boy replied, "It would be easier for me to empty the ocean into this hole than it would for you to make your congregation understand the Blessed Trinity." Then he revealed himself as an Angelic messenger from God.

The Angels

#16 Who are the angels?

Well, let's start with who the angels are not. They aren't the souls of our deceased loved ones, which is the popular opinion of the entertainment media, such as Clarence in the movie *It's a Wonderful Life*. And they aren't cute little children with wings.

The angels are pure spirits who possess intelligence and free will. They don't have a body, but God has seen fit at various times throughout history to allow angels to assume a physical presence in dealing directly with man. (cf. the book of Tobit, Genesis 18 and 19) Also, the angels are more perfect than we are and more like God, because they are pure spirits. This makes them superior to us in the order of creation.

#17 How do we know the angels exist?

The existence of angels has been revealed to us through the Bible and Sacred Tradition, which is the totality of Divine Revelation. The Bible is chock full of angelic references: Luke 1:11-20; 2:9-13; 22:43; Matthew 1:20; 2:13; 2:19; Acts 8:26; 10:3; 12:7 and loads more in the Old Testament.

I always read a few of these passages to my students, because I'll be promoting devotion to the holy Angels before I'm done telling the student about them.

#18 Are all the angels good?

God made all the angels good, but some became evil and rebelled against Him when He tested them (II Peter 2:4). These rebellious angels are called devils, evil spirits, or demons. God cast them into hell for their disobedience. Because they have become enemies of God, the demons desire to harm us by tempting us to sin against God. We can resist them, though; not of ourselves, but with God's help (I Peter 5:8-9).

Read these two passages above.

#19 Did God reward the good angels?

Absolutely! God granted the faithful angels the same reward He will give to us if we persevere in serving Him well; that is, the reward of the eternal happiness of heaven where we will live with the angels to see God as He truly is, and to love and adore Him forever.

#20 Do the good angels care for us?

Yes, the good angels pray for us, protect us, and serve us as guardian angels (Psalm 91:11). At the moment God creates each human soul, He assigns to us a guardian angel to be with us in this life and throughout all eternity. Our guardian angel protects us from spiritual dangers, guides our minds to know what is right, prays for us, and presents our prayers to God. Although our guardian angel is superior to us in the order of creation, he serves us in this life and will continue to be our servant in heaven. This is the way of God: that the least shall be first, and the greatest becomes the servant of all. (cf. Tobit and Matthew 18:10)

I wholeheartedly recommend developing a devotion to your guardian angel. I'll bet if you think about it, you can come up with a dozen instances in your life—a near accident, an actual accident, an injury or illness—that when it was over you realized you should have been dead. And if not for your Angel, you probably would have been!

Your guardian angel has been with you, protecting and helping you, since you were conceived in your mother's womb. But your angel doesn't want his relationship with you to be all one-sided. He longs to have a personal relationship with you.

You may not believe this right now, but if you take the challenge I'm about to make, you can develop the sort of relationship with your angel that will allow you to actually carry on conversations with him.

Get in the habit every morning of talking to your guardian angel. Talk to him the way you would your best friend. Tell him about all your problems, your joys, and even the goings-on in your life. Then just sit there for about 15 minutes. Think of nothing except your angel. Angels love silence—including mental silence. So if any thought besides your angel comes into your mind, start over thinking of nothing but him.

It takes about two weeks of this to silence the "white noise" in your mind. But if you'll persevere with this, after a couple of weeks you will hear your angel begin to speak to you. And wouldn't it be great to have that sort of relationship with a being as powerful as your guardian angel?

To get an idea of how close and intimate your guardian Angel can be, I'd suggest you read the book of Tobit. It will only take about an hour.

I will never suggest such things in this book unless I've done them myself, and they are approved by the Church. This whole concept of communicating with your guardian angel is probably something you never heard of before, so I can understand if you're a little skeptical. In addition to the suggestions above, if you're interested in looking into this, please purchase the book The World and Work of the Holy Angels *by Fr. Robert J. Fox (RIP). I knew Fr. Fox the last 20 years of his life, and I was very skeptical about talking to my guardian angel when he first told me about it, to say the least. But it works!*

Unless you are willing to undertake this yourself with your guardian angel, simply omit the last four paragraphs of the above answer.

Man and His Fall

#21 What is man?

Man is a creature composed of a physical body and a spiritual soul. The soul possesses intelligence and free will, and it is created in the image and likeness of God. The soul is also immortal, which means that it will live forever, and each soul is individually created by God.

The soul is what gives us life. This means when we look at a friend or loved one we are not really seeing that person, but rather we are looking at the "house" in which that person lives. It is the soul which possesses the personality, free will, intelligence, and reasoning ability. This is why there is so much emphasis on the soul in Christianity.

#22 Why did God create us?

This is the question man of every age has asked himself since the dawn of time. The Jews of old have known the answer to this question for at least 5,000 years, and we Catholics—who are merely New Covenant Jews—have known it for 2,000 years.

God created us to know Him, love Him, and serve Him in this life so we may be happy with Him forever in the next life. Once we come to know God, we can't help but love Him. After we learn to love Him, we want to serve Him. If we persevere in our service to God for love of Him, He will reward us with eternity with Him in heaven.

#23 Why did God give us free will?

God created us with free will so we would love Him by our own choice. What good is the love of a robot that is programmed to love? It serves no purpose. By giving us free will, He allows us to choose—with His help—to do what is good and to avoid evil. In this way He can reward us for our good choices.

I used to have a computer of mine set up so that when I booted it up, a female voice would say, "Good morning, Joe. I love you."

Did that computer love me? Of course not. What good is a machine that is programmed to tell me it loves me?

The same is true of the human person in his relationship with God. For Him to reward us, we have to express a freely willed love for Him.

#24 Who were the first human beings God created?

The Bible tells us they were Adam and Eve, the first persons of mankind from whom the entire human race descended.

At this point there is often a student who brings up Adam and Eve's sons marrying women that are not the offspring of our first parents. This argument is called polygenesis. While some students are genuinely baffled by this, most will bring it up in an attempt to have a "gotcha" moment. You have to be prepared to answer a charge of polygenesis, which is a heresy. So I'll answer it for you here.

To begin, prior to the fall of man, there was no such thing as linear time. This is because man was created to live forever, without aging or knowing illness. Time is part of the punishment for original sin. So while Scripture indicates Adam lived 930 years after the fall, we really have no idea how long he'd lived before the fall. There was no measurement of time, because linear time didn't exist for humans. He and Eve may have lived thousands of years prior to the fall.

The very first command God gave Adam and Eve was to be fruitful and multiply. In other words, to make lots of babies (Genesis 1:28). And you should recall that prior to the fall of man there was no pain in child bearing (Genesis 3:16). So Adam and Eve had a lot of time (perhaps thousands or millions of years) to make a lot of babies.

Regarding Cain, Abel and Seth, just because the Bible mentions only them as Adam's sons, doesn't mean he and Eve didn't have thousands or even millions of children. The Bible never talks about the ordinary, but only the extraordinary. The people, places and things mentioned in the Bible are only those things central to the message the sacred writers. They had no desire to mention those things that were not central to their message. The reason why there was focus on the three sons was because when Moses wrote Genesis it was because he wanted to show a direct link to what would one day be called the Children of Israel.

To put all this together, there was no polygenesis. Cain, Abel and Seth clearly married women who were either sisters or (more likely) distant cousins.

#25 What gifts did God give our first parents?

The greatest of the gifts God gave our first parents was the gift of *sanctifying grace*; that is, a sharing in His divine life, which made them holy, and gave them a right to heaven.

Some other gifts God gave our first parents were superior knowledge, control of the passions by use of reason, and freedom from suffering and death.

Through being given superior knowledge, our first parents had dominion over all the earth. With control of the passions by use of reason, Adam and Eve were not driven by the desires of the flesh; in other words, they did not know lust or anger. Freedom from suffering and death means they were meant to live forever.

#26 What is original sin?

Original sin is the sin transmitted by Adam to all the human race. It is called "original" because it has been passed to all men from its *origin*, which is Adam. We know original sin is real from the Bible (Genesis 3:1-24; Romans 5:12-19), and from the teachings of the Church.

#27 If our first parents were created holy, how could they sin?

Our first parents were not yet in heaven, where a person sees God and can't sin. They still lived on earth, so they lived by faith. Also, they had free will, meaning they could choose good over evil. When the devil tempted them, they knowingly (with superior knowledge) and willfully (with free will) disobeyed God.

Because of their sin, our first parents lost their sanctifying grace and the right to heaven. They lost their other gifts, too, becoming inclined toward evil and subject to ignorance, suffering and death. This means that original sin, which has been passed down to us from Adam, causes us to enter the world with the absence of sanctifying grace and the right to heaven. It also causes us, like it did Adam and Eve, to be inclined to evil and subject to ignorance, suffering and death (Romans 5:12).

However, original sin does not make our nature totally corrupt. Our mind can still know truth and our will is still free; therefore, we can still do good and avoid evil, but with greater effort and God's help.

#28 Isn't God unjust in punishing us for Adam's sin?

Not at all. Sanctifying grace was a free gift of God. No one has a right to a gift. When Adam sinned he forfeited his gift, thus losing it and God's other gifts for himself and us as well.

Let's explain it this way. If your parents were wealthy people, you could expect to inherit that money when they died. You would have a right to that wealth because it had been secured to be left to you. But what if your parents made some bad investments and lost all their wealth just before they died? All the money would be gone.

Now let's say after your parents died you went to the bank and said to the banker, "Okay, here I am. Give me Mom and Dad's money." What do you think the banker would say? After he quit laughing, he'd tell you all that money was lost by your parents, so it's not there for you either. They lost their own wealth and, by necessity, lost what would have been yours. The same is true with original sin.

#29 Is there any remedy for original sin?

Yes, Jesus Christ, the God-man, died on the cross to redeem us from sin and restore sanctifying grace to us. The ordinary means of removing original sin from the soul is by way of Baptism, which we will examine in a later lesson.

Notice the word "ordinary". In Catholic theology, any time you see the word "ordinary," the word "extraordinary" won't be far behind. You'll see this repeatedly in here. I always tell my students the very same thing I wrote here about ordinary and extraordinary in Catholic theology.

#30 Is there any remedy for the _effects_ of original sin?

The effects of original sin may be partially remedied. This is done by Scripture reading, religious instruction (such as this), prayer, devout reception of the sacraments, voluntary penance, and obedience to God's law.

#31 Was any human person ever preserved from original sin?

Students will often insist that Jesus is the answer. That would be right, if we did not specify a human person. Besides, Mary's Immaculate Conception was needed for Christ's preservation from original sin.

I highly recommend that you use these diagrams when teaching students about the Immaculate Conception. I've found that they tend to get confused or not get the concept altogether if you don't use visual aids.

Yes, the Blessed Virgin Mary was preserved from original sin from the moment of her conception in view of the merits of Jesus Christ. This privilege is called the *Immaculate Conception*.

Because Jesus is God and could have no sin, and since original sin is passed to our descendants, it was necessary for the Blessed Virgin Mary to be preserved from original sin. This made her a pure vessel, a worthy Ark of the New Covenant. So that we may better understand how God accomplished this, we will look at the following illustrations.

First, we have God overlooking the history of man, from creation to apocalypse. For us, time is linear. For Him, there is no time, so He sees everything in history—past, present, and future—all at once.

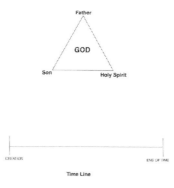

Next we see God looking down on His Son's sacrifice of the cross for the redemption of the entire human race. It was on the cross that He redeemed us and brought sanctifying grace in the world—the sort of grace everyone must have to be holy and attain heaven—even Mary.

In a manner of speaking, the Father reached down to His Son and took the sanctifying grace the Son won for us with His sacrifice and...

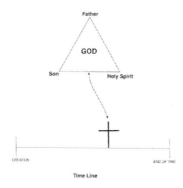

applied it to the soul of the Blessed Virgin Mary at the

moment of her natural conception in her mother's womb. This is how Jesus was given a perfectly clean vessel to grow in as He came into the world. This is the *Immaculate Conception*.

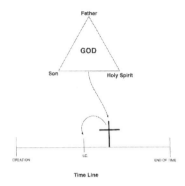

FOUR

THE SECOND ARTICLE OF THE CREED

"Jesus Christ His only Son our Lord"

The Incarnation—True God and True Man

> *People are astounded that I spend less time on this article than any other. If you think about it, though, it makes sense. After all, all of Catholic teaching is ultimately about Jesus. We only deal with things about Him here that aren't dealt with anywhere else.*

#32 What is the Incarnation?

The Incarnation is when God became man; that is, when God the Son became man to redeem us (John 3:16-17). His very name as man, as foretold by the archangel (Luke 1:31), means savior.

#33 Why is Jesus both true God and true man?

Jesus is true God because He has the same divine nature as God the Father. He's true man because He was born of a woman, just like any man. Also, like any other man, Jesus has a human body and a human soul. Although Jesus is true man, He was still free from all sin, both original and personal, because He is also true God—and God can't sin.

#34 How many Persons are there in Jesus Christ?

There is only one Person in Jesus Christ. He is the second Person of the Blessed Trinity. That means His Person is divine—God Himself.

#35 How many natures are there in Jesus Christ?

There are two natures in Jesus Christ. One of His natures is divine, the other is human.

It's important a student grasp the differences between Jesus' Personhood and His natures. This is because a good understanding now will save the student some confusion and you a lot of headaches as potential questions come later. So if need be, spend time making this very clear. The next question and answer may help.

#36 If Jesus possesses a human nature, how is it that we can call Mary the Mother of God?

Did your mother give birth to a person or a nature? She

gave birth to a person, of course. (A nature is merely something possessed by a person.) Since Jesus is a divine Person, the second Person of the Blessed Trinity, she conceived and gave birth to the second person of God. This makes her the Mother of God. Mary's divine motherhood is the greatest privilege ever given to a human person (cf. Luke 1:43)

#37 Was the Son of God always man?

No, He was not. He became man at the Incarnation when He united a human nature to His divine nature (called the *hypostatic union*). The Son of God is eternal; He has always existed. Jesus Christ, as God *and* man, has only existed for 2,000 years.

FIVE

THIRD ARTICLE OF THE CREED

"Conceived by the Holy Spirit, born of the Virgin Mary."

Son of God and Son of Mary

#38 When did the Incarnation take place?

The Incarnation took place on the day the Son of God was conceived in the womb of the Virgin Mary. We call this event the Annunciation, because the archangel appeared to Mary to announce to her the opportunity to become the Mother of God by offering her this special privilege.

#39 Who is the father of Jesus Christ?

The only true father of Jesus Christ is God the Father. St. Joseph was Jesus' foster father and the husband of the Blessed Virgin Mary. St. Joseph loved and cared for Jesus as any father would do, but God is His true Father.

#40 When and where was Jesus Christ born?

Jesus Christ was born in Bethlehem 2,000 years ago in a small cave, or grotto, where animals are fed. Bethlehem means "house of bread" and a manger (from the French verb "to eat"), where the Christ child was laid, was used to hold food for the animals.

The above has great significance for the Church's teaching on the Eucharist later.

It's important to realize that Jesus could have been born under any circumstances He chose. Because He is God and King of the universe, Jesus deserved to be born into wealth and royal splendor; however, He chose to be born poor. He chose this because He wanted to teach us to be detached from earthly goods and to concentrate on the riches of heaven. It isn't at all wrong to have wealth and possessions. What is wrong is to care more for them than the things of God.

THE BLESSED VIRGIN MARY

#41 Was Mary always a virgin?

Yes. Mary was a virgin before, during, and after the birth of Christ. This is called the perpetual virginity of Mary.

As odd as it might seem, in the hundreds of students I've had, I don't recall one ever questioning this. That's not to say you won't be questioned on it, as I know some of my godchildren have been questioned while doing this. So I suggest you brush up on the apologetic for this one.

#42 If Mary was perpetually virgin, why is it that the Bible speaks of the "brethren of the Lord"?

I added this question the very first year I began doing this, as every single student I had asked this question themselves before I added it.

The word "brother" in itself proves nothing, as it had a very wide meaning among the Jews. It was used in the Old Testament for relatives in general (Job 42:11; 19:1314), nephews (Genesis 29:15-16), distant cousins (Leviticus 10:4), and first cousins (I Chronicles 23:21). Besides, there is no word in Hebrew for cousin, so that Old Testament writers were forced to use the word "ah," brother, to describe different degrees of kindred. For example, Jacob, speaking of his cousin Rachel, calls himself her father's brother, rather than style himself the son of her father's sister, the only way he could describe the relationship in Hebrew (Genesis 29:12). It is certain, then, that if Jesus had cousins, especially if they were born of the same mother, they had to be called His brother in the Aramaic tongue. Therefore, the phrase "brethren of the Lord" in no way threatens the doctrine of the perpetual virginity.

#43 Why is Mary the Mother of God?

The Bible plainly declares in many passages that the Blessed Virgin Mary is the Mother of God. The angel Gabriel said to Mary: "And behold you shall conceive in your womb, and bear a son, and you shall call his name Jesus... The Holy Spirit will come upon you, and the power of the Most High will overshadow you; therefore, the child to be born will be called holy, *the Son of God*" (Luke 1:31, 35). The saintly Elizabeth greeted Mary with these words: "Whence is this to me that the *mother of my Lord* shall come to me?" (Luke 1:43) St. Paul says that, *"God sent his son, born of a woman"* (Galatians 4:4, cf. Romans 1:3-4).

The belief was so firmly accepted as divinely revealed that the Council of Ephesus (A.D. 431) made it the standard of orthodoxy.

#44 Why is Mary the Mother of the Church?

The Church is the Mystical Body of Christ; we are its members and He is its head (cf. Romans 12:4; I Corinthians 12:12; Ephesians 1:22-23, 5:23; Colossians 1:18). By the mere fact that the Church is a divine organism, and that a mother cannot give birth to a head without giving birth to the whole body, Mary is the Mother of the Church.

Because Jesus is God, all the events associated with His crucifixion, particularly the words He spoke, were of great significance to all men of all times in all places. "When Jesus saw his mother, and the disciple whom he loved standing near, he said to his mother, 'Woman, behold your son!' Then he said to the disciple, 'Behold your mother!'" (John 19:26-28) Since these words were intended universally, John was representing the Church while Mary was who she is—the Mother of God. It was at this moment that our Savior gave Mary as the Mother of the Church.

#45 Does devotion to Mary diminish our devotion to Christ?

Certainly not! Indeed, devotion to Mary has quite the opposite effect. No man is ever honored by failing to honor his mother. In honoring Mary we imitate Jesus Christ, who loved her as a mother. We pray to her so that she will help us to know her Son, lead us to Him, and help all mankind to accept Him.

#46 Did Jesus always know that He was God?

Yes. How can an infinite God ever not know He is God? Even though Jesus has two natures, He is only one Person— the second Person of the Blessed Trinity, the Son of God. Because of this, Jesus knew He was God even while he was a zygote in Mary's womb.

#47 Did Jesus know all things; that is, the past, present, and future?

Again, Jesus is an infinite God. From the moment of the Incarnation and throughout His life He knew all things. There is nothing He did not know. Some people argue that Jesus only came to gradually know who He was, but that isn't at all logical, reasonable, or possible.

#48 Did Jesus say that He was God?

He made this claim repeatedly (cf. John 8:58, *et alia*).

#49 Did Jesus prove He was God?

Yes. Jesus proved He was God by the miracles He worked through His own power (cf. John 11:1-44), by His prophecies (cf. Matthew 17:23), by His holiness of life, and by His sublime teachings. The crowning testimony of His divinity was that He rose from the dead by His own power.

SIX

FOURTH ARTICLE OF THE CREED

"Suffered under Pontius Pilate, was crucified, died and was buried."

#50 What do we mean when we call Jesus Christ our Redeemer?

To say that He is our Redeemer is to say that He offered Himself to God the Father in sacrifice, shedding all His blood for the forgiveness of our sins. For love of us, Jesus suffered betrayal by one of his close friends (Matthew 26:20-25, 47-50), suffered an agony of spirit (Luke 22: 39-44), was falsely accused by the very people He loved and came to save (Matthew 27:15-23), was scourged and mockingly crowned with thorns (Matthew 27:27-30), was forced to carry a heavy cross through the streets of Jerusalem (Matthew 27:31), and was finally crucified by having nails driven through His flesh and died with the humiliation of being stripped naked (Matthew 27:35-36).

#51 When and where did Christ die?

Jesus was executed on Good Friday, outside Jerusalem on a hill called Golgotha, a Hebrew name meaning "place of the skulls." The same hill was called in Greek, Calvary. We know this to be true from the Gospels, and from various historians of that time. In fact, St. John the Evangelist, who wrote the last Gospel, was present at Jesus' crucifixion.

#52 Did Jesus suffer and die as God or as man?

Jesus suffered and died in His human nature, because as God He could neither suffer nor die. It is important to note that Jesus died just like every man, as His human soul separated from His human body. However, His divine nature remained united to His body and His soul.

#53 Did Jesus <u>have</u> to suffer and die for our sins?

No, nothing compelled Jesus to suffer and die. He did so of His own free will for love of us (John 10:17-18). Because Jesus is God the Son, He is infinite. This means that all His sufferings have infinite value. The slightest suffering of God the Son (diaper rash as an infant? a scraped knee as a toddler?) could have been accepted by God the Father as adequate for the redemption of all mankind. However, Jesus chose to suffer the immense pains of His passion and death because He wanted to make full reparation to the Father, teach us how evil sin is, and show us the depth of His love for us.

SEVEN

FIFTH ARTICLE OF THE CREED

"He descended into hell, the third day he rose again from the dead."

Christ's Descent and Resurrection

#54 What does "He descended into hell" mean?

When we say that Jesus descended into hell we mean that after His death on the cross, while His body remained in the tomb, Jesus' soul descended into the "lower parts of the earth" (Ephesians 4:9). Since the gates of heaven were closed with Adam's original sin, and could not be reopened until the Redemption, the patriarchs and other just of the Old Testament (i.e., Abraham, Isaac, Jacob, Moses, David, *et cetera*) who were not condemned to the hell of eternal punishment were sent to the so-called vestibule of hell, what tradition agrees to call the *limbo of the Fathers*.

#55 Why did Christ descend to the dead?

He descended into the abode of the dead to show Himself to the souls of the just who were waiting for their redemption. He told them that their time of waiting was over and the Redemption had been accomplished.

The doctrine of Christ's descent to the dead, which was defined by the Fourth Lateran Council, is explicitly taught in the Bible. "But God has raised him up, having loosed the sorrows of hell, because it was not possible that he should be held fast by it" (Acts 2:24; cf. 31). "Now this, he ascended, what does it mean but that he also first descended into the lower parts of the earth?" (Ephesians 4:9) "In which also he went and preached to those spirits that were in prison" (I Peter 3:19).

In the New Testament, Christ Himself refers by various names and figures to the place or state which Catholic tradition has agreed to call the limbo of the Fathers. In Matthew 8:11 it is spoken of under the figure of a banquet or in Matthew 25:10 under the figure of a marriage feast. He also calls it "Abraham's bosom" in His parable of Lazarus and Dives (Luke 16:22), and "paradise" when addressing the penitent thief on the cross (Luke 23:43).

I often point out here [when I think the student needs or can handle it] that the parable of Lazarus and Dives may not have been a parable at all. This is merely my theory/opinion, as I've never read an official commentary on this. There are two reasons why I theorize this: 1) this is the only parable recorded in Scripture where Jesus used an actual person's name, and 2) Lazarus was raised from the dead by Jesus [John 11:1-44]. The reason I relate this is that students seem to better grasp the concept of the limbo of the Fathers when I do.

#56 What do we mean when we say that on the third day Jesus rose from the dead?

This means that on the third day Jesus reunited His human soul with His human body and rose from the dead, as He had predicted (cf. Matthew 17:23). We know that Jesus truly rose from the dead because this historical fact was witnessed by hundreds of Christ's followers and recorded in the Bible.

The most telling evidence of Christ's resurrection is the apostles themselves. First of all, Christ's resurrection was the central theme of their preaching. They preached His resurrection as proof of His divinity.

Secondly, the resurrection is proved by the apostles' lives and deaths. All but one of the apostles was martyred. At any given point, the denial of Christ's resurrection would have spared them horrible deaths. Besides, no reasonable person is willing to die for a lie. If the apostles had made up the story of Christ's resurrection, it is reasonable that at least one of them would have admitted the resurrection was a lie in order to save his own life. The fact is, none of them did. They all had seen Him, touched Him, spoken with Him, and died for that truth.

Various villages, towns and cities claim to possess the remains of nearly every person mentioned in the New Testament. But no one claims the remains of Jesus and His mother Mary. If Jesus had not resurrected from the dead, surely at least one location would boast possession of His remains.

#57 What did Jesus do after His resurrection?

Jesus remained on earth for forty days after His resurrection to prove that He had truly risen and to complete the teaching of His apostles.

#58 Why is Christ's resurrection important?

The resurrection is important because it proves He is God. Since He proved that He is God, we are obliged to obey all He has commanded us through His Church.

Another reason the resurrection is important is because of the way it inspires us. The resurrection strengthens our faith and gives us courage to suffer and serve for the love of Him. It is this way that we can one day join Him in heaven.

EIGHT

SIXTH ARTICLE OF THE CREED

"He ascended into heaven, and sits at the right hand of God, the Father Almighty."

The Ascension

#59 What do we mean by the words, "He ascended into heaven"?

By this we mean that forty days after His resurrection, in the presence of many of His followers, Jesus ascended into heaven of His own power. It was not merely a spiritual ascension, but He actually ascended body and soul (Acts 1:9-11).

#60 Why did Jesus ascend into heaven?

Jesus ascended into heaven to fulfill the promises He had made: to prepare a place for us (John 14:3); to be our mediator with God the Father (Hebrews 9:24); to send the Holy Spirit to the apostles (John 16:7).

#61 Did Jesus ascend into heaven alone?

No. Although they were not visible to those who

witnessed the Ascension, the souls of the just who were in the limbo of the Fathers accompanied Him to heaven.

#62 What does "sits at the right hand of God the Father Almighty" mean?

Since God the Father is pure spirit, we know that this phrase is symbolic rather than literal. It means that, as God, Jesus has the same power as God the Father, and that as man, He is King over all creation.

#63 Is Jesus now only in heaven?

Of course not! Because He is God, Jesus is most certainly everywhere (omnipresent). As the God-man, Jesus has ascended into heaven to await His second coming, and He is present for our love, worship, and adoration in millions of tabernacles throughout the world in the Most Holy Eucharist.

NINE

SEVENTH ARTICLE OF THE CREED

"From thence He shall come to judge the living and the dead."

Judgment

#64 What does "from thence He shall come to judge the living and the dead" mean?

This phrase refers to Christ's second coming (Acts 1:11). At the time appointed by God the Father, Jesus will return to earth to judge all people who have ever lived. For some this will be the most glorious and happy day they have ever known. For others it will be the most terrible day of their pitiful existence.

#65 How many judgments are there?

There are two judgments. One takes place immediately after death, and it's called the particular judgment. The other takes place at the end of time, and it's called the general judgment.

The General Judgment

#66 Why will there be a general judgment?

God is both perfectly just and perfectly merciful, and all mankind has the right to see the perfection of His justice and mercy. All will see that He was right in rewarding those who trusted in His infinite goodness. Conversely, we will see how He was just in punishing those who rejected Him with their sins and refused to repent.

The same identical eternal destiny will be pronounced in the general judgment that was pronounced in the particular judgment. There are no second chances after death, so it is to our benefit to do as God asks now. **Remember: Throughout all eternity you will be reminded of the words you have read here! It can be to your eternal joy or your eternal torment.**

#67 On what will we be judged in the general judgment?

In all of the Bible there is only one time that Jesus gives us the criteria by which we will all be judged at the general judgment. These criteria are found in Matthew 25:34-46.

Jesus gives us six things on which we will be judged:

1. feeding the hungry
2. giving drink to the thirsty
3. sheltering the homeless
4. clothing the naked
5. visiting the sick
6. visiting the imprisoned

He tells us we are (quite literally, the Church believes) treating Him however we treat others in these circumstances. But don't make the mistake of thinking helping people with these needs alone will save you. It's important to note there is a thin line between secular humanistic philanthropy and Christian humanism in these things. If you are meeting the needs of others for any reason besides love of Jesus alone, you may very well hear the words, "Depart from me, you cursed, into the eternal fire prepared for the devil and his angels..." (Matthew 25:41). Think about it.

The Particular Judgment

#68 On what will we be judged in the particular judgment?

Christ's judgment of us will be very exacting. Each individual soul will be judged on the good and evil we have done—every thought, desire word, action, and (my personal favorite) omission—from the time we reached the use of reason; i.e., when we were old enough to know the difference between right and wrong—about age seven.

Once each soul is judged, the soul will either be rewarded with eternal life in heaven, punished in purgatory until cleansed perfectly for heaven, or condemned to eternal damnation in hell. The reward or punishment deserved by each soul will be carried into effect immediately after this particular judgment.

TEN

EIGHTH ARTICLE OF THE CREED

"I believe in the Holy Spirit."

The Divinity of the Holy Spirit

#69 Who is the Holy Spirit?

The Holy Spirit is the third Person of the Blessed Trinity, and He proceeds eternally from the Father and the Son. The Holy Spirit is indeed God, completely equal to the Father and the Son. Like the Father and the Son, the Holy Spirit is almighty, eternal, and infinite.

#70 How do we know about the Holy Spirit?

We learned about the Holy Spirit via Divine Revelation from Jesus Christ, who placed Him on an equal level with the Father and the Son.

#71 Are there other names for the Holy Spirit?

Yes, there are many other names. He is called Advocate, Sanctifier, Spirit of Truth, Soul of the Church, Paraclete, Soul of My Soul, and Delightful Guest to name a few.

The Holy Spirit and the Apostles

#72 When did Jesus promise to send the Holy Spirit?

He made the promise on numerous occasions. See Luke 24:49, John 14:26, John 15:26, Acts 1:8, *et alia*.

#73 When did the Holy Spirit come upon the apostles in a visible way?

The Holy Spirit first manifested Himself in a visible way as tongues of fire on the first Christian Pentecost Sunday. Through this manifestation of the Holy Spirit, the apostles received the light to understand all that Jesus taught them. This new light, which is the power of the Holy Spirit, gave the apostles the zeal to preach what Jesus taught without fear.

#74 What is the role of the Holy Spirit in the Church?

The Holy Spirit is the soul of the Church, making her holy by the grace of Jesus Christ. The Holy Spirit enables the Church to teach all that Jesus taught without the possibility of error (this is called infallibility). Finally, He transforms the members of the Church into witnesses for Christ. The Holy Spirit was sent by the Father and the Son to live in the Church until the end of time.

#75 What is the role of the Holy Spirit in our lives?

Provided we are in a state of grace, the Holy Spirit dwells in our souls to make us holy with sanctifying grace—hence the reason He is sometimes called Soul of My Soul. He enlightens our minds to know God, strengthens our wills to carry out God's will, and sets our hearts on fire to love God and our neighbor.

We should practice devotion to the Holy Spirit by praying to Him and asking Him to teach us to respond eagerly to His inspirations.

ELEVEN

NINTH ARTICLE OF THE CREED

"I believe in the holy Catholic Church, the communion of saints."

> *There are three places in the catechism when you're likely to see your non-Catholic student convert. The first place is when presenting arguments for the existence of God. This is the second place you're likely to see them convert. Once Jesus Christ's divinity is established, when you prove that He founded the Catholic Church, you'll find students often feel compelled to become Catholic at this point.*

The Visible Church

#76 What is the Catholic Church?

The Church is the society of the baptized faithful who

believe the same faith, receive the same sacraments, and obey the pope, who is the successor of St. Peter. She is also the communion of life, charity and truth and is used by Christ to continue His work of redemption in the world until the end of time.

#77 Who founded the Catholic Church?

Jesus Christ founded the Catholic Church. He brought it into being, structured it, and passed on to it His own mission to continue His work of redemption.

#78 How did Jesus found the Catholic Church?

Jesus founded the Catholic Church on St. Peter. He set Peter as its rock and foundation, and to him alone did Jesus give in a special way the powers of binding and loosing everything on earth, of strengthening his brethren, and feeding the whole flock (Matthew 16:18-19; Luke 22:31; John 21:15-17).

#79 Who is the head of the Catholic Church?

Jesus is the head of all the Catholic Church. But the pope, who is the successor of St. Peter, is the head of the Catholic Church on earth.

#80 Is there any biblical evidence that Jesus made Peter the first pope?

Yes, the biblical evidence is overwhelming. Following the logical presentation of Karl Keating in his classical work *Catholicism and Fundamentalism*,[1] we find the evidence to be irrefutable.

Keating notes first that St. Peter was almost always named first in the Gospels' listings of the apostles (Matthew 10:1-4; Mark 3:16-19; Luke 6:14-16; Acts 1:13), and that sometimes the apostles were referred to only as "Peter and those who were with him" (Luke 9:32). He points out that

Peter was the first of the apostles to preach, the first to perform a healing miracle, and the one to whom the revelation came that Christianity was for Gentiles as well as Jews (Acts 2:14-40, 3:6-7, 10:46-48).

Keating goes on to tell us that "Peter's preeminent position among the apostles was symbolized at the very beginning of his relationship with Christ, although the implications were only slowly unfolded. At their first meeting, Christ told Simon that his name would thereafter be Peter, which translates as Rock (John 1:42). The startling thing was that in the Old Testament only God was called a rock. The word was never used as a proper name for a man. If one were to turn to a companion and say, 'From now on your name is Asparagus', people would wonder. Why Asparagus? What is the meaning of it? Indeed, why Peter for Simon the fisherman? Why give him as a name a word only used for God before this moment?

"Christ was not given to meaningless gestures, and neither were the Jews as a whole when it came to names. Giving a new name meant that the status of the person was changed, as when Abram was changed to Abraham (Genesis 17:5); Jacob to Israel (Genesis 32:28); Eliacim to Joakim (2Kings 23:34); and Daniel, Ananias, Misael, and Azarias to Baltassar, Sidrach, Misach, and Abednago (Daniel 1:6-8). But no Jew had ever been called Rock because that was reserved for God. The Jews would give other names taken from nature, such as Barach (which means lightening; Jos 19:45), Deborah (bee; Genesis 35:8), and Rachel (ewe; Genesis 29:16), but not Rock. In the New Testament James and John were surnamed Boanerges, Sons of Thunder, by Christ (Mark 3:17), but that was never regularly used in place of their original names. Simon's new name supplanted the old."[2]

St. Peter's name has been firmly established by Christ as a name synonymous with God. Throughout Jesus' and Peter's relationship the reason became gradually clearer, but it becomes crystal clear in Matthew 16:17-19. Immediately after Peter proclaims Christ's divinity, Jesus says, "Blessed are you, Simon Bar-Jona! For flesh and blood has not revealed this to you, but my Father who is in heaven. And I tell you, you are Peter, and on this rock I will build my church, and the powers of death[3] shall not prevail against it. I will give you the keys of the kingdom of heaven, and whatever you bind on earth shall be bound in heaven, and whatever you loose on earth will be loosed in heaven."

This passage seems obvious to most readers. As Keating points out, the verse could be re-written as: "You are Rock, and on this rock I will build my church".[4] It makes perfect sense that Jesus is here giving St. Peter supreme authority; however, those who desire to debunk the papacy prefer to claim that the rock refers to Christ instead of Peter.

To settle this objection, we turn once more to Keating: "According to the rules of grammar, the phrase 'this rock' must relate to the closest noun. Peter's profession of faith ('Thou art the Christ, the Son of the living God') is two verses earlier, while his name, a proper noun, is in the immediately preceding clause. As an analogy, consider this artificial sentence: 'I have a car and a truck and it is blue.' Which is blue? The truck, because that is the noun closest to the pronoun 'it'. This identification would be even clearer if the reference to the car were two sentences earlier, as the reference to Peter's profession is two sentences earlier than the term rock."[5]

Not only is the reference to rock clear, but we see also that Jesus is giving Peter more authority than God had ever given any man, along with some specific promises. Immediately after stating that he will build the Church on Peter (the Rock), Jesus goes on to make a promise and explain why He will do this.

The promise is that "the power of death" (or the more common "gates of hell") will not defeat the Church built on Peter. This is a promise that the Church will not be destroyed by Christ's enemies, and that she will stand until the end of time. Consider this: numerous Roman emperors, Attila the Hun, Napoleon, Hitler, and many other mighty enemies of the Church have tried to destroy her, yet she continues to live while they are but dust and ashes. Indeed, there is not one nation on earth today that existed when the Church began, yet here she is, as youthful and vibrant as she was 2,000 years ago!

Next we find Jesus using the symbol of the keys. This symbol has always implied power and authority, and the giving of keys implies a transfer of that power and authority. This is not lost on us today. The owner of a business possesses both the keys to the business and the authority to run it. When he passes those keys to a new manager, he also passes over the power and authority.

Finally, there is what we call the power of binding and loosing. Fr. Bertrand Conway writes: "'Binding and loosing' among the Rabbis of our Lord's time meant to declare something 'prohibited' or 'permitted'. Here it plainly means that St. Peter, the Steward of the Lord's house, the Church, has all the rights and powers of a divinely appointed steward. He does not, like the Jewish Rabbis, declare probable, speculative opinions, but he has the right to teach and govern authoritatively, with the certainty of God's approval 'in heaven'... A law giving power is certainly implied by these words."[6]

#81 Who is the pope?

The pope is the visible head of the Church and the successor of St. Peter. He is the Vicar of Christ, and he possesses the power of jurisdiction over the universal Church in matters of faith, morals, discipline, and government.

#82 What is meant by the hierarchy of the Church?

According to the Vatican II document *Lumen Gentium*, "In order to shepherd the People of God and to increase its numbers without cease, Christ the Lord set up in His Church a variety of offices which aim at the good of the whole body. The holders of office, who are vested with a sacred power, are, in fact, dedicated to promoting the interests of their brethren, so that all who belong to the People of God... may attain to salvation."[7]

Now, these office holders are the Church's leaders in different levels of authority. They are, in the order of authority, first the pope, then the bishops (including cardinals and archbishops), priests (including monsignors), and deacons (including permanent and transitional).

#83 Who are the bishops?

The bishops are the successors of the apostles. They take the place of the apostles in the modern Church. Jesus made the bishops the authentic teachers of the faith, and only the pope's power is superior to theirs.

#84 Who are priests?

All baptized persons participate in the common priesthood of the faithful, but there is a difference in essence, and not merely degree, between the priesthood of the faithful and the priesthood of Holy Orders.

"In what sense? While the common priesthood of the faithful is exercised by the unfolding of baptismal grace—a life of faith, hope, and charity, a life according to the Spirit—the ministerial priesthood is at the service of the common priesthood. It is directed at the unfolding of the baptismal grace of all Christians. The ministerial priesthood is a means by which Christ unceasingly builds up and leads his Church. For this reason it is transmitted by its own sacrament, the sacrament of Holy Orders."[8]

The two most important responsibilities of a priest are to offer the Holy Sacrifice of the Mass, and to reconcile sinners to God by way of the sacrament of Penance. Priests are also collaborators with their bishop, and are subject to him.

#85 Who are deacons?

Deacon comes from a Greek word meaning *"kicking up dust,"* which gives us some idea of the busy life a deacon leads. Deacons are men who truly live their Catholic faith, and they are ready for every good work that leads to the salvation of souls. They are ordained for a ministry of service to the Church and Her faithful. Deacons are helpers of bishops and priests, and they obey the authority of bishops and priests by fulfilling the duties assigned to them.

There are two types of deacons: transitional and permanent.

Transitional deacons are men who are studying for the priesthood. They are usually ordained to the diaconate one year before being ordained to the priesthood.

Permanent deacons are men who serve the Church in the life-long capacity of the diaconate. Permanent deacons may be married, if their marriage took place prior to ordination. If a deacon's wife dies, the deacon cannot marry again.

#86 Who are religious?

Religious are men and women who live a consecrated life as members of religious orders, such as the Salesians,

Benedictines, Carmelites or Franciscans. They are neither clerical nor lay, except those who are also priests. They are called by God to live the evangelical counsels of poverty, chastity, and obedience. They renounce the world and dedicate themselves to life-long service to God and His Church. They imitate the poor, chaste, and obedient Christ, who founded the religious state.

#87 Who are the laity?

That would be all the rest of us. The laity are the baptized faithful who are neither bishops, priests, deacons, or religious. The laity possess the responsibility of aiding the bishops and priests in spreading and sharing the faith, insofar as their God-given talents permit. They are also subject to the pope, and the bishops who are in union with him, in matters of faith and morals.

The Church as Mystery

#88 When did the Church become known as Catholic?

Although the name Catholic is not applied to the Church in the Bible, Christ and the apostles had the concept of catholic in mind, as catholic comes from a Greek word (*katholikos*) meaning universal. The Catholic Church is certainly universal; that is, for all people of all times, and in all places.

St. Ignatius of Antioch (A.D. 107) writes in his *Letter to the Smyrnæans*:

Where the bishop is, there let the multitude of believers be; even as where Jesus Christ is, there is the Catholic Church.[9]

Notice that St. Ignatius didn't write of the Catholic

Church as if he were giving it a new name, but rather as though the name had long been in use and his readers would recognize it. It's reasonably safe to assume, then, that the Church was probably called Catholic during the latter part of the first century. Indeed, it is likely that St. John the Apostle (who was a friend of St. Polycarp, who was a friend of St. Ignatius) had heard the Church called by the name Catholic and had done so himself, since he died around the year A.D. 100.

#89 Are there other names for the Catholic Church?

Yes, the Catholic Church has many other names. Among them are the scripturally based names of The Way, the Bride of Christ, the Kingdom of Heaven, and the Body of Christ.

#90 Why is the Church called the Body of Christ?

St. Paul refers to the Church as the Body of Christ repeatedly (cf. I Corinthians 12:12), but in order to understand why he does so, as well as its significance, we need to focus on Paul's own conversion (Acts 9:1-6).

St. Paul was a Pharisee and a persecutor of Christians. At the time of his conversion, he was on his way to Damascus to arrest Christians when Jesus appeared to him in His glorified state.

"Now as he journeyed he approached Damascus, and suddenly a light from heaven flashed about him. And he fell to the ground and heard a voice saying to him, 'Saul, Saul, why do you persecute me?' And he said, 'Who are you, Lord?' And he said, 'I am Jesus, whom you are persecuting.'" (Acts 9:3-5)

This encounter with Jesus apparently formed Paul's

theology on the Church. Paul saw the Church as divinely instituted, with Jesus as its head and we as its members. Indeed, Paul saw that Jesus and His Church are one and the same! Notice that Jesus didn't ask "Why do you persecute my followers?" or "Why do you persecute my Church?" He asked, "Why do you persecute *Me?*"

Jesus had ascended to heaven a long time before Paul met Him on the road to Damascus, so Paul could not have been persecuting Jesus in the ordinary sense. The persecution was of His followers. But that isn't what Jesus says. Christ's words are clearly indicative that *to persecute His followers is to persecute Him.* This is why Paul taught that we are the members of the Body of Christ—the Church— and He is its head. You can't attack any one part of a body without the entire body suffering. Paul understood that Jesus and His Church are one.

#91 Who is the soul of the Church?

The Church is the Body of Christ. For a body to live— and the Church is a living, breathing body—it must have a soul. The Holy Spirit, then, is the soul of the Church. He remains with the disciples of Christ for all times (cf. John 14:16); He leads them to all truth (cf. John 16:13); He lives in them as in a temple (cf. I Corinthians 3:16; 6:19); He helps to preserve the deposit of faith entrusted to the Church (cf. II Timothy 1:14); He directs the Church authorities in their activity (cf. Acts 15:28).

The Church's Mission

#92 What mission did Jesus Christ give His Church?

Jesus gave His Church His own mission. He willed that

the successors of St. Peter and the other apostles—that is, the pope and the bishops—should preach His Gospel faithfully, administer the sacraments, and shepherd His people with love.

The mission of Christ is not left solely to the pope, bishops, priests and deacons. Although the laity can't perform those functions that are specific to possessors of Holy Orders, we are still obliged to help bring souls into the Church as the Holy Spirit gives us aid. Since the laity *are* the Church, we must participate in the Church's mission. "As the 'convocation' of all men for salvation, the Church in her very nature is missionary, sent by Christ to all nations to make disciples of them".[10]

#93 From where does the Church draw her teachings?

All of the Church's teachings are drawn from Divine Revelation.

#94 What is Divine Revelation?

Divine Revelation is what God has spoken to us about Himself, the purpose of our life, and His plan for our salvation. He spoke to us first through the prophets of the Old Testament, then through His Son. Jesus gave the totality of Divine Revelation to His apostles, who continue to this day (through their successors, the bishops) to teach all that Jesus had taught them. Thus Divine Revelation ended with the death of the last apostle, St. John. The Church does not and cannot accept a new public revelation as pertaining to the divine deposit of faith.

#95 Where do we find Divine Revelation?

We find Divine Revelation in Sacred Scripture and Sacred (or Apostolic) Tradition.

#96 What is Sacred Tradition?

Due to the common usage of "tradition," students have a tendency to get confused here. Make sure there is no doubt in your mind that they perfectly understand what the Church means by Tradition. Tradition in this sense is not legend, mythological accounts, nor transitory customs that come and go. Tradition means the teachings and teaching authority of Jesus and the apostles.

Sacred Tradition is the word of God entrusted by Jesus Christ and the Holy Spirit to the apostles. The apostles, in turn, handed those sacred truths down to their successors (successive popes and bishops) in the fullness of purity (cf. John 21:25; II Timothy 1:13-14; II Thessalonians 2:15). The apostolic successors, by proclaiming the word of God handed down by word of mouth, preserve the truth faithfully, explain it, and make it more widely known.

The Fathers of Vatican II explained it more clearly when they wrote:

Hence there exist a close connection and communication between sacred Tradition and sacred Scripture. For both of them, flowing from the same divine wellspring, in a certain way merge into a unity and tend toward the same end. For sacred Scripture is the word of God inasmuch as it is consigned to writing under the inspiration of the divine Spirit. To the successors of the apostles, sacred Tradition hands on in its full purity God's word, which was entrusted to the apostles by Christ the Lord and the Holy Spirit. Thus, by the light of the Spirit of truth, these successors can in their preaching preserve this word of God faithfully, explain it, and make it more widely known. Consequently it is not from sacred Scripture alone that the Church draws her certainty about everything which has been revealed. Therefore both sacred Scripture and sacred Tradition are to be accepted and venerated with the same devotion and reverence.[11]

#97 What is the magisterium?

The magisterium is the living teaching authority of the Church. It is exercised when the pope, and the bishops in communion with him, authentically interpret the word of God, whether written or handed down, guarding it scrupulously and explaining it faithfully in accord with a divine commission and with the help of the Holy Spirit. Therefore, the fullness of divinely revealed truth comes to us by way of Sacred Tradition, Sacred Scripture, and the magisterium, which is the Church's teaching authority.

#98 How many forms of the magisterium are there?

There are two forms of the magisterium. The most common is the *ordinary* magisterium, which consists of the daily teachings of the pope and the bishops in communion with him.

The second form is the solemn or *extraordinary* magisterium, which consists of dogmatic definitions. It adds nothing to Divine Revelation, but only explains it and creates a new obligation to believe.

The Marks of the Church

#99 How can we know the Catholic Church is the Church founded by Christ?

There are roughly 40,000 Christian churches in America, and that alone tells us they can't all have been founded by Christ. We can we know the Catholic Church is the

Church founded by Christ because it is the only one with the characteristics (marks) Jesus gave to His Church; that is, He made it *one*, *holy*, *catholic* (universal) and *apostolic*. Other churches may have one or more of these marks, but only the Catholic Church has all four.

One

We say the Catholic Church is one because all its members profess the *same* faith, participate in the *same* sacraments, and obey the Roman Pontiff, the Vicar of Christ (Ephesians 4:4-5).

Jesus never spoke of a plurality of churches, but of "my Church," when He first promised Peter that He would make him the rock foundation of the Church He was about to establish (Matthew 16:18-19). The Church is always pictured in the New Testament as visibly one, presided over by Peter, who represents Christ, telling all men until the end of time to believe what He and His apostles taught, to obey His and their commands, and to worship as He ordered (cf. John 10:16).

Christ plainly foretold that the gates of hell would never prevail against His Church, and that He would provide for its unity by His own presence and the power of the Holy Spirit. It is granted that the private judgment of the individual naturally brings about disunion in the Church, but Christ ensured its unity by a special supernatural grace, which He asked of His Father the night before He died. His prayer for unity was:

"That they may all be one; even as thou, Father, art in me, that they may become perfectly one." (John 17:21-23)

St. Paul insists on the unity of the Church in all his epistles. Although he mentions individual local churches in certain cities (called dioceses today), he teaches clearly that they are parts of the one Church in every place (I Thessalonians 1:8; I Corinthians 1:2; II Corinthians 2:14). The Church is not a mere organization that may be divided and subdivided like a nation or a club, but a divine organism with its own inherent principle of life. It is Christ's Mystical Body, of which He is its head and all Christians are members. It is founded by *one* Lord, given life by *one* Spirit, entered into by *one* baptism, ruled by a *united* body of bishops, and having one aim, the glory of God and the salvation of men's souls (Romans 12:4-8; I Corinthians 12:12-27; Ephesians 4:3-16).

Holy

The Catholic Church is holy because Jesus, its Founder, and its Soul, the Holy Spirit, are holy. The Church teaches holy doctrine and gives its members the means of living holy lives, thus producing saints in every age (Ephesians 5:25-27). The founders of other churches—Luther, Calvin, Zwingli, Wesley, *et cetera*—were but men, and in no way remarkable for heroic virtue.

The Catholic Church is holy, because of her intimate union with Christ as His Bride (Ephesians 5:23-32) and His Mystical Body (I Corinthians 12:27; Ephesians 1:22; 4:12; 5:30). Catholics are a "chosen people" and a "holy nation" because they are branches of the true Vine, Jesus Christ (John 15:5). Although people outside her fold may, through invincible ignorance, be members of the Church in desire, and thus share in her divine life, their churches are "cast forth as a branch and withers" (John 15:6).

Catholic

The Catholic Church is catholic, or universal, because it is for all peoples of all times, because all mankind is called by the grace of God to salvation (Mark 16:15). The Catholic Church alone is universal in time, doctrine, and extent. She has existed in perfect continuity from the time of Christ, and she will last until His second coming. She teaches all His Gospel, and administers all His divine means of salvation. She is not confined to any particular region or nation, but is widespread among all the nations of the world. Indeed, until the year 1517, there was no other Christian religion beside the Catholic Church. All others are merely shoddy imitations of the real thing.

Apostolic

To say the Church is apostolic implies that the True Church is the Church which Christ commissioned His apostles to establish under the supremacy of St. Peter. The True Church must trace its origin in unbroken line to Jesus and His apostles. Before giving His divine commission to the apostles, Christ insists upon His divine commission from His Father: "As the Father has sent me, even so I send you" (John 20:21).

The only Church that can rightly claim its origin is not due to a break with the past is the Catholic Church. The European continental Protestants broke with the apostolic Church at the time of Luther's revolt (1517-1520), and the English Protestants (1559), when King Henry VIII made Parker the first Protestant Archbishop of Canterbury.

When the early Catholics wished to use a most convincing argument to prove the True Church, they always appealed to the fact of its apostolic origin. We find them compiling authentic lists of legitimate bishops with regard to the Apostolic See of Rome. As early as the second century we find the Syrian Hegesippus and the Greek Irenaeus, Bishop of Lyons, maintaining that the source and standard of the faith is the apostolic Tradition, handed down in an unbroken succession of bishops.

But since it would be very long in such a volume as this to count up the successions [i.e., series of bishops] in all the churches, we confound all those who in any way, whether through self-pleasing or vainglory, or through blindness or evil opinion, gather together otherwise than they ought, by pointing out the tradition arrived from the apostles of the greatest, most ancient, and universally known Church, founded and established by the two most glorious apostles, Peter and Paul, and also the faith declared to men which through the succession of bishops comes down to our times.[12]

Indefectibility and Infallibility

#100 What does indefectibility mean?

Indefectibility means that the Catholic Church will remain until the end of time, that it cannot be destroyed by any force in the world or from hell. Jesus said:

"And I say to thee, thou art Peter, and up on this rock I will build my church, and the gates of hell shall not prevail against it." (Matthew 16:18)

Since Christ promised that not even the gates of hell shall prevail against His Church, we have the steadfast assurance that the Church will continue until the end of the world.

#101 What does infallibility mean?

Infallibility means the impossibility of falling into error.

The perpetual assistance of Christ and the Holy Spirit guarantees the purity and integrity of the faith and morals taught by the Church.

Would a good God, "who desires all men to be saved and come to the knowledge of the truth" (I Timothy 2:4), fail to provide His revelation with a living, infallible teacher? Would a just God command us to believe under penalty of hell (Mark 16:16), and at the same time leave us to the mercy of every false teacher and lying teacher, preaching a Gospel opposed to His (II Peter 2:1; Galatians 1:8)?

No, the Church Christ founded is everywhere spoken of in the New Testament as a divine, infallible teaching authority.

#102 Is the pope infallible?

According to *Lumen Gentium* of the Second Vatican Council:

The Roman Pontiff, head of the college of bishops, enjoys this infallibility in virtue of his office, when, as supreme pastor and teacher of all the faithful—who confirms his brethren in the faith—he proclaims by a definitive act a doctrine pertaining to faith or morals.[13]

This does not mean the pope is infallible in all things. For example, the pope would not be exercising the charism of infallibility if he were to, say, predict the winner of the World Series. Karl Keating says that "the inability of the Church to teach error is infallibility, and it is a *negative* protection. It means what it is officially taught will not be wrong, not that the official teachers will have the wits about them to stand up and teach what is right when it needs to be taught."[14]

The pope is infallible only under the following conditions:

1. **When he speaks ex cathedra**, i.e., when he speaks officially as supreme pastor of the universal Church. He is not infallible when acting as supreme law maker, judge, or ruler. Nor is he infallible as a simple priest or as the local Bishop of Rome.

2. **When he defines a doctrine regarding faith and morals.** This means to settle a doctrine definitively, finally, and irrevocably. To omit defining a doctrine may cause great harm or be negligence on the part of the pope, but that would not nullify the charism of infallibility.

3. **When he speaks of faith and morals, which includes the whole content of Divine Revelation.** It follows that the pope is also infallible in judging doctrines and facts so intimately connected with revelation that they cannot be denied without endangering revelation itself.

4. **When he intends to bind the entire Church** and the intention to bind all the faithful must be clearly stated. If he fails to express the intention to bind the consciences of the faithful, it is not infallible.

#103 Are the bishops infallible?

Individually the bishops are not infallible. However, they do teach infallibly in an ecumenical council (such as Vatican II) when, with the approval of the pope, they set forth teachings of faith and morals to be held by the entire Church. The bishops can also teach infallibly when, in union with the pope, outside of an ecumenical council, they all teach the same doctrine of faith and morals.

#104 Does infallibility mean the pope can do no wrong?

No, infallibility does not mean that the pope cannot commit sin. This is called impeccability. He may commit sin like any other Catholic, and he is bound to seek forgiveness like any other Catholic through the sacrament of Penance. Infallibility is not a personal charism, but rather a divine and official charism, given by Christ to Peter and his successors to keep them from error in the defining the content of the deposit of faith.

#105 Why did Jesus make His Church infallible?

Jesus made the Church infallible so that she would not compromise with the ideas of changing times nor yield to pressures within or without, but would teach always and only the faith entrusted to her by her divine founder, who is Christ.

Almost without exception, other Christian religions have changed their theological views, particularly as regards morals. For instance, 50 or 60 years ago some Fundamentalist sects did not teach that the use of tobacco was wrong. Today, however, they teach that the use of tobacco, even in moderation, is sinful. Does that mean that a modern Fundamentalist's grandfather smoked and went to heaven, but the modern Fundamentalist will go to hell if he smokes? That seems to be the implication. The Catholic Church, on the other hand, teaches that using tobacco products in moderation is normally not sinful.

A more vivid example would be the events that have unfolded in Christendom since 1930. At one time, all

Christian religions taught that artificial contraception is a sin worthy of eternal punishment. In England, at the Lambeth Conference of 1930, the Bishops of the Anglican Church were under immense pressure to rule that artificial contraception is acceptable. Although those Protestant bishops admitted artificial contraception is wrong, they granted permission for its use by Anglican followers. Resultantly, the floodgate of permissiveness was opened. Today, the Catholic Church stands virtually alone in condemning the use of artificial contraception.

Jesus made His Church in infallible to protect the fullness of divinely revealed truth. Because Jesus, who is God, is the same yesterday, today, and forever (Hebrews 13:8), His moral laws and doctrines of faith must also remain the same.

#106 How should Catholics feel toward the Church?

Jesus called for unconditional obedience to the Church (Luke 10:16, Mark 16:16). Because of this, and the fact that Jesus and His Church are one, Catholics should allow themselves to be guided by the Church, assent to her teachings, love her, respect her priests and bishops, and pledge their fidelity to the supreme pontiff, who represents Jesus on earth.

#107 What is heresy?

Heresy is the deliberate denial of one or more truths of the Catholic faith. If a person intentionally holds to what is known to be heresy, that person risks eternal punishment. An example of this would be a direct denial of, say, the Real Presence, or for a Catholic to become a Baptist.

#108 What is schism?

Schism is the deliberate refusal of a Catholic to submit

to the authority of the pope. This, too, presents the risk of eternity separated from God. An example of this would be for a Catholic to become a member of the Eastern Orthodox Church.

#109 What is apostasy?

Apostasy is the complete rejection of one's Catholic faith. Like heresy and schism, the apostate risks and eternity in hell. An example of this would be for a Catholic to convert to Islam.

The Church and Non-Catholics

#110 Since Jesus Christ founded the Catholic Church to continue his mission of salvation, are all people obliged to it?

The Fathers of the Second Vatican Council explained it this way:

Basing itself on Scripture and Tradition, the Council teaches that the Church, a pilgrim now on earth, is necessary for salvation: The one Christ is the mediator and the way of salvation; he is present to us in his body which is the Church. He himself explicitly asserted the necessity of faith and Baptism [Mark 16:16], and thereby affirmed at the same time the necessity of the Church which men enter through Baptism as through a door. Hence they could not be saved who, knowing that the Catholic Church was founded as necessary by God through Christ, would refuse either to enter it or to remain in it.[15]

However, those same Council Fathers went on to say:

Those who, through no fault of their own, do not know the Gospel of Christ or his Church, but who nevertheless seek God with a sincere heart, and, moved by grace, try in their actions to do his will as they know it through the dictate of their conscience—those too may achieve eternal salvation.[16]

I follow this up by saying the following...

Let's say there's a little blue-haired lady down in Podunk, Arkansas, and she has never been out of the county her entire life. She's a member of the First Baptist Church of Podunk because her grandparents belonged to the group of founding families a hundred years ago. Her parents were married in this church, she was baptized here as a young girl, she married her husband here. Later she had her children all baptized here, and after they were grown she buried her husband from this church. Because she's never been out of Podunk, and since the town doesn't have a Catholic parish, the only things she knows about Catholicism are those things her pastors over the years have told her. Yet she lives her Baptist faith as best as she can.

Now, do you think God would send that sweet little old lady to hell just because she had no knowledge of the Catholic faith, or a way to get that knowledge? Of course not!

Or let's consider my little indigenous buddy, Mgawai. He lives in the deepest, most remote part of the jungle, and he worships Mgumba. Mgawai's never heard of Jesus Christ, much less the Catholic Church. But his worship of Mgumba is devout; Mgumba teaches Mgawai it's wrong to steal, wrong to lie, wrong to unjustly take an innocent life, wrong to have more than one spouse, et cetera. He knows Mgumba created all the world, and he knows He loves Mgawai.

In essence, Mgawai already worships God, but he calls God Mgumba. Do you think God will send little Mgawai to hell just because he knows nothing of Jesus Christ... despite that he's living better than most Christians? No!

#111 What is the difference between the Catholic Church and all other Christian churches?

Catholics and the members of other Christian churches are brothers who believe in Jesus Christ, are baptized, and possess in common many means of grace and elements of truth; however, our separated brethren are not yet blessed with the unity that Jesus Christ bestowed on his followers (John 17:20-21).

#112 May a Catholic belong to a secret society?

Catholics are discouraged from seeking membership in secret societies, and the Church forbids membership to any secret society that in any way plots against the Church or state. This means a Catholic may not become a member of the Masonic Order, or Freemasons.[17]

The Church and State

#113 What does the Catholic Church claim from the state?

The Catholic Church claims religious freedom, which

is necessary that she may be faithful to her divine commission.

#114 Should the state fear the Church?

The state should not fear the Church.

It is the duty of citizens to work with civil authority for building up society in a spirit of truth, justice, solidarity, and freedom.

However...

Citizens are obliged in conscience not to follow the directives of civil authorities when they are contrary to the demands of the moral order.[18]

The Communion of Saints

#115 What do we mean when we say, "I believe in the communion of saints?"

The communion of saints is the spiritual union which unites the Church Militant (the faithful on earth), the Church Suffering (the souls in purgatory), and the Church Victorious (the Saints in heaven) in one Mystical Body, the Church, and the participation of all in the one supernatural life. The saints, by their closeness to God, obtain from Him many graces and favors for the faithful on earth and the souls in purgatory; the faithful on earth, by their prayers and good works, honor and love the saints, and give relief to the suffering souls by their prayers and the Holy Sacrifice the Mass; the suffering souls in purgatory also pray for those still on earth.

TWELVE

TENTH ARTICLE OF THE CREED

"The forgiveness of sins."

This article lays a foundation for Christian morality, so it's vital you make everything you teach here as clear and precise as possible.

#116 What does "the forgiveness of sins" mean?

This means that in his infinite mercy Jesus Christ has given His Church the power to forgive all sins, no matter how serious they are or how often they have been committed, if the sinner is truly sorry (John 20:22-23).

#117 Doesn't Jesus speak of an unforgivable sin against the Holy Spirit (Matthew 12:31-32)?

No sin is unforgivable, either by God or the Church that forgives in God's name. God wills all men to be saved (I Timothy 2:4), and His mercy is infinite. Matthew 12:31-32 refers to the sinner who refuses to repent, despite the graces God gives him. Such a person does not actually receive God's pardon because he neither asks for it nor is willing to fulfill the conditions necessary to obtain it.

The sin mentioned by Christ is the willful rejection by the Pharisees of the miracles He performed as proof of His divine mission. Instead, they credited Christ's miracles to Satan. In other words, they were obstinate in their sin.

#118 What is actual (personal) sin?

Actual sin is any sin we commit ourselves by any free and willful thought, desire, word, action, or omission that is against the law of God.

#119 How many kinds of actual sin are there?

You can lighten things up and have a little fun right here. When I ask this question, I get a kick watching a mild panic come over the student; they think you're about to ask them to enumerate sins. They're relieved to hear the answer you give.

There are two kinds of actual sin; mortal (deadly) and venial. (I John 5: 16)

#120 What is a mortal sin?

A mortal sin is any serious offense against God's law (i.e., murder, masturbation, adultery, artificial contraception, fornication, etc.). It causes the soul to lose sanctifying grace, destroys the merit of all a person's good acts, and makes the person deserving of eternity in hell, unless the sinner repents.

#121 When is a sin mortal?

A sin is mortal when three conditions are present:

1. Serious matter (the thought, desire, word, action, or omission must be seriously wrong or thought to be seriously wrong).
2. Sufficient reflection (the person knows it is seriously wrong).
3. Full consent of a free will to doing what the person knows is seriously wrong.

All three of these conditions must be simultaneously present for a sin to be mortal.

#122 What is a venial sin?

A venial sin is a less serious offense against God. It does not deprive the soul of sanctifying grace, but it does weaken the will toward mortal sin. Venial sin does not make the sinner deserving of eternal punishment; however, because God is infinitely just, punishment is still exacted, either in this life or in purgatory.

#123 What makes a sin venial?

A sin is venial when it lacks one or more of the elements which constitute a mortal sin: serious matter, sufficient reflection, and full consent of a freely full will. If only one or two of these three conditions for a mortal sin is present, the sin is only venial.

Sources and Occasions of Sin

#124 What are the main sources of sin?

The main sources of sin are seven vices, called the capital sins: pride, covetousness, lust, anger, gluttony, envy, and sloth. They are called the capital sins because they are the chief source of actual sins. Of these, pride takes the first position.

#125 What is the source of all capital sins?

Original sin is the source of all the capital sins.

#126 What are occasions of sin?

Occasions of sin are persons, places, or things which lead one to sin. They are *near occasions* of sin when they will certainly, or almost certainly, lead a person to sin. They are *remote occasions* of sin when the danger of sinning is only slight.

#127 Are we obliged to avoid the occasions of sin?

We're obliged to avoid all near occasions of sin as far as possible. Here is a practical example.

Let's say Mike has confessed to his priest five weeks in a row that he's got drunk once. The wise priest sees an obvious problem, and he resolves to help Mike work it out. When Mike confesses drunkenness the sixth week in a row, Father asks him why this is happening. Mike says, "Well, Father, I stop off after work on payday to have one drink. But there are lots of bars on my way home, and I get good and thirsty after one drink, so I end up stopping at many of the bars before I get home."

Father instructs Mike to get a map of the city, and to highlight the various routes he can take home from work. Mike brings Father the map below. On it the "H" represents Mike's home, the "W" represents his place of work, and the "A" "B" and "C" represent the three possible routes home from work.

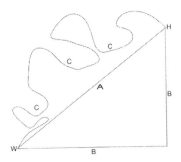

Father: Which route do you take home from work, Mike?

Mike: I take "A", Father. After all, it's the closest and quickest.

Father: Apparently not on Friday nights, Mike. What is "B" like? Are there many bars?

Mike: Not as many, Father, but uh...

Father: What is it, Mike?

Mike: Well, Father, all those places are where women stand up on a stage and...

Father: Oh! Well, we'll not have you driving down a lane like that! What's wrong with "C", Mike?

Mike: Aw, Father, that road will take me an extra 20 minutes each way.

Father: Which is better: an extra 20 minutes here, or eternity in hell?

Mike: Okay, Father. You've made your point.

For Mike, the route he took home from work on payday was a near occasional of sin. The "B" route represents a remote occasion of sin. The "C" route will clearly help Mike avoid the remote (route "B") and near (route "A") occasions of sin associated with the other two routes. Listening to his wise confessor's advice will be pleasing to God, and can save Mike from eternal punishment.

#128 What are temptations?

Temptations are inclinations to sin that come to us from the world, the flesh, and the devil. We can always resist temptations, but not by our own power alone. God gives us all the grace we need to resist temptation, so we should ask Him to do so with confidence (I Corinthians 10:13).

Situation Ethics and Fundamental Option

These two erroneous schools of thought [heresies] have crept into Catholic thinking and must be dealt with in today's culture and society.

#129 What is situation ethics?

Situation ethics contends that moral decisions should not be based on universal moral laws, but on the specific particular situation in which a person finds himself. Since this situation is unique and unrepeatable, the person's conscience alone is to determine the right moral decision, apart from any principle or law. The fundamental error of situation ethics is that it is incompatible with the fact that God gave us an objective moral norm to judge what is right and what is wrong: the ten Commandments. The Church has always taught that there are some acts which are intrinsically good and some which are intrinsically evil, apart from any circumstances.

An example of this would be for a married couple to use artificial contraception, because as newlyweds they are not yet financially capable of caring for children. Artificial contraception is always evil.

#130 What is fundamental option?

Fundamental option is the theory of those who hold of the person commits a mortal sin only when he has the intention of rejecting God. An example of this would be when a couple engages in premarital sex, believing themselves to be expressing love rather than rejecting God. However, the Church teaches that when a person knowingly and willfully does anything which is seriously against God's law, a mortal sin is always committed no matter the sinner's intention.

The Sacraments of Forgiveness

#131 How does the Church forgive sin?

Christ made His Church the "sacrament of salvation" and gave her two sacraments for the forgiveness of sins committed after Baptism: Penance and the Anointing of the Sick. These are called the sacrament of healing.

#132 What must we do to avoid sin?

To avoid sin we must pray constantly, receive the sacraments often, remember that God sees us, recall we are temples of the Holy Spirit, keep busy with work or legitimate recreation, promptly resist temptations, and avoid the near occasions of sin.

THIRTEEN

ELEVENTH ARTICLE OF THE CREED

"The resurrection of the body."

Bodily Resurrection

#133 What does the resurrection of the body mean?

It means that the bodies of all people—both good and evil—will rise from the dead at the end of the world and will be reunited to their souls for all eternity (I Corinthians 15:51-53).

#134 Why will our body rise?

It is natural to the human person to be a material body and a spiritual soul. The body participated with the soul in all the good and evil done in life, so it is only just that both body and soul should share in the eternal reward or punishment earned in life.

#135 Will each of us have our own body when we rise from the dead?

Yes, the body we will have at the resurrection is the

same body we had on earth. Assuming we are judged worthy of heaven, the only difference between our earthly body and resurrected body is that the latter will be in a glorified state; that is, it will be exceedingly beautiful and forever free from pain and death (I Corinthians 15:43-44). We know that the Blessed Virgin Mary was at least 50 years old at the end of her earthly life, yet visionaries invariably describe her as youthful and exceedingly beautiful.

#136 Has anyone already entered heaven with a glorified human body?

Yes, Jesus Christ is in heaven with His glorified body. Also, His Mother, the Blessed Virgin Mary, is living in heaven, body and soul. This is called the Assumption.

According to the Catechism of the Catholic Church:

The Immaculate Virgin, preserved free from all stain of original sin, when the course of her earthly life was finished, was taken up body and soul into heavenly glory, and exalted by the Lord as Queen over all things, so that she might be the more fully conformed to her Son, the Lord of lords and conqueror of sin and death. The assumption of the Blessed Virgin is a singular participation in her Son's Resurrection and an anticipation of the resurrection of other Christians.[1]

Reincarnation

#137 What is reincarnation?

Reincarnation is the false belief that the souls of the dead keep returning to earth in different forms or bodies. Various scriptural references show that reincarnation is not possible. Among the most striking is when Paul wrote that "it is appointed for men to die once, and after that comes judgment" (Hebrews 9:27).

FOURTEEN

TWELFTH ARTICLE OF THE CREED

"And life everlasting."

Eternal Life

#138 What is meant by life everlasting?

This refers to the eternal blissfulness of the saints in heaven, and the eternal torments of those damned to hell (cf. Matthew 25:34, 41).

#139 What is meant by the immortality of soul?

This means that the soul will never die, that it will live forever. The soul can either live eternally and heaven (usually after a period of purification in purgatory) or hell.

Hell

#140 What is hell?

Hell is a place of eternal punishment for those who refused to repent of their wicked ways during life. They will suffer forever with every sort of torment, with no relief. The worst of these torments will be the eternal separation from God (cf. Mark 9:48; Matthew 13:41-42).

#141 How can a loving God send anyone to hell?

In actuality, God does not send anyone to hell, but rather we send ourselves. He created us with free will, then gave us an objective set of more norms by which to live. He respects the free will He gave us. If we choose to ignore Him and abuse the gift of a free will by unrepentant mortal sin, then we choose hell.

Purgatory

It is very, very important you have a firm understanding of purgatory—the entire concept. Unless you do, you won't be able to properly teach it or answer questions about it. Why is an understanding of purgatory so important? A heretical Protestant doctrine has almost been universally accepted as true: That all "saved" souls go to heaven immediately after death. [These days it is generally accepted that both the "saved" and "unsaved" will go to heaven.]

This is a major heresy, and one that causes countless souls to languish in purgatory much longer than they need to, because there is no one praying or offering Masses for them. If nothing else motivates you to get this right, remember you (probably) will one day be suffering in purgatory.

I think this is so important that I recommend

you read the book Purgatory: Explained by the
Lives and Legends of the Saints, *by Fr. F. X.
Schouppe, S.J. This book—a classic—describes
God's justice in purgatory throughout the first half
of the book, and His mercy in the second half. It's a
remarkably astonishing book! I read it 25 years ago,
and it's still fresh in my mind.*

#142 What is purgatory?

"All who die in God's grace and friendship, but still
imperfectly purified, are indeed assured of their eternal
salvation; but after death they undergo purification, so as to
achieve the holiness necessary to enter the joy of heaven.
The Church gives the name Purgatory to this final purification of the elect, which is entirely different from the punishment of the damned."[1] It is in purgatory and that the last
vestiges of love of self are transformed into love for God.

Purgatory is a testimony to God's mercy and justice.
Because He is infinitely merciful, as well as an infinitely
just, purgatory is a necessity. If God were more merciful
than just, He would be imperfect. He is perfectly merciful,
but that mercy can be perfect only if it is balanced by His
perfect justice.

Although purgatory is not explicitly mentioned by that
name in the Bible, the concept of a place of purification is
certainly implied. Jesus said, "I tell you, *you will not get out*
till you have paid the very last penny" (Luke 12:59). Christ
mentions the sin for which "there is no forgiveness, either in
this world *or in the world to come*" (Matthew 12:32). This
implies that venial sins can be forgiven in the next world.
Where? Hell is eternal punishment. "Nothing unclean shall
enter heaven" (Revelation 21:27), and even venial sin

causes the soul to be unclean. The implication is clearly purgatory.

Paul tells us that at the day of judgment each man's work will be tried. This trial happens after death. What happens if a man's work fails the test? "He will be the loser; and yet he himself will be saved, though only as men are saved by passing through fire" (I Corinthians 3:15). Now this loss, this penalty, cannot refer to consignment to hell, since no one is saved there; and heaven cannot be meant, since there is no suffering ("fire") there. Purgatory alone explains this passage.[2]

The Church has always believed in purgatory. The Bible mentions the need to pray for the dead: "It is a holy and wholesome thought to pray for the dead, that they might be loosed from their sins" (II Maccabees 12:46). There are also inscriptions of prayers for the dead in the catacombs, where Christians stayed largely hidden during the great Roman persecutions of the first three centuries. Finally, we have the writings of the early Christians such as Tertullian (160-240), Cyprian (200-258), Cyril of Jerusalem (315-386), Ambrose (340-397), John Chrysostom (344-407), and Augustine (354-430) to tell us about purgatory and the need to pray for the dead.

I tell this story to drive home the point of God's justice and mercy...

Let's say you borrow your friend's car to run some errands because yours is in the shop. Your friend is happy to let you use his car, but he insists you have it back by three o'clock because he also has to be somewhere.

Your errands take longer than you'd planned

and you're afraid you're going to be late, so you drive more quickly than you ordinarily would. In your haste, you take a corner a little too quickly and a little too sharply, and you crease the car's fender on a corner fire hydrant.

When you pull into your friend's driveway, you immediately draw his attention to what you've done. You tell him, "I'm sorry I damaged your car. Will you forgive me?"

You friend is a good Catholic, so he responds, "Sure, I forgive you... now pay for my fender."

The damage has been done—a damage you're responsible for—and has to be paid for. That's only right and just. This sense of justice is one given to us all by God. If God authors this simple sense of justice in us, how much more exacting will the justice of an infinite God be?

When we sin against God, there has to be reparation—we have to make it right. We can make reparation for our venial sins and forgiven mortal sins in this life, or we can make reparation in purgatory.

#143 Will purgatory last forever?

No, purgatory will not last forever. After the general judgment there will be only heaven and hell.

Heaven

#144 What is heaven?

Heaven is a place of everlasting possession and vision of God (called the *beatific vision*), in which the souls of the just will be fulfilled with a complete happiness that is totally free from suffering for fear of loss (cf. I Corinthians 2:9; Romans 8:18; I John 3:2; Revelation 21:3-4).

#145 Who will be eternally rewarded in heaven?

The souls rewarded in heaven are those who did good works and died in a state of grace, and who are, after their purgatory, free from all venial sin and purified of all punishment due to sin (cf. Matthew 6:20; 16:27).

#146 What must we do to attain heaven?

To attain heaven we must fulfill the purpose for which God made us; that is, to know Him, to love Him, and to serve Him in this life. For those who are aware that the Catholic Church is the Church Christ founded, this means they must become Catholic and live in obedience to Christ and His Church, who has had Christ's mission and authority passed on to her.

FIFTEEN

DIVINE GRACE

God's Free Gift

Grace: What It Is, What It Does

#147 What is grace?

Grace is a supernatural (above nature = divine) gift which God freely gives us for our salvation. All grace comes to us through the merits of Christ's Passion—His suffering from Holy Thursday night until His death on the cross—and is offered to us by His Church.

To say that Grace is a supernatural gift implies two things. The first is that as a gift we have no right to it, but God grants Grace because He loves us. The second is that Grace has a supernatural purpose, which is the attainment of heaven.

#148 How many types of grace are there?

There are three primary types of grace. One type, sacramental grace, we will discuss when we study an overview of sacraments. The other two, sanctifying grace and actual grace, we will discuss now.

Sanctifying Grace

#149 What is sanctifying grace?

Simply stated, sanctifying grace is God's life in us (GLIU). It is a supernatural quality infused into our soul at Baptism. Sanctifying grace gives us a share in the divine life and allows us to become a temple of the Holy Spirit, God's friend, and an heir of heaven. It also makes possible the ability for us to merit heavenly rewards for our good actions (cf. I Corinthians 6:11; II Peter 1:4; I Corinthians 3:16; John 15:15; I John 3:1; Romans 8:16-17; Romans 2:6).

#150 Why is sanctifying grace also called habitual grace?

Because it inheres permanently in our soul, provided we are free of mortal sin.

#151 Is sanctifying grace necessary for our salvation?

Sanctifying grace is necessary for our salvation because it makes us pleasing to God, and this type of grace alone makes possible the attainment of heaven.

#152 What does it mean to be in a state of grace?

To be in a state of grace means to be in a state of friendship with God; that is, to have sanctifying grace in the soul and be worthy of heaven.

#153 Can sanctify in grace be lost?

Yes. We lose sanctifying grace each time we commit a mortal sin. One whose soul lacks sanctifying grace because of a mortal sin risks eternal damnation at death.

#154 Can sanctifying grace be recovered?

Yes. The ordinary means of recovering sanctifying grace

is by making a good confession and receiving absolution through the Sacrament of Penance.

#155 Can sanctifying grace be increased?

Certainly! And we should strive always for its increase, because increased sanctifying grace makes us closer to God. Sanctifying grace can be increased by good works, prayer, and devout reception of the sacraments, most especially the Holy Eucharist. Increasing sanctifying grace is how we journey on the road to holiness.

Other Divine Gifts

#156 Do we receive any other supernatural gifts along with sanctifying grace?

Absolutely! Along with sanctifying grace, God infuses into our soul the theological virtues of faith, hope, and charity (to be discussed in a later lesson), which makes us capable of performing ordinary acts of Christian virtue. God also infuses the gifts of the Holy Spirit, which allow us to respond easily and joyfully to actual graces and to perform heroic acts of virtue.

#157 What are the gifts of the Holy Spirit?

There are seven gifts of the Holy Spirit: wisdom, understanding, counsel, fortitude, knowledge, piety, and fear of the Lord. You can find them in I Corinthians 12.

Actual Grace

#158 What is actual grace?

Actual grace is a divine enlightenment of our mind and strengthening of our will to help us to choose what is good and avoid evil (cf. Psalm 32:8; Hebrews 13:20-21).

#159 Is actual grace necessary?

Yes. Without actual grace it is impossible for us to do anything that is pleasing to God. We are bombarded by actual grace every waking moment. We respond to God's actual grace every time we do good and avoid evil. By the mere fact that you are going through this, you are responding well to God's actual grace (cf. Philemon 2:13; John 15:5).

#160 Does God give sufficient grace to all?

Yes, God gives sufficient grace for the salvation of all. He gives enough grace for us to always keep His command-ments, and He gives enough grace for sinners to be converted (cf. Ezekiel 33:11).

#161 Can God's grace be resisted?

God gave all people a free will, and He respects the free will He gave us. God will never force Himself on us. We can reject God's grace, but by doing so we reject His love.

#162 Is there any way we can dispose ourselves to respond positively to actual grace?

To become attuned to actual grace we must become attuned to God. This is done by constant prayer.

SIXTEEN

THE SACRAMENTS IN GENERAL

An Overview

This overview is really what you'd call the "mechanics" of the sacraments. Sacramental theology is a theology all its own—it's very deep, complex, and fascinating. For this reason, it's important you don't take lightly teaching this part. If you get the mechanics right here, all the seven sacraments sort of fall into place—especially the Holy Eucharist and Penance.

Grace-Giving Signs

#163 What is a sacrament?

"The sacraments are perceptible signs (words and actions) accessible to our human nature. By the action of Christ and the power of the Holy Spirit they make present efficaciously the grace that they signify."[1]

#164 How many sacraments are there?

There are seven sacraments: Baptism, Confirmation, Holy Eucharist, Penance, Anointing of the Sick, Holy Orders, and Matrimony.

#165 Were all seven sacraments instituted by Christ?

Yes, all seven sacraments were instituted by Christ. As we shall soon see, there is ample scriptural evidence of this.

#166 Do all the sacraments give grace?

Provided they are received with the right disposition, which means with the intent to receive grace, all the sacraments give grace.

#167 Which graces do the sacraments give?

All of the sacraments give or increase sanctifying grace. They also give sacramental grace.

#168 What is sacramental grace?

Sacramental grace is the special grace proper to a particular sacrament which gives us the right to those actual graces that will help us attain the sacrament's purpose. For example, the sacramental grace of Matrimony helps us to live always in fidelity to our spouse, to raise our children well, and to help our spouse become holy.

Kinds of Sacraments

#169 How may the sacraments be grouped?

The sacraments may be divided into three groups. They are the sacraments of initiation, the sacraments of reconciliation, and the sacraments of vocation.

Encourage the student to learn these groups, as this will be the easiest way for most to memorize the seven sacraments.

#170 What are the sacraments of initiation?

The sacraments of initiation are Baptism, Confirmation, and Holy Eucharist. They are called sacraments of initiation because they are the sacraments through which we begin the Christian life.

#171 What are the sacraments of reconciliation?

The sacraments of reconciliation are Penance and Anointing of the Sick. They are called sacraments of reconciliation because they reconcile us to God. The primary work of the Anointing of the Sick is to bring spiritual healing to the soul and often also the natural healing of the body.

#172 What are the sacraments of vocation?

The sacraments of vocation are Holy Orders and Matrimony. They are called sacraments of vocation because the priestly state and the married state are life-long vocational commitments.

#173 Can some sacraments be received only once?

Yes. The sacraments of Baptism, Confirmation, and Holy Orders can be received only once because they place an indelible mark, called a character, on the soul. This character is eternally visible to God, his angels and saints, and the demons. For those who persevere and win the crown of eternal glory, these characters will forever edify the angels and saints in heaven, and glorify God. They also increase our capacity for joyfulness in heaven. For those who do not persevere, the demons will use these characters to add to the eternal punishment the damned deserve.

Elements of a Sacrament

#174 What constitutes a true sacrament?

Two elements are necessary to constitute a true sacrament. They are *matter* and *form*.

#175 What is matter?

Matter is some sensible, concrete thing or action. Examples would be the pouring of water or anointing with oil.

#176 What is form?

Form refers to the essential words used by the minister of a sacrament. For example, "I absolve you from your sins."

#177 Must the matter and form be united?

Yes, they must be united. The matter must be used at the same time that the words of the form are spoken, and both must be done by the same minister.

#178 Who is the minister of a sacrament?

The minister of a sacrament is a person who has received from Jesus the authority to act for Him in giving that particular sacrament.

#179 Does the effectiveness of a sacrament depend on the holiness of the minister?

---

*If the student appears astute enough, after reading the answer below, I explain first that the minister of a sacrament acts **in persona christi**; that is, the minister acts in the person of Christ. Then I explain that the reason the effectiveness of a sacrament doesn't depend on the holiness of the minister is because the sacraments work **ex opere operato**— which means by the work performed. So even an* *atheist can be the minister of Baptism in an emergency.*

No. The only limiting factor to the measure of grace Jesus imparts through a sacrament is the disposition of the person receiving the sacrament.

#180 How should we be disposed when receiving the sacraments?

We should receive the sacraments with an intensity of faith and love, but also with trust in God's mercy and sorrow for our sins.

#181 Is the state of grace necessary for the reception of the sacraments?

The state of grace is absolutely necessary for four of the sacraments. They are Confirmation, Holy Eucharist, Holy Orders, and Matrimony. The state of grace is normally necessary for the Anointing of the Sick.

SEVENTEEN

BAPTISM

Gateway to Life in the Spirit

The First Sacrament

#182 What is Baptism?

"Holy Baptism is the basis of the whole Christian life, the gateway to life in the spirit, and the door which gives access to the other sacraments. Through Baptism we are freed from sin and reborn as sons of God; we become members of Christ, are incorporated into the Church and made sharers in her mission: 'Baptism is the sacrament of regeneration through water in the word.'"[1]

#183 Did Jesus make Baptism obligatory?

Yes. Jesus told His apostles to "go into all the world and preach the Gospel to the whole creation... *he who believes and is baptized will be saved*; but he who does not believe will be condemned" (Mark 16:15-16). It is with these words that Jesus made Baptism obligatory (cf. John 3:5).

#184 Does Baptism remove all sin?

Yes. Baptism removes the stain of original sin and all actual sins we have committed. It also removes all of the eternal punishment due to our sins.

#185 What does the character of Baptism do for us?

The character or seal of Baptism confers on us a permanent relationship with Christ which will identify us as Christians in this life and into eternity.

#186 Who usually baptizes?

The ordinary minister of Baptism is a priest or deacon.

Emergency Baptism

#187 In case of emergency, who can baptize?

In case of emergency (i.e., imminent death), anyone, even an atheist, can baptize.

#188 How is emergency Baptism given?

For emergency Baptism to be validly given, the following conditions must be met:

1. The person baptizing must have the Church's intention; that is, that the Baptism take away sin.

If an atheist is asked by a dying person to baptize him/her and that atheist agrees, the atheist has the Church's intention.

---

1. The person baptizing must pour water on the

head three times in such a manner that it flows over the skin

2. At the same time as the water is being poured, the person baptizing must say: "I baptize you in the name of the Father, and of the Son, and of the Holy Spirit."

#189 If the person survives, should the Baptism be repeated?

No. A re-Baptism is not necessary, nor is it possible, since Baptism can be administered only once. Should the newly baptized survive, the ceremonies surrounding Baptism should be performed in a parish church by a priest or deacon.

Importance of Baptism

#190 Is Baptism necessary for salvation?

Yes. Jesus made Baptism absolutely necessary for salvation. He indicated this to Nicodemus (John 3:5) and to His apostles (Mark 16:15-16).

#191 Should infants be baptized?

This is an important one, as nearly all Protestant denominations teach that infant Baptism is wrong. I highly recommend that you get your apologetic fixed well in your mind. The best place to start on this would be Karl Keating's modern classic Catholicism and Fundamentalism *published by Ignatius Press.*

The early Christian Fathers are unanimous in insisting upon infant Baptism, basing it on the universal command of Christ to baptize all (Matthew 28:19; Mark 16:15-16; John 3:5), and on its divine power to cleanse original sin from the soul. Irenaeus (A.D. 130-205) writes:

He came to save all through Him are born-again unto God; infants, and children, boys and youths, and elders.[2]

Origen (A.D. 185-254) declared infant Baptism an apostolic institution.[3] St. Cyprian and the Bishops of the Third Council of Carthage (A.D. 253) taught that children should be baptized as soon as possible after birth. Yes, infants should be baptized, as the Church has taught for 2,000 years.

#192 What happens if an infant dies without Baptism?

There are two major schools of reputable thought in speculative theology on this subject. The first comes from those who hold that an infant who dies without Baptism goes to *limbo*. This school, espoused by St. Thomas Aquinas, teaches that limbo is a place of perfect natural happiness, but minus the vision of God. This is reasonable, since the unbaptized infant still possesses the stain of original sin, but has no actual sin.

The second school of thought is much more modern, albeit just as valid. It contends that the Holy Spirit enlightens the soul—which is capable of instantaneous enlightenment under divine direction (cf. Acts 1-16; 2:1-47) —at the moment of death to the totality of Catholic truth. Then the free will of the soul, which is not influenced by the commission of actual sin, makes the decision to accept that truth, and passes into the next life with perfect contrition; therefore, being saved and made worthy of heaven, but without the seal of Baptism.

In either case, the child is left to the infinite mercy of God.

#193 Can an adult who has died without Baptism be saved?

An adult who dies unbaptized because he does not know about Baptism or its importance can be saved if he lived his life trying to do good and avoiding evil. This is called *Baptism of desire*. Indeed, the Church embraces as her own those who are studying the faith with the intention of being received into the Church, so that they receive Baptism of desire should they die prior to reception into the Church.

There are also those who may suffer martyrdom for the faith, although they are not Catholic. Such a person would be the recipient of *Baptism of blood*.

Here I tell the following story...

In the early days of the Church, during one of the ten great Roman persecutions, a group of ten Christians were captured. They were told that they were about to be speared to death for practicing Christianity, but they could save themselves if they would only deny Christ and make a sacrifice to the emperor as a god.

The Roman centurion asked each Christian if they would renounce the faith, and all refused... except the last man. He renounced Christ and was allowed to leave in order to make the required sacrifice. Then the twist.

A Roman soldier threw down his spear and took the place of the Christian traitor. He said, "I don't know who this Jesus of Nazareth is, but any God who inspires such courage in His followers is a God I wish to follow." Then he was killed with the Christians, baptized in his own blood!

Godparents or Sponsors

#194 What are the responsibilities of godparents?

Although it is a great honor to become the godparent of one who is to be baptized, it should not be viewed as a position or office of honor. It should instead be viewed as an active participation in the life of a soul for the purpose of helping the soul to obtain spiritual perfection and perfect unity with God. Being a godparent is an awesome responsibility, and God will judge a godparent on the basis of how seriously he undertook this responsibility.

As the godparent of an infant, it is the godparent's responsibility to see to it that the godchild is raised as a good Catholic if the natural parents become lax in their God-given responsibilities. However, it is important to remember that the parents have a far greater role in the life of the child than the godparent.

In the case of an adult convert, the godparent should see to it that the godchild has all he or she needs to grow in the spiritual life and a deeper understanding of what the Church teaches. The important thing to remember in this case is that the godchild's free will must be respected.

I add here that, as the godfather of 84 adults, I take this responsibility much more seriously than the text above implies. I tell students that I am willing to die for the souls of my godchildren. Although I obviously haven't had to sacrifice my life, I have thought on several occasions I would have to. So this exclamation of willing sacrifice is not hollow or speculation. I've been tried by fire on this; and, no, I'll not tell what happened. But I very strongly suggest that this is something you need to consider long and hard before you become the godparent of an adult.

#195 Who should be chosen as godparents?

The parents of an infant should choose as godparents only those who *know and live* their Catholic faith. Candidates for godparents must be at least 16 years old. The same criteria should be considered by adult converts when selecting godparents.

#196 What promises do we make in Baptism?

The promises we make in Baptism (done for a child by his parents) are to reject Satan and everything contrary to the law of God, and to live according to the teachings and example of Jesus Christ. These promises are important because they are our guide on the road to salvation.

EIGHTEEN

CONFIRMATION

The Sacrament of the Holy Spirit

Sacrament of Witness

#197 What is Confirmation?

Confirmation is the sacrament instituted by Christ that makes baptized persons "more perfectly bound to the Church and... enriched with a special strength of the Holy Spirit. Hence [baptized persons] are, as true witnesses of Christ, more strictly obliged to spread and defend the faith by word and deed."[1]

#198 What else does Confirmation do for us?

Confirmation increases sanctifying grace in our soul, increases the supernatural virtues, and gives an increase in the gifts of the Holy Spirit. It imprints on the soul an indelible spiritual mark and for this reason cannot be repeated. It enables us to courageously profess our faith, even under the threat of death. Indeed, without the sacrament of Confirmation there would be far fewer martyrs in the Church's glorious history.

#199 How do we know that Jesus instituted the sacrament of Confirmation?

Although it is not called by the name Confirmation, we see it clearly in use by the apostles in the historical passages of the New Testament (cf. Acts 8:14-17; 19:6). Since the apostles did and taught all and only that which Christ commanded, we are assured by their actions that Jesus instituted this sacrament.

#200 Who is the minister of Confirmation?

The ordinary minister of Confirmation is the diocesan bishop, but priests may also confirm under certain conditions. For example, in case of emergency (impending death) or with the bishop's prior permission (institutional situations, such as prisons or nursing homes), a priest may confirm.

#201 How is Confirmation given?

Confirmation is given by tracing a cross on the person's forehead with a blessed oil, called holy chrism (a mixture of olive oil and an aromatic substance, blessed by the bishop), while reciting the form: "Be sealed with the gift of the Holy Spirit."

A cross is traced on the person's forehead as a symbol of the faith that the confirmed must live and profess, even under the direst of circumstances.

I tell students about my Confirmation. I was confirmed by Archbishop Oscar Lipscomb, Emeritus Archbishop of Mobile. The way he administered Confirmation was unforgettable! I don't recall his Homily or much else about that Mass, but I do recall how His Excellency gave me the sacrament. His eyes were intensely boring into mine, his face only about six inches from mine. While farrowing my forehead very hard with his thumb, he slowly and somberly said, "Be sealed with the gift of the Holy Spirit." I **know** *I was confirmed.*

Importance of Confirmation

#202 Who can receive Confirmation?

Confirmation may be received by any baptized person who has never been confirmed, after having been properly instructed in the duties and responsibilities of the Christian life.

#203 How should one prepare for Confirmation?

One prepares for Confirmation by being in the state of grace and knowing the main truths and duties of the Catholic faith.

#204 Is Confirmation valid if received by one who is in a state of mortal sin?

Yes, Confirmation will be valid, but illicitly received. God will withhold the special graces of Confirmation until the confirmed is reconciled to God by way of a good confession. Furthermore, if Confirmation is received in a state of mortal sin, the confirmed commits the additional mortal sin of sacrilege. This, too, must be confessed, along with all the Communions received since the last good confession and the sacrilege attached to them. It's actually easier to just remain in a state of grace.

#205 Who should be confirmed?

All Catholics have an obligation to be confirmed at the appropriate time. In the case of children, parents have the grave obligation to see to it that their children are properly instructed before receiving Confirmation.[2] In the case of adult converts, both the convert and his godparent have a grave obligation to ensure complete and proper instruction.

#206 Are we obliged to continue to study our Catholic faith after Confirmation?

Absolutely! Every Catholic has an obligation to study the faith for the entirety of his life. This is how we prepare ourselves to share the faith with others, thus responding positively to the sacramental graces of Confirmation. Failure to study is a rejection of the graces God gives us through Confirmation.

I explain that we're expected to continue our studies in accordance with our abilities. For example, for most people that might mean an occasional book along with reading a few Catholic magazine articles a week. For some, it might mean just reading good Catholic articles or watching good Catholic videos.

I point out the fact that I have taught the catechism at least once a week for the last 30 years. In fact, I have gone years at a time when I taught it daily, and I frequently run across something that makes me say to myself, "Wow! I had forgotten that." So learning and studying the faith doesn't end with Confirmation, nor should it.

#207 Who should be chosen as godparent for Confirmation?

Practicing and knowledgeable Catholics should be chosen as godparents for Confirmation. It is preferable for the Confirmation godparent to be the same as that of Baptism.

NINETEEN
HOLY EUCHARIST

The Heart and Soul of Our Faith

This is the third place where a student is most likely to convert. I made the intellectual decision to convert at the 9th article of the Creed, but I made the emotional decision here.

The Holy Eucharist is the very heart of our holy and ancient faith. Christianity makes absolutely no sense without this sacrament. Indeed, I can't imagine what attraction any form of Christianity has for those who don't believe in the Real Presence. Surveys show that 70% of Catholics no longer believe in the Eucharist. I don't believe that; I believe they were never taught in the first place. It is your responsibility to change that.

Real Presence

#208 What is the Holy Eucharist?

In the Holy Eucharist Jesus gives us Himself, under the appearances of bread and wine, fully and completely; He is truly present in his body, blood, soul, and divinity, in order to give Himself to the Father for our salvation, and to give Himself as divine nourishment for our souls.

#209 When did Jesus institute the Holy Eucharist?

Jesus instituted the Holy Eucharist on Holy Thursday night at the Last Supper, the night before He was crucified. The Last Supper was the very first Mass.

At the first Mass during the Last Supper, He took bread in His sacred hands, gave the Father thanks and praise, broke the bread and said: "Take, eat; this is my body." Then He took the cup of wine, gave thanks and said: "Drink of it, all of you; for this is my blood of the covenant, which is poured out for many for the forgiveness of sins" (cf. Matthew 26:26-29; Mark 14:22-25; Luke 22:17-20).

#210 When Jesus said, "This is my body" and "This is my blood," what happened to the bread and wine?

When Jesus said "This is my body," the substance of the bread was changed into the true body of Jesus Christ. Only the appearances (called accidentals) of the bread and wine remained; that is, all that remained of the bread are those things which affect the five senses: in this case, taste, appearance, touch, and smell.

The same is true of the wine. When Jesus said "This is my blood," the entire substance of the wine was changed into His real blood. Therefore, Jesus' body and blood are really present in the Holy Eucharist.

We speak of "the body of Christ" and "the blood of Christ" to distinguish the two appearances. In fact, both are the same identical substance: Christ's body, blood, soul and divinity, which is Christ whole and entire.

#211 Why do Catholics believe that they receive the living Christ in Communion?

What follows is not only the Church's teaching on the Holy Eucharist, but a substantial part of the apologetic for it as well. If you will learn this in your general memory, you will always have a good defense of why we believe in the Real Presence.

We believe in the Real Presence of Jesus Christ in the Holy Eucharist because He promised to give us His flesh as food and His blood as drink. Now we will demonstrate why Catholics believe this.

And he said to them, "I have earnestly desired to eat this passover with you before I suffer..."

This is how St. Luke begins his narrative of the Last Supper. The immediate question that comes to mind is, why would Jesus be so anxious to have this singular meal with His apostles when He knows that this will be his last meal? Does a death row inmate look forward to his last meal? For all intents and purposes, that's what's happening here. So why is Jesus actually looking forward to His last meal? To answer this we must begin by reading the sixth chapter of John.

The sixth chapter of John opens with a miracle where

Jesus feeds 5,000 people on five barley loaves of bread and two fish (John 6:1-14). After preaching to the people, Jesus instructed his apostles to get into the boat and cross over the Sea of Capernaum, but He Himself slipped into the mountains to pray alone—unbeknownst to the people (John 6:15).

In the middle of the night, when the apostles were about halfway across the sea on their journey, Jesus performed His second miracle in this chapter: He came walking across the water (verse 19). When Jesus got into the boat with the apostles, the third miracle of John 6 took place: the boat was immediately at the land where they were going (verse 21).

Because the people wanted to be with Jesus, they spent the night going across the Sea of Capernaum to where the apostles would land their boat, because they knew that Jesus was would eventually show up wherever the apostles were. They were amazed to see Jesus with the apostles, since they knew He did not get into the boat with them (verses 22-24).

When they found him on the other side of the sea, they said to him, "Rabbi, when did you come here?" (verse 25). But Jesus ignored their question and cut right to the heart of the matter. *Jesus answered them, "Truly, truly, I say to you, you seek me, not because you saw signs, but because you ate your fill of the loaves. Do not labor for the food which perishes, but for the food which endures to eternal life, which the Son of man will give you; for on him God the Father has set his seal."* (26-27)

Then Jesus went on to begin telling them what they had to do to inherit eternal life.

Although ordinarily a wonderfully innovative people, the Jews of Jesus' day were theological airheads. They asked,

"Then what sign do you do, that we may see, and believe you? What work do you perform? Our fathers ate manna in the wilderness; as it is written, 'He gave them bread from heaven to eat.'" (30-31)

It is unbelievable that the Jews would challenge Jesus after the miracle of feeding them all the day before and the apparent miracle that occurred in the middle of the night, as was evident when they found Jesus on the other side of the sea in the morning. Astonishing!

Jesus said to them, "I am the bread of life; he who comes to me shall not hunger, and he who believes in me shall never thirst." (John 6:35)

He went on to explain through verse 40 that He was the bread sent from heaven by the Father.

Up to that point, Jesus' followers understood him to be speaking symbolically. But He went on to tell them that He was the bread they would have to eat to inherit eternal life.

The Jews then disputed among themselves, saying, "How can this man give us his flesh to eat?" So Jesus said to them, "Truly, truly, I say to you, unless you eat the flesh of the Son of man and drink his blood, you have no life in you; he who eats my flesh and drinks my blood has eternal life, and I will raise him up on the last day. For my flesh is food indeed, and my blood is drink indeed. He who eats my flesh and drinks my blood abides in me, and I in him. As the living Father sent me, so he who eats me will live because of me." (John 6:52-57)

No longer did Jesus' followers believe He was being symbolic. They now understood Him to be speaking literally. He said, "my flesh is food indeed, and my blood is drink indeed" (verse 55); the word "indeed" made His statement imperative. He prefaced His entire statement with the phrase "truly, truly," which He always used to emphasize the importance of what He was about to teach. The followers' literal understanding of what Jesus said repulsed them:

After this many of his disciples drew back and no longer went about with him. (John 6:66)

If they misunderstood by taking Jesus' words literally, why didn't He stop them and explain what He meant? Any other time they misunderstood He would explain, so why not now? He did not go after them because He intended for them to take Him literally.

Jesus said to the twelve, "Will you also go away?' Simon Peter answered him, 'Lord, to whom shall we go? You have the words of eternal life; and we have believed, and have come to know, you are the holy one of God." (John 6:67-69)

The apostles had been with Him from the beginning. They also understood what He said to be literal. They did not know *how* He would do what He said, but they believed that He would eventually show them.

Jesus finally explained the how to them at the Last Supper. In Luke 22:15 Jesus said, "I have earnestly desired to eat this passover with you before I suffer." He had *earnestly desired* to give them His flesh and blood since He first made the promise. In verses 16 through 20 Jesus proceeded to give them what He had promised at the first Mass.

These passages, as well as others, explain why Catholics believe in the Real Presence of Jesus Christ and the Holy Eucharist. The short of it is that we believe in the Real Presence because Jesus said so!

It is at any time from this point on that I tell the student about verified Eucharistic miracles. The most famous one with the easiest story to tell is the

Eucharistic Miracle of Lanciano. There are a lot of books, videos and online information about this, and you should learn all you can about it. An excellent YouTube video can be viewed here: https://youtu.be/DKg--OVT39w.

Effecting Christ's Real Presence

#212 How does Jesus become present in the Holy Eucharist?

Jesus becomes present in the Holy Eucharist by a change called *transubstantiation*.

#213 What is transubstantiation?

Transubstantiation is the change of the entire substance of the bread and the entire substance of the wine into the real body and blood of Jesus Christ.

#214 Didn't you Catholics invent transubstantiation in the 13th century?

This is a false charge leveled against the Church that usually finds its origin in a book by Lorraine Boettner called *Roman Catholicism*.[1] This book is often referred to as the "anti-Catholic Bible."

Boettner chargers that transubstantiation was an invention by the pope in the year 1215. "The implication is that transubstantiation was not believed until 1215—that it was, indeed, an 'invention'. The facts are otherwise. Transubstantiation is just the technical term used to describe what happens when the bread and wine used at Mass are turned into the actual body and blood of Christ. The belief that this occurs has been held from the earliest times. It stems from the sixth chapter of John's Gospel, the 11th chapter of

I Corinthians, and the several accounts of the Last Supper. As centuries passed, theologians exercised their reason on the belief to understand more completely how such a thing could happen and what it's happening would imply. Because some of them, in trying to explain the Real Presence, developed unsound theories, it became evident that more precise terminology was needed to ensure the integrity of the belief. The word *transubstantiation* was finally chosen because it eliminated certain unorthodox interpretations of the doctrine, and the term was formally imposed at the Fourth Lateran Council in 1215. So the use of the technical term was new, but not the doctrine."[2]

Total Presence

#215 Is the whole Christ truly present in the Holy Eucharist after the transubstantiation?

Yes, the whole Christ in His Body, Blood, Soul, and Divinity—true God and true man—is truly present after the transubstantiation. Indeed, the whole Christ is present in each particle of the consecrated Host and each drop of the consecrated Wine.

#216 Is the Real Presence of Christ in the Holy Eucharist a mystery of faith?

Yes, the Eucharistic Presence of Christ is a mystery of faith. Again, a mystery of faith is a truth we can't fully understand (doesn't violate reason), but we accept it on the authority of the one who revealed it—in this case God.

#217 How is Jesus able to change ordinary bread and wine into His Body and Blood?

Jesus is able to change ordinary bread and wine into His Body and Blood because He is God and can do all things.

The Mass

#218 What is the Holy Sacrifice of the Mass?

The Holy Sacrifice the Mass (also called the Eucharistic Celebration) is at one and the same time: the sacrifice of the cross made present on our altars; a memorial of Jesus' death, resurrection, and ascension; and a sacred banquet at which we receive Him and Holy Communion.

#219 Who can celebrate the Holy Sacrifice of the Mass?

Only a validly ordained priest can celebrate the Holy Sacrifice of the Mass, because he alone has been given the power of Christ to perform the consecration. In other words, only a validly ordained priest can change the bread and wine into the body and blood of Jesus.

You frequently hear lay people say they celebrated the Mass. This is a misnomer, as it's impossible for a layman to celebrate the Mass. Lay people can *participate* in the celebration of the Mass, but they can't actually *celebrate* it.

#220 When did Jesus give priests the power to celebrate the Holy Sacrifice of the Mass?

Jesus gave the priesthood the power to celebrate the Holy Sacrifice of the Mass in the upper room on Holy Thursday night at the Last Supper when He said to His apostles: "Do this in remembrance of me" (Luke 22:19; cf. I Corinthians 11:24).

#221 When does the change of the bread and wine into the body and blood of Christ take place?

This change of the substance of the bread and wine (transubstantiation) into the body and blood of Christ takes place at the consecration when the priest repeats Christ's words of institution: "This is my body" and "This is my blood."

#222 What is a sacrifice?

A sacrifice is the offering of a victim by a priest to God. Throughout the Old Testament we find sacrifices of flesh, cereal (various grains and bread), and wine (read all of Leviticus).

#223 Is the Mass a true sacrifice?

Yes, because Jesus Christ offers Himself to the Father through the priest as a victim under the appearances of bread and wine.

#224 Is the Mass the same sacrifice as that of the cross?

Absolutely! The Mass and Jesus' sacrifice on Calvary are one and the same; because in the Mass Jesus makes Himself present on the altar so that we can celebrate the memory of the cross, as well as applying its saving power for the forgiveness of our sins. According to the *Catechism of the Catholic Church*: "The sacrificial character of the Eucharist is manifest in the very words of institution: 'This is my body which is given for you' and 'This cup which is poured out for you is the New Covenant in my blood.' In the Eucharist Christ gives us the very body he gave up for us on the cross, the very blood which he 'poured out for many for the forgiveness of sins.'"[3]

#225 In which ways are the sacrifice of the cross and the Holy Sacrifice of the Mass the same?

In both the Holy Sacrifice of the Mass and the sacrifice

of the cross, the victim is Jesus Christ. He acted as High Priest who offered Himself to the Father from the cross; He continues to act as High Priest of the same sacrifice in the Mass, but does so now through the ministry of His priests.

#226 How do the Holy Sacrifice of the Mass and the sacrifice of the cross differ?

The difference is in the manner of presentation. Christ "who offered himself once in a bloody manner on the altar of the cross is contained and is offered in an unbloody manner"[4] on the altar of the Mass.

#227 At what point in the Mass does Jesus offer Himself to His Heavenly Father as a victim for our salvation?

Jesus offers Himself as a victim to the Father in the consecration of the Mass. The double consecration of the bread and wine represents the mystical separation of His Body and Blood. When body and blood are separated, death results. Reception of the Holy Eucharist is our participation in Christ's redemptive sacrifice on the cross.

Purpose and Effects of Mass

#228 What is the purpose of the Sacrifice of the Mass?

The purpose of the Sacrifice of the Mass and the sacrifice of the cross are one and the same. They both give glory, praise, and worship to the Father; they both provide expiation and reparation for our sins and the sins of all mankind; they both appeal to God for the natural and supernatural favors we need, particularly those which help us to become holy.

#229 Is the Mass offered to God alone?

Yes, the Mass is offered to God alone. People are often confused by "Masses for the saints," believing Masses are offered to the saints. Masses are sometimes offered in honor of, but not to, saints. Saints are honored because of their holiness in the way they lived in imitation of Christ, and priests offer Masses in their honor to thank God for them, and hold them up as an example to all people. The Mass is the highest form of divine worship, so it is offered to God alone.

#230 Can the Mass be offered for the poor souls in purgatory?

> I can't say this often enough: thanks to watered-down catechesis over the last 50 years allowing massive Protestant errors to infiltrate Catholic thought, most modern Catholics think that dying equates to going to heaven. Few people die as saints... very few. By thinking souls go straight to heaven after death, those souls languish in purgatory because no one will pray for them. So I've always believed it is imperative that prayers and Masses for holy souls in purgatory become as natural for Catholics as waking up in the morning. Consequently, I repetitively teach this ad nauseam.

Not only can the Mass be offered for the poor souls in purgatory, but it should be offered for them on a *frequent* basis. The Mass both forgives sin and the punishment due for sin. The poor souls in purgatory have had their sins forgiven, which is why they are there; however, they are repaying God's justice for their sins with punishment in purgatory. Having Masses celebrated for them can get them liberated from purgatory so they can join God in heaven.

Too many people fool themselves by believing their departed loved ones go straight to heaven, which is seldom the case. It is a genuine act of love to have Masses celebrated often for our departed friends and loved ones. Those Masses are not wasted, even if the person for whom they are offered is already in heaven, as God applies the merits of these Masses to other poor souls in purgatory. A good practice would be to have Masses celebrated each November (the month traditionally set aside for that purpose), the anniversary of the person's birth, and the anniversary of the person's death.

#231 What are the personal effects of the Sacrifice of the Mass?

The Mass remits all venial sins and the punishment due to forgiven sin (mortal and venial), provided we participate in the Mass with the proper dispositions. It also increases sanctifying grace, the infused virtues of faith, hope, and charity, and the gifts of the Holy Spirit. Again, we receive these benefits according to our own dispositions.

#232 How should our participation and dispositions be in the Mass?

I always take time here to talk about Mass etiquette and dispositions after reading the question's answer. For example, I will always mention the place for socializing is not in the church, but rather outside. I talk about proper genuflections, why, and to Whom. You get the idea. If you're not as brushed up on this as you should be [don't worry; most modern

Catholics aren't], so you need to visit JoeSixpackAnswers.com to learn what you need to know.

We should participate in the Mass by being attentive and joining our prayers with those of the priest. We should maintain the same dispositions we would've had at the foot of the cross on Calvary, of which the Mass is a perpetuation.

Parts of the Mass

#233 How is the Mass divided?

The Mass is divided into two parts: the *Liturgy of the Word* (also called the *Liturgy of the Catechumens*), and the *Liturgy of the Eucharist*. In the first part, Jesus speaks to us through the Bible. In the second part, Jesus offers Himself to the Father for our salvation.

The two-part division of the Mass has its origins in the ancient Roman persecutions. When the Church was forced into the catacombs by the persecuting Roman emperors, the Church's leaders had to be cautious of infiltration by spies. Catechumens (those just learning in order to convert) were permitted to stay during the first part of the Mass, but were asked to leave during the second part for more learning. This was done as a safeguard to prevent Roman spies from desecrating Our Lord in the Eucharist. Hence the reason the first part of the Mass was called the *Liturgy of the Catechumens.*

Holy Communion

#234 What is Holy Communion?

Holy Communion is the nourishment of our souls by receiving the Body, Blood, Soul, and Divinity of Jesus Christ and the Holy Eucharist (John 6:53). Christ mandated that we receive Him in the Eucharist for the life of our soul.

There are numerous fruits of Holy Communion. The chief fruit, of course, is an intimate, interior union with Christ. Just as Matrimony is the sacrament that weds a man and woman, the Eucharist is the sacrament that weds us to Christ.

Holy Communion also produces other fruits. If produces an increase in sanctifying grace, and increases in the theological virtues of faith, hope, and charity. It also remits venial sin. Holy Communion weakens concupiscence, the propensity to sin that comes from our broken human nature. It also adds strength to the force of our will, preserves us from falling into mortal sin, and helps us to joyfully accept the duties and sacrifices that our Catholic life demands.

Finally, Jesus pledged to us in John 6:54 that by receiving Holy Communion worthily we can be assured of the resurrection and heavenly bliss. Holy Communion is the single greatest love story in the history of man, and that love affair is between God and man.

#235 What are the necessary conditions for receiving Holy Communion worthily?

Two conditions are necessary for us to receive Holy Communion worthily. They are to be in a state of grace, and to have the right intention.

#236 What does it mean to in a state of grace?

To be in a state of grace means that we are in a state of friendship with God. This means to be in a state that is free of mortal sin.

#237 If a person is in a state of mortal sin and receives Holy Communion, does he still receive Jesus?

The state of a person's soul in no way affects the presence of Christ in the Eucharist, since His presence is the result of the words and actions of the priest during Mass. A person who knows he is in a state of mortal sin when receiving Communion commits the additional mortal sin of sacrilege, and risks condemning his soul to hell for all eternity. In order to rectify this, the communicant must make a good confession, including the sin of sacrilege.

#238 What if a person recalls that he has a mortal sin he forgot to confess, but only remembers while awaiting Communion or just after having received Communion?

In a case where the person truly forgot to confess a mortal sin, the communicant should not feel guilty for receiving Communion, as no sin of sacrilege is committed; however, that communicant has a grave obligation to make a good confession as soon as possible.

#239 What does it mean to have the right intention?

Having the right intention means receiving communion to show God we love him. We must be careful to avoid other intentions. We are not receiving Communion for the respect of others, nor to make ourselves feel holy. By the mere fact that we are all sinners, none of us is worthy to receive Communion, but Jesus deems us worthy if we are free of mortal sin; therefore, we receive Him only with the intention of showing God our love for Him.

#240 Are there any other dispositions we should have before receiving Communion?

Yes. We should be free, as far as possible, from fully deliberate venial sins. We should also make acts of faith, hope, charity, sorrow (for our sins), and desire (to receive Communion).

#241 Is there a fast to be observed before receiving Communion?

Ignorance of the law is no excuse in civil and criminal law. However, such is not the case when it comes to divine and Church law. Invincible ignorance pardons us from the guilt of sin when we unknowingly violate divine and Church law. I frequently remind students of this when teaching, but I'm also quick to point out that ignorance is, by its nature, a depravity and must be corrected. In this case, to knowingly violate the fast before Communion and then receive Communion anyway is a grave sin. And I point out that even chewing gum and breath mints violate the fast.

Yes, the Church requires a fast for one hour prior to receiving Communion. We may not eat or drink anything, except water and prescription medication. The elderly, those with serious illnesses, and those who care for them are exempt from this Eucharistic fast.

#242 What should we do after receiving Holy Communion?

We should always offer an act of thanksgiving. This means that we should adore Jesus present in us, thank Him for coming, express our love and the desire to do his will, and ask for his blessings.[5]

#243 How can we gain the greatest spiritual benefits from Holy Communion?

Because the graces we receive from Communion are in direct proportion to the dispositions we maintain, the greatest spiritual benefits are derived from a good preparation and thanksgiving.

#244 Is there any time when we are obliged to receive Holy Communion?

Yes, the Church commands that we must receive Holy Communion at least once a year, during the Easter time. The law in the United States is expanded from universal law to be inclusive of the time from the first Sunday of Lent until Trinity Sunday. This is called the Easter Duty.

For a grave—*repeat,* **grave**—reason this duty may be fulfilled at another time during the year. Failure to fulfill our Easter Duty is a mortal sin.

The law in the United States is so accommodating that I usually tell my students you almost have to be in a coma or stranded on a desert island to not be able to fulfill your Easter Duty.

I also explain that just because you go to Communion even every day doesn't mean you have fulfilled your Easter Duty. You must make the intention that a particular Communion during the time-frame established by the Church is your Easter Duty Communion. I always tell students I form the intention of making my Easter Duty Communion on the first Sunday of Lent in order to ensure that I don't forget, so I'm not left doubting or wondering later during the Lenten or Easter seasons whether I met my obligation.

Many people say I'm being too legalistic with this. Well, I suppose I can see where someone may think that. The rhetorical questions I ask in response to that accusation are: "Did Jesus establish the Catholic Church? Did he give her His own authority? Does the Church have an Easter Duty requirement? Does she tell us to form an intention to fulfill the Easter Duty?" Since the answers to these questions are all in the affirmative, I'm not being at all legalistic. After all, either Jesus and His Church mean what they say or they don't.

#245 Is it good to receive Communion frequently?

Absolutely! Holy Mother Church recommends that we receive Communion weekly at Sunday Mass, but she is most pleased to allow the faithful daily Communion so we may grow in grace and holiness.

#246 When are we obliged to begin receiving Communion?

The obligation to begin receiving Holy Communion begins at the age of reason; that is, approximately at the age of seven. It is vital that a proper preparation is made before receiving First Holy Communion. This means a thorough instruction in the Church's teachings on the Eucharist, and preparation for a good confession prior to First Holy Communion.

---

*Here is where I express a personal preference and why. I tell the students that it is their right to receive Communion in the hand, and I even instruct them as to the proper way to do it. I tell them the way most people do it is to receive in the hand; however, I go on to tell them I have **never** received any way except on the tongue, and I tell them why. You yourself may not even know the history of Communion in the hand, so I'll explain it for you.*

*Prior to Vatican II, we had no Extraordinary Lay Ministers of the Holy Eucharist and no one was permitted to touch the Host except by receiving Him on the tongue. In fact, for quite a while after Vatican II no one but a priest was permitted to touch the Host. The reason for this is that **no one** is worthy to touch the Body of Christ, or the chalice containing His Precious Blood. The only reason a priest was deemed worthy was because in the rite of ordination the bishop gives the hands of the priest a special anointing to make his hands worthy to handle the sacred species. This is still done today, although the bishops have been forced by circumstances to change the wording of the official explanation for this anointing.*

Sometime after Vatican II, certain priests and a few bishops encouraged liturgical experimentation, against Canon Law and in violation of liturgical norms, which included communicating the laity in the hand. This was unlawful and, for the priests and bishops who did it, a sin (not for the laity, since they didn't know any better).

By the time Pope Paul VI found out about this scandalous abuse, it was already widespread in the Occidental world. Since the people had come to accept it as the norm, and since there may have been Church-wide rebellion and confusion if the Holy Father had definitively corrected the situation, he opted—albeit reluctantly—to legalize the practice of Communion in the hand.

The history behind this practice is clearly indicative of the reality that it **is not** in the heart of the Church to practice Communion in the hand. In fact, even though he re-wrote Canon Law and liturgical norms to allow Communion in the hand, St. John Paul II never communicated in the hand when he celebrated the Mass. And that's why I refuse to do so myself—I've never touched a consecrated Host.

However, no matter my personal feelings on the subject, **a student has the right to know the legitimate options available to him**.

TWENTY
PENANCE

A Sacrament of Healing

#247 What is the sacrament of Penance?

The sacrament of Penance, also called Reconciliation or Confession, is the sacrament instituted by Christ through which He forgives sins committed after Baptism and the penitent confesses them to the priest and the priest grants absolution.

#248 Isn't the sacrament of Penance just an invention of the Church?

This is vitally important! This is also an excellent apologetic for auricular confession. You'd do well to commit it to memory. Anti-Catholics often accuse the Church of "inventing" confession in A.D.1215 at the Fourth Lateran Council.

No. That the sacrament of Penance was instituted by Christ can be proven in Sacred Scripture. In John 20:20-23 we find Jesus addressing the apostles in the upper room on the evening of the first Easter Sunday:

"'Peace be with you. As the Father has sent me, even so I send you.' And when he had said this, he breathed on them, and said to them, 'Receive the Holy Spirit. If you forgive the sins of any, they are forgiven; if you retain the sins of any, they are retained.'"

In this special commission to the apostles we find several interesting elements. The first is that Christ makes Himself clear that what He is giving the apostles is indeed a commission mandate when He tells them that He is sending them as the Father sent Him. In other words, He's passing on to them His own mission of redemption.

The second important element is that he breathed on them. In all of human history, this is only the second time that God breathed on man. The first time God breathed on man was when He gave life to Adam (Genesis 2:7). God is giving a new type of life to man here, as He is telling the apostles that they now have his power to forgive the sins of those who are repentant and sorrowful, or not to forgive the sins of those who are not repentant and sorrowful.

Anti-Catholic writer Loraine Boettner, author of *Roman Catholicism*, a book that Catholic apologist Karl Keating calls the *anti-Catholic bible*, writes that "auricular confession to a priest instead of God" was invented by Pope Innocent III and the bishops of the Fourth Lateran Council in the year 1215.[1] This is the most generally held position by those who claim the Church invented the sacrament of Penance. Even if the Church's opponents were to completely discount the scriptural references to confession

—which they do—we should expect a find no historical evidence of the sacrament's existence prior to 1215. This is not the case.

There are many, many writings of the early Christians dating to hundreds of years before the Fourth Lateran Council. St. Gregory the Great (A.D. 590-604) in his homily on John 20:23 writes:

The apostles, therefore, have received the Holy Spirit in order to loose sinners from the bonds of their sins. God has made them partakers of his right of judgment; they are to judge in His name and in His place. The bishops are the successors of the apostles, and, therefore, possess the same right.[2]

St. Caesarius of Arles (A.D. 470-542) writes:

It is God's will that we confess our sins not only to him but to men, and since it is impossible for us to be free from sin, we must never fail to have recourse to the remedy of confession.[3]

In a sermon on the last judgment the saint tells us

to escape damnation by making a sincere Confession from the bottom of [our] hearts, and to fulfill the penance given by the priest.[4]

St. Leo the Great (A.D. 370-461) writes:

God in his abundant mercy has provided two remedies for the sins of men; that they may gain eternal life by the grace of Baptism, and also by the remedy of Penance. Those who have violated their vows of Baptism may obtain the remission of their sins by condemning themselves; the divine goodness has so decreed that the pardon of God can only be obtained by sinners through the prayer of the priests. Jesus Christ has Himself conferred upon the rulers of the Church the power of imposing canonical penance upon sinners who confess their sins, and of allowing them to receive the Sacra-

ments of Christ, after they have purified their souls by a salutary satisfaction... Every Christian, therefore, must examine his conscience, and cease deferring from day to day the hour of his conversion; he ought not to expect to satisfy God's justice on his deathbed. It is dangerous for a weak and ignorant man to defer his conversion to the last uncertain days of his life, when he maybe unable to confess and obtain priestly absolution; he ought, when he can, to merit pardon by a full satisfaction for his sins.[5]

The great bishop St. Augustine (A.D. 354-430) tells his flock

not to listen to those who deny that the Church has the power to forgive all sins.[6]

St. Ambrose (A.D. 340-397) declares that priests pardon all sins, not in their own name, but as "ministers and instruments of God."[7]

Paulinus of Milan (A.D. 395), a biographer of St. Ambrose, explicitly mentions the fact the saint heard confessions. He writes:

As often as anyone, in order to receive penitents, confessed his faults to him, he wept so as to compel them to weep... But he spoke of the causes of the crimes which they confessed to known the Lord alone.[8]

Origen (A.D. 185-254) in his commentary on Psalm 28 writes:

When you have eaten some indigestible food, and your stomach is filled with an excessive quantity of humor, you will suffer until you have gotten rid of it. So in like manner sinners, who hide and retain their sins with in their breasts, becomes sick therefrom almost to death. If, however, they accuse themselves, confess their sins, and vomit fourth their iniquity, they will completely drive from their souls the principal evil. Consider carefully whom you choose to hearken to your sins. Know well the character of the physician to whom you intend to relate the nature of your sickness.... If he judges that your sickness is of such a nature that it should be revealed publicly in church for the edification of the brethren and your own more effective cure, do not hesitate to do what he tells you.[9]

The great preponderance of evidence shows that Confession was not a 13th-century invention of the Church, but that it had already been in place for centuries before the Fourth Lateran Council was convoked. Still, opponents of the Church on this issue, although they cannot explain these early writings, continued to have a problem reconciling John 20:23 to anything other than Confession.

Many claim that Jesus is merely repeating His precept that we must forgive one another. But this presents a problem. It is true that Jesus taught throughout the Gospels that we are to forgive others who sin against us, but that is not what John 20:23 says. In this passage, Jesus speaks only to His apostles. He gave them the power to choose whether to forgive sins. Either He was contradicting Himself in this passage from the previous admonishments to forgive "seven times seventy," or He was giving the apostles a power never given to man before. Since He would soon be ascending to heaven and no longer personally present to forgive sins as He had during His ministry, He gave this power to His priesthood by way of the apostles. As Karl Keating writes: "If there is an 'invention' here, it is not the sacrament penance, but the notion that the priestly forgiveness of sins is not to be found in the Bible or in early Christian history."[10]

#249   Does   the   priest   actually   forgive our sins?

Yes. The *Catechism of the Catholic Church* says that "[s]ince Christ entrusted to his apostles the ministry of reconciliation, bishops who are their successors, and priests, the bishops' collaborators, continue to exercise this ministry. Indeed bishops and priests, by virtue of the Sacrament of Holy Orders, have the power to forgive all sins 'in the name of the Father, and of the Son, and of the Holy Spirit.'"[11]

In any sacrament in which a priest or bishop is the minister, he acts *in persona Christi*; that is, in the person of Christ. To put it in this purely secular terms for a better understanding, bishops and priests hold a sort of special ambassadorship.

If the U.S. ambassador to Japan works out a certain agreement with the Japanese and signs that agreement, it is the ambassador's negotiations and signature which makes that agreement binding. However, the ambassador has acted in the person of the President of the United States.

So, too, does a priest or bishop act in the sacrament of Penance. He hears the penitent's sins and makes a judgment call regarding those sins, the penitent's contrition and willingness to repent—a power granted by Christ in John 20:23—then he grants absolution for those sins.

#250 Why do we have to confess our sins to the priest in order to obtain forgiveness?

As previously stated, Jesus gave His priesthood the power to forgive or retain sins in John 20:23. In order for the priest to be able to exercise the power of absolution, he must first hear the sins to determine if the penitent is contrite and intends to avoid those sins and their near occasions in the future.

#251 What are the matter and form of the sacrament of penance?

The matter consists of the penitent's sins and the acts required of the penitent. There are three such acts: contrition (sorrow), confession of sins, and acceptance of the penance.

The formula of absolution used in the Latin church expresses the essential elements of the sacrament: the Father of mercies is the source of all forgiveness. He effects the reconciliation of sinners through the Passover of his Son and the gift of his Spirit, through the prayer and ministry of his Church:

"God, the Father of mercies, through the death and resurrection of his Son, has reconciled the world to himself and sent the Holy Spirit among us for the forgiveness of sins; through the ministry of the Church may God give you pardon and peace, and I absolve you from your sins in the name of the Father, and of the Son, and of the Holy Spirit."[12]

#252 *What does the sacrament of Penance do for us?*

If well-received, the sacrament of Penance "brings about a true 'spiritual resurrection,' restoration of the dignity and blessings of the life of the children of God, of which the most precious is friendship with God."[13]

The sacrament of Penance:

- restores or increases sanctifying grace
- forgives our sins
- obliterates eternal punishment due for mortal sins
- helps us with an additional strength to avoid future sins
- restores all the merits that have been lost by the commission of mortal sins

#253 What is required to make a good confession?

There are five elements necessary for us to make it a good confession:

1. We must make a good examination of conscience
2. We must be truly sorry for our sins
3. We must resolve not to sin again (called a firm purpose of amendment)
4. We must confess our sins to a priest
5. We must accept the penance the priest assigns us

#254 What does it mean to make a good examination of conscience?

In order to make a good examination of conscience, we must make a deliberate recalling all the sins we have committed since our last good confession. This is done by going over in our minds all that is required of us by God's Commandments and the Church's laws. The Church recommends that we undertake a brief examination of conscience each night before bedtime, which makes it much easier to do before confession.

There are a number of prayer books and leaflets available that have a printed examination of conscience. They merely list God's Commandments and the Church's laws in order. Under each commandment or law are questions we should ask ourselves, as they pertain to each commandment and law. The two best printed forms of an examination of conscience I have seen are found in the *Queen of Apostles Prayerbook*,[14] and the *Handbook of Prayers*.[15]

#255 What is contrition?

No better answer is found anywhere than in the *Catechism of the Catholic Church*, which echoes the Council of Trent:

Among the penitent's acts, contrition occupies first place. Contrition is 'sorrow of the soul and detestation for the sin committed, together with the resolution not to send again.'[16]

Contrition is absolutely necessary in order to receive absolution.

#256 How many kinds of contrition are there?

There are two kinds of contrition: perfect and imperfect.

#257 What is perfect contrition?

Perfect contrition—more formally called contrition of charity—is sorrow for our sins with the purest of motives. Perfect contrition is hatred for our sins solely for the love we have for God and the offense our sins cause him. "Such contrition remits venial sins; it also obtains forgiveness of mortal sins *if it includes the firm resolution to have recourse to sacramental confession as soon as possible.*"[17]

#258 What is imperfect contrition?

Imperfect contrition—more formally called attrition—is sorrow for our sins for less pure motives. Like perfect contrition, imperfect contrition is still a gift of God, a prompting of the Holy Spirit. We experience imperfect contrition when we are sorry for our sins because we fear hell, or because of the inherent evil of sin.

#259 Which kind of contrition must we have to receive the sacrament of penance well?

Although perfect contrition is the better of the two,

and certainly most pleasing to God, we may receive the sacrament well if we at least have imperfect contrition. That is the contrition we will all have almost 100% of the time.

#260 Should we also be sorry for our venial sins?

We should be sorry for all our venial sins primarily because all sins offend God, even venial sins. We should also be sorry for venial sins because they weaken our will to resist mortal sin, and they make us deserving of temporal punishment.

#261 What does it mean to be firmly resolved to sin no more?

A firm resolution to sin no more (called a *firm purpose of amendment*) is simply a determination not to sin, and to avoid all the near occasions of sin.

#262 When should we express our contrition to God?

The rite of the sacrament of Penance allows for recital of the prayer called the act of contrition, of which there are many, and we should be sincere in the recitation of this prayer. Of course, we are free—even encouraged—to make an impromptu act of contrition if we wish.

#263 What is confession?

Confession is the actual telling of our sins to a priest. This is the only way he can absolve all our sins, as he has no way of knowing what to absolve without first hearing them.

The confession (or disclosure) of sins, even from a simply human point of view, frees us and facilitates our reconciliation with others. Through such an admission man looks squarely at the sins he is guilty of, takes responsibility for them, and thereby opens himself again to God and to the communion of the Church in order to make a new future possible.[18]

#264 How should we go to confession?

I offer the following because most people don't know how to make a proper confession. Most priests won't bother to correct a penitent because they're just happy to get people in the confessional.

The following is the proper liturgical format for going to confession:

1. Greet the priest; make the Sign of the Cross.
2. Say "Amen" to the prayer of the priest, or a Bible reading, if any. Then say, "It has been [*one week, one month, etc.*] since my last confession; these are my sins." Or you can use the old form, if you're more comfortable. The old form is, "Father, forgive me, for I have sinned. It has been [*one week, one month, etc.*] since my last confession; these are my sins."
3. Tell your sins to the priest, at least *all mortal sins*, according to their kind (nature) and the number of times committed. And it's good to tell all your venial sins, even the smallest.
4. Ask any questions, if you have any.
5. Conclude by saying, "Father, for these and all the sins of my past life I am heartily sorry."
6. Listen to any counsel the priest may give, pondering it later.
7. The priest will next assign the penance.

Remember what it is, as you're obliged to fulfill it.

8. The priest will say, "Now make a good act of contrition." Recite it aloud.

9. The priest will next grant absolution. Your only response is "Amen," but you will make the Sign of the Cross while he says, "I absolve you of your sins in the name of the Father, and of the Son, and of the Holy Spirit."

10. The priest will say, "Give thanks to the Lord for He is good."

11. You respond, "His mercy endures forever."

12. The priest will say, "God has freed you from your sins. Go in peace."

13. You respond, "Thank you, Father."

#265 Must we confess every sin?

We must confess every mortal sin.

Without being strictly necessary, confession of every day faults (venial sins) is nevertheless strongly recommended by the Church. Indeed the regular confession of our venial sins help us form our conscience, fight against evil tendencies, let ourselves be healed by Christ and progress in the spirit.[19]

#266 Is there any sin God will not pardon?

Absolutely speaking, no sin is unpardonable by either God or the Church. It is God's will that all men be saved (I Timothy 2:4), and His mercy is infinite. Provided that we are truly sorrowful, make a good confession and are fully resolved to avoid sin in the future, we will always be pardoned by God's unfathomable mercy and love.

Many people quote Christ in Matthew 12:32, where He says:

"And who ever says a word against the Son of Man will

be forgiven; but whoever speaks against the Holy Spirit will not be forgiven, either end of this age or in the age to come." (*cf. Mark 3:30; Luke 12:10*)

This passage is a reference to the sinner who refuses to repent, despite the graces God offers him. Such a person doesn't actually receive God's pardon, because he fails to ask for it, or fulfill the necessary conditions to obtain it.

The sin mentioned by Christ in the above passage referred to the willful rejection by the Pharisees of the miracles He performed as proof of His divine mission, and their maliciousness in crediting them to the power of Satan.

#267 Should fear or shame ever prevent us from confessing a mortal sin?

Speaking from a purely human psychological standpoint, it's easy to understand how a penitent would be tempted to withhold a mortal sin in confession from a sense of embarrassment or fear. However, from the standpoint of theology, logic and reason, such feelings are superfluous. The priest to whom we confess our sins is acting in the person of Christ. It is actually Christ to whom we are confessing.

Furthermore, the priest is bound by the *seal of confession*. That means he can never tell a soul—including his own confessor—anyone's confession. In the 2,000-year history of the Church, only once has this seal been broken; it even hasn't ever been broken by renegade priests such as Martin Luther, the man responsible for the Protestant Revolt. Indeed, many priests have been jailed, tortured, and murdered rather than divulge the contents of a penitent's confession.

The seal of confession even extends to the point that a priest cannot use the knowledge from a confession for any reason. Following is an example.

Let's say that Fr. Patrick has appointed Judas Avarice to oversee the parish finances. One day, Judas goes to Father in confession and tells him that he has embezzled $250,000 from the parish funds. Since Judas must replace the money to satisfy God's justice, Fr. Patrick tells him to repay the money. However, there are two things Father *cannot* do. He cannot tell the police and have Judas prosecuted, as that would break the seal of confession. Furthermore, Father cannot later replace Judas in his position, as this would be acting on the knowledge obtained in confession. The seal of confession is that strict!

#268 What if someone deliberately omits confessing a mortal sin?

If a penitent deliberately omits the confession of a mortal sin, he commits the additional mortal sin of sacrilege, risking eternal punishment in hell; furthermore, he leaves the confessional without having any of his sins forgiven. In order to be forgiven and reacquire God's sanctifying grace, the penitent must confess the sin of sacrilege, any Holy Communion he has received since his sin of sacrilege (which is itself a sin of sacrilege to be confessed), all of the sins from his sacrilegious confession, and all of the mortal sins he has committed since. It is much easier—emotionally and spiritually—to make a good confession in the first place.

If you are ever tempted to withhold a mortal sin in confession, immediately tell the priest and ask his help. The temptation will flee!

#269 What should we do if we forget to confess a mortal sin?

Should we genuinely forget to confess a mortal sin, it is okay to receive Communion, as God forgave the sin, because we made a good confession and did not deliberately omit a mortal sin; however, we are obliged to confess the forgotten mortal sin the next time we go to confession.

#270 May a priest refuse to give absolution?

Yes, he may, provided the penitent shows no sign of sorrow for the mortal sin he has confessed, or if he indicates that he will not break with the sin.

For example, a man confesses several acts of adultery because he has a mistress. The confessor tells the man he must break off the adulterous relationship. The man refuses. The priest would have an obligation to refuse absolution.

Satisfaction for Sin

#271 Why do we receive a penance after confession?

We receive a penance to make at least some satisfaction for our sins, thus decreasing the punishment we deserve for those sins.

#272 What should we do after confession?

We should first take time to thank God for the graces to make a good confession. Then, as soon as possible, we should perform the penance assigned with thoughtfulness, love, and devotion.

#273 Does the Sacrament of Penance remove all punishment due to sin?

The Sacrament of Penance always removes all the eternal punishment in hell that is deserved by mortal sin, but it does not necessarily remove all the temporal punishment.

#274 Why is temporal punishment required by God?

If God is infinitely merciful, He must also be infinitely just. He cannot be perfect—in other words, cannot be God —if He is more merciful than just, and vice versa. To be more of one than the other would make him unbalanced, and thus imperfect. Therefore, He must demand justice.

This is where I add an analogy to make it easier to understand God's perfectly balanced mercy and justice. In many ways, we are a reflection of God. So we get our human sense of justice from Him.

This particular analogy usually helps students understand why God demands justice. Also, since Protestants don't believe in purgatory and therefore believe they will go straight to heaven when they die, this analogy explains the reasonableness of purgatory. I gave this same analogy in the section on purgatory, but I give it again here because repetition is the best teacher. So here is the analogy:

Let's say your car is out of commission, so you need to borrow your friend's car to run some important errands. Your friend tells you he is happy to loan new his car, but he needs you to return it by a certain hour because of his own commitments.

As you near completion of the errands you borrowed the car for, you look at your watch and realize you're behind schedule. In trying to get everything done and get back to your friend in time, you take a corner a little too quickly and a little too sharply. You crease the fender of your friend's car on a fire hydrant at the corner.

When you get back to your friend's house with his car, you show him the damage from the accident you had with the fire hydrant. You say, "I'm sorry. Can you forgive me?"

Your friend is a good practicing Catholic, so he says, "Sure, I forgive you." Then holding out his hand palm up, he says, "Now pay for my fender."

Because our own human justice is a mere reflection of divine justice, and we imperfect humans demand such simple justice from each other, how can we expect God to demand less?

#275 How can we satisfy the debt of temporal punishment we owe to God for our sins?

The debt of temporal punishment can only be satisfied either in purgatory or on earth. Since there is no merit in purgatory, and since purgatory is not a pleasant place, we are far and away better off satisfying the debt in this life.

The means of satisfying this debt, which also contributes to our own sanctification, are voluntary acts of penance, devout participation in the Mass, prayer, fasting, almsgiving, earning indulgences, performing the spiritual and temporal works of mercy, and patiently accepting the trials and sufferings of God chooses to permit in our lives.

First Penance

#276 When should children begin to go to confession?

Children should begin the habit of frequent confession when they reach the use of reason, which is usually at about seven years of age.

#277 Should first Penance precede First Holy Communion?

Absolutely! A first penance *must* be made prior to First Holy Communion. This practice helps to preserve the child's innocence, aids in spiritual growth, and strengthens the child's will against temptations.

Indulgences

#278 What is an indulgence?

Fewer than 10% of Catholics know what indulgences are, and fewer than 1% even bother to use them. This is another consequence of the aftermath of Vatican II. Indulgences shouldn't be taught just because they are a part of our faith (although that alone is reason enough), but primarily because they are given to us by the Catholic Church so that we may avoid the pains of purgatory and grow in holiness. Therefore, you need to teach this in order to let your students see the true heart of the Church and to have a better chance of spiritual growth. What you need to realize, though, is that you cannot teach anything you are not doing yourself. So you need to start using indulgences yourself, if you are not already doing so. Furthermore, I recommend that you take time to read Indulgenarium Doctrina by St. Pope Paul VI.

An indulgence is the remission before God of the

temporal punishment due sins already forgiven as far as their guilt is concerned, which the follower of Christ with the proper dispositions and under certain determined conditions acquires through the intervention of the Church which, as minister of the Redemption, authoritatively dispenses and applies the treasury of the satisfaction won by Christ and the saints.[20]

In simpler terms, an indulgence is a remission of the whole or part of the temporal punishment due to forgive a sin, granted by the pope and the bishops out of the Church's spiritual treasury, which is made up of the infinite redemptive merits of Jesus Christ, in the superabundant merits of the saints. It is more than a mere remission of canonical words of penance, for it really remits the whole or part of the punishment due the sinner by God, either here or in purgatory...

The divine power of the Church to grant indulgences may be better understood if we compare it with the state's custom of pardoning the whole or part of a punishment inflicted by civil law upon a criminal. The president has the right to grant a complete pardon to any criminal within the confines of the United States; the governor to any criminal in his state. The state, moreover, remits part of a criminal's punishment for good behavior while in prison.

State officials may grant a criminal pardon, even if he is not sorry for his crime, out of deference to powerful friends; the Church, on the contrary, never remits the punishment unless the sinner has manifested his sorrow.

Indulgences are granted in two forms: plenary and partial. A plenary indulgence remits all of the punishment due to forgiven sins. A partial indulgence remits some portion of the punishment due to forgiven sins.

#279 *For whom and how can we gain an indulgence?*

We may gain an indulgence for ourselves or the poor souls in purgatory. We must be in a state of grace, have the desire to gain the indulgence, and perform the good acts required by the Church.

TWENTY-ONE

ANOINTING OF THE SICK

Another Sacrament of Healing

Instituted by Christ

#280 What is the Anointing of the Sick?

The Anointing of the Sick is the sacrament instituted by Christ which gives spiritual health, and sometimes—within the providential will of God—physical healing, to persons who are in danger of death due to a serious illness, injury, or old age.

#281 How do we know that Jesus instituted the Anointing of the Sick?

All the proof we need for this is found in the biblical writings of the Apostle James:

Is any among you sick? Let him call the elders of the church, and let them pray over him, anointing him with oil in the name of the Lord; and the prayer of faith will save the sick man, and the Lord will raise him up; and if he has committed sins, he will be forgiven. (James 5:14-15)

Of course, we also see in the Gospels where Christ sends His apostles and other disciples to perform this act while preaching (Mark 6:12-13).

#282 What does the Anointing of the Sick do for us?

The Anointing of the Sick increases sanctifying grace, allows the sick person the grace of uniting himself more closely to Christ's Passion (thus giving suffering new meaning), "strengthens against the temptations of the evil one, the temptation to discouragement and anguish in the face of death [cf. Hebrews 2:15]," removes temporal punishment due to sin, removes venial sin, and "lead[s] the sick person to healing of the soul, but also of the body if such is God's will [cf. Council of Florence (1439): DS 1325]."[1]

#283 How is the Anointing of the Sick a sacrament of reconciliation?

This sacrament reconciles sinners to God in that it remits venial sins. Also, if the sick person is unable to make a good confession prior to receiving the sacrament (e.g., coma, delirium, paralysis, *et cetera*) it will remit mortal sins as well, provided the sick person has at least imperfect contrition. If the sick person regains his health he is obligated to make a good confession if he was not in a state of grace prior to receiving the Anointing of the Sick.

#284 Who can confer the Anointing of the Sick?

Only a validly ordained priest may confer the Anointing of the Sick.

#285 Who may receive the Anointing of the Sick?

Anyone may receive the Anointing of the Sick who is baptized, has reached the use of reason, and is in danger of death—but not necessarily at the point of death—from sickness, old age, or injury.

#286 How should one prepare to receive the Anointing of the Sick?

In order to best receive this sacrament, and if possible, one should prepare by making a good confession and making acts of faith, hope and charity, and be completely resigned to God's holy will.

#287 What is the matter of the Anointing of the Sick?

The proximate matter is the actual anointing. The remote matter is plant oil (usually olive oil) which has been blessed by the bishop or an authorized priest. Any priest may bless the plant oil in the event of an emergency.

#288 How is the Anointing of the Sick conferred?

The celebration of the sacrament includes the following principal elements: the "priests of the Church" [James 5:14] —in silence—lay hands on the sick; they pray over them in the faith of the Church [cf. James 5:15]...; they then anoint them with oil blessed, if possible, by the bishop.[2]

#289 May the anointing be administered to a person about to undergo surgery?

Yes, the sacrament may and should be administered to anyone about to undergo surgery, if the surgery is for a serious condition, or if general anesthetic is being used. (No matter how minor the surgery, general anesthetic can always be a risk to life. That said, this is a priest's pastoral call.)

#290 May a person be anointed more than once?

Yes, a person may be anointed more than once, if his

condition worsens, or if he gets better then has a relapse. The elderly, whether sick or in good health, may receive the Anointing of the Sick at regular intervals.

#291 May an unconscious person receive the Anointing of the Sick?

An unconscious person may and should receive the anointing, if he is in danger of death.

#292 Should a priest be called even if someone is already apparently dead?

If any doubt at all exists that a person is already really dead, resolve the doubt by calling a priest.

Just because there are no brain waves, no heartbeat or no respiration doesn't necessarily mean the person is already dead. The theological definition of death is when the soul separates from the body. There have been innumerable instances in history demonstrating that people weren't really dead.

This is where I relate a true story from the 1950s relating to this. It goes as follows:

A certain man was lying in a bed in a large hospital of a major city. He was comatose when the doctors made their final examination. He had no vital signs, so the physicians pronounced him dead. The poor man could hear all of this, but was incapable of alerting the doctors!

At that moment, a priest responding to an earlier call came into the room. The doctors told the priest he was wasting his time, that the patient was already dead. But the good priest, obedient to the teachings of the Church, ignored the doctors and began administering the Anointing of the Sick.

Suddenly the man regained consciousness and sat up in bed! He thanked the priest for his faithfulness, and explained what he'd experienced.

This true story teaches us that the Anointing of the Sick not only cures the sick—when God so wills —but that apparent death is not necessarily real death. Be sure to call a priest to administer the anointing, even if the person has appeared to be dead for several hours.

TWENTY-TWO
HOLY ORDERS

An Extraordinary Vocation

I teach this sacrament with great reverence and respect. The priesthood took a major hit in the early 2000s because of a few bad apples. But that was grossly unfair to all the great priests who hold their priesthood and its commitments in the highest esteem.

People often accuse me of clericalism, but I think that's because they don't understand what that is. Apparently they think anyone who believes priests are very special men who deserve extraordinary respect adheres to clericalism. That simply isn't the case.

Time was when a cassock-clad priest with biretta would walk through his parish neighborhood, talking to everybody—Catholic and non-Catholic alike. Being a man, he was subject to stop in a parishioner's bar on Saturday night for a whiskey and cigar [nothing feminine about priests of yesteryear], reminding the men to stop drinking and eating at midnight so they could go to Communion the next day. But you could always count on a priest to spend much of his time before the tabernacle praying for all the parishioners in his parish. I think you can still count on that.

Yes, priests who are true to their priesthood are real men. If we want our priests to rise to the heights of their vocation and be true fathers of our souls, it's time to treat them like the special men they are. It all begins with how we teach about this sacrament. How you teach a student will determine how the student treats a priest, and extra-special treatment of a priest will restore the courage of their commitments and their confidence—the confidence stolen from them by the horrid dominant culture we live in.

Above all else, teach your students to love the priesthood... and make sure you set the example.

Three Holy Vocations

#293 What is Holy Orders?

Holy orders is the sacrament through which the mission entrusted by Christ to his apostles continues to be exercised in the Church until the end of time: thus it is the sacrament of apostolic ministry. It includes three degrees: episcopate [bishop], presbyterate [priest], and diaconate [deacon].[1]

#294 Who can administer Holy Orders?

Only a validly consecrated bishop can administer Holy Orders, and only with papal permission for each ordination.

#295 Who may receive Holy Orders?

"Only a baptized man (vir) *validly receives sacred ordination."* [1983 *Code of Canon Law, can.* 1024] *The Lord Jesus chose men* (veri) *to form the college of the twelve apostles, and the apostles did the same when they chose collaborators to succeed them in their ministry... The Church recognizes herself to be bound by this choice made by the Lord himself. For this reason, the ordination of women is not possible. No one has a* right *to receive the sacrament of Holy Orders... he is called to it by God."*[2]

The male candidate for the priesthood must be a good Catholic, prepare himself by the necessary studies, have the intension of giving his life to God's service, and be accepted by his bishop or a religious superior for ordination.

#296 What are the effects of Holy Orders?

The effects of this sacrament are many. As with all of the sacraments after Baptism, Holy Orders increases sanctifying grace, gives a sacramental grace, and imprints an indelible character on the soul.

The increase in sanctifying grace is necessary for all people, as this is how we strive to fulfill Christ's command that we are to "be perfect, as your heavenly Father is perfect" (Matthew 5:48). This is important in a special way to the recipient of Holy Orders, as this man must be a Christ-like example to the souls he shepherds, as well as save his own soul.

The sacramental grace of Holy Orders benefits not only the ordained, but also the lay faithful. This is so because the sacramental grace of this sacrament allows the priest[3] or deacon to truthfully proclaim the Gospel, fulfill the ministry of the word of truth, and remove the people by the "bath of rebirth" (Baptism). The priest also offers the Holy Sacrifice of the Mass, and reconciles sinners to God by way of the sacrament of Penance.

The sacramental grace of Holy Orders is especially evident in the confessional. When a penitent goes to the same confessor with regularity and frequency, the priest comes to know the penitent's soul intimately. The sacramental grace he received in Holy Orders helps the priest to lead that soul on a journey to perfection in God.

There are also special benefits for a bishop from sacramental grace of Holy Orders. Thanks to this grace, bishops have the ability to govern their dioceses (territories assigned to the bishops by the pope), as well as to present Church teachings in a manner that best benefits the souls of their flocks.

Finally, the priest, by virtue of the sacrament of Holy Orders, acts *in persona Christi* in the fulfillment of his liturgical sacramental duties. St. Thomas Aquinas says that

Christ is the source of all priesthood: the priest of the old law was a figure of Christ, and the priest of the new law acts in the person of Christ.[4]

#297 What are the chief supernatural powers of the priest?

Of these chief supernatural powers there are two: the power to change ordinary bread and wine into the Body and Blood of Jesus Christ in the Holy Sacrifice the Mass; and to forgive sins in the sacrament of Penance.

#298 Why is it that priests do not marry?

All the ordained ministers of the Latin Church... are normally chosen from among men of faith who live a celibate life and who intend to remain celibate *"for the sake of the kingdom of heaven." Called to consecrate themselves with*

*undivided heart to the Lord and to "the affairs of the Lord,"
they give themselves entirely to God and to men. Celibacy it
is a sign of this new life to the service of which the Church's
minister is consecrated; accepted was a joyous heart celibacy
radiantly proclaims the Reign of God.*[5]

#299 Do some Catholic priests marry?

In accord with their ancient traditions, and with
approval from the Holy See, some priests of the various
Eastern rite Catholic Churches do marry. However, if they
plan to marry, they must do so before ordination.

#300 What is the role of the deacon?

Deacons are helpers of bishops and priests, and are
subject to their authority. Deacons may officiate at
weddings, perform baptisms, carry Communion to the sick,
preside at graveside funeral services, and serve in various
other non-liturgical capacities.

#301 May deacons marry?

A man who is already married may become a deacon,
but he cannot remarry if his wife dies, nor can a married
deacon become a priest.

#302 How should we regard bishops and priests?

In this age of rudeness, disrespect, and crass familiarity,
bishops and priests are often treated with grave disrespect
and irreverence. Catholics who are guilty of this should be
ashamed, and all others should be scandalized. The
humility of priests and bishops often prevents them from
chastising people for acts of disrespect, so lay people should
work to correct the situation. After all, each of these men of
Holy Orders daily perform miracles that the laity cannot.
By their hands and words alone the Creator of the Universe
comes down from heaven to the altar. By their words and

intentions alone are your sins forever obliterated from God's holy record.

A priest should be addressed as Father, because he is our spiritual father. A bishop should be addressed as Your Excellency, in keeping with old European court manner, as the highest form of respect. It is not wrong to kiss a priest's hand, because his along brings us the Body of Christ. It is not wrong to bow and kiss a bishop's ring in greeting, as this is a gesture of fidelity and respect to his apostolic office. In this era of evil and uncertainty, we should return to the concreteness of reality that is the holy priesthood.

#303 Why do Catholics call the priest "Father" when Jesus commanded us not to call anyone father, except God in heaven?

The implied objection in this question refers to Christ's words in Matthew 23:9 when he said:

"And call no man your father on earth, for you have one Father, who is in heaven."

People who make an objection to Catholics calling their priests "Father" do not consider our Lord's words in context, nor do they consider the totality of Sacred Scripture.

Christ tells us in Matthew to call no man father, yet God gives us the fourth commandment: "Honor your father and your mother" (Exodus 20:12). Either there exists a contradiction between God the Father and God the Son, which is impossible, or those who say Catholics are wrong to call priests Father wrongly interpret Jesus' words in Matthew.

Christ was not finding fault with either as a word rabbi (teacher) or father, but rather was teaching us that God alone is the source of all authority. The rebuke Jesus gave was not of the use of the word father, but of the pride of the Pharisees (cf. Matthew 23:2-10). If the rebuke was for use of the words father and teacher, no one would be right to call his male parent father.

The early Christians never interpreted these words literally. St. Paul refers to himself as Timothy's father in Philippians 2:22 and I Timothy 1:2. He also refers to himself as the spiritual father of his converts:

For though you have countless guides in Christ, you do not have many fathers. For I became your father in Christ Jesus through the Gospel. (I Corinthians 4:15)

In writing to other Christian leaders, the Apostle John call them fathers:

I am writing to you, fathers, because you know him who is from the beginning. (I John 2:13)

Are we to believe these two great apostles, who were promised to remember all Christ had taught them with the assistance of the Holy Spirit, would directly and blatantly disobey Christ? The objection made against Catholics from Matthew 23:9 is without foundation.

TWENTY-THREE

HOLY MATRIMONY

Christian Marriage

#304 What is Matrimony?

Matrimony is the sacrament instituted by Christ which unites for life a baptized to man and a baptized woman for the purposes of fulfilling their lawful responsibilities to God, for which God gives grace.

#305 What is the purpose of marriage?

Unity and procreation is that two-fold purpose of marriage. By unity we mean that the bond of the sacrament of Matrimony lasts until death, and that the man and woman are to live together as one (Matthew 19:5-6). By procreation we mean the begetting and rearing of children in the fear and love of God. In short, the two-fold purpose of marriage is the giving of love and the giving of life.

The dominant culture is actually attempting to

make marriage go the way of the dinosaur. That being the case, if your student is married, this is an excellent place to make comments or ask questions designed to encourage a conversation about the life-long bond of matrimony, NFP, and procreating children. (BTW, if you're married and practicing artificial birth control, this is the point where you need to either make up your mind to stop practicing artificial birth control and live as Christ commands or forget about evangelization. You don't have any business teaching what you don't live, or omitting any Catholic teaching.)

#306 Is there another dimension to Christian marriage?

As a natural extension of the giving of love, God gives the spouses all the graces necessary to help one another grow in holiness. Just as children produced in the matrimonial bond are a manifestation of marital love, so too is a positive response to God's graces by the parents to help their children become holy, a manifestation of that love.

#307 When is marriage a sacrament?

Marriage is a sacrament when both husband and wife are baptized. If one or both are not baptized at the time of marriage, the marriage is non-sacramental. The marriage becomes retroactively sacramental as soon as both husband and wife are baptized.

#308 How do we know that Jesus instituted the sacrament of Matrimony?

God instituted matrimony in the Garden of Eden, when He created Adam and Eve. Before the coming of Christ, matrimony was a *sacred contract*, but not a sacrament. Jesus raised Matrimony to the level of a sacrament.

Jesus taught the indissolubility of marriage (cf. Matthew 19:6), and this requires supernatural help (grace). Paul compares Christian marriage to the permanent union between Christ and His Church (cf. Ephesians 5:22-23) and stresses its importance, reinforcing the sacramental character of Matrimony. Also, early Christian writers refer to Christian marriage as something supernatural, which confers grace upon those who receive it. Finally, the Church has defined Matrimony as one of the seven sacraments instituted by Christ.

At the marriage feast at Cana, Christ worked his first public miracle, thus manifesting the holiness of the married state. In the marriage contract, God has made a natural relation a means of grace for Christians.

#309 How is the sacrament of Matrimony conferred?

A baptized man and a baptized woman confirm this sacrament upon each other by exchanging their marital vows of mutual consent before the Church.

#310 What are the matter and form of Matrimony?

The matter is a mutual consent of the spouses to give themselves to each other. The form consists in the words or actions through which the spouses express their consent.

#311 Who is the minister of the sacrament of Matrimony?

---

*This question's answer always blows my students'
minds. They usually tell me the priest is the*

minister of the sacrament of Matrimony. I make certain, however, to stress that the bride and groom are the ministers, as this affords me the opportunity to stress how heavy a decision it is to marry, as well as how permanent it is.

The ministers are the bride and groom themselves. Each confers the sacrament on the other, in the presence of a witnessing priest or deacon.

#312 What is necessary for the worthy reception of Matrimony?

Matrimony should be received by persons in the state of grace, who understand the responsibilities of married life and follow the marriage laws of the Church.

#313 What is the ordinary law regarding Matrimony?

The ordinary law of the Church requires that a Catholic be married in the presence of a priest or a deacon and before two witnesses.

#314 Why does the Church make laws regarding the marriages of Catholics?

The Church makes marriage laws because she has authority from Christ over all the sacraments and other spiritual matters that affect baptized persons.

#315 What is a Nuptial Mass?

A Nuptial Mass is a Wedding Mass with special prayers to obtain God's blessing for the couple. Like the marriage feast at Cana, a Nuptial Mass makes Jesus truly present. A Nuptial Mass is not obligatory, but it is the most appropriate setting for the celebration of Matrimony.

#316 What are the effects of Matrimony?

First, there is, as in all the sacraments after Baptism, an increase in sanctifying grace. Next, there is a *"marriage bond* [that] has been established by God himself in such a way that a marriage concluded and consummated between baptized persons can never be dissolved,"[1] except by death.

Finally, there is the sacramental grace of Matrimony.

This grace... is intended to perfect the couple's love and to strengthen their indissoluble unity. By this grace they 'help one another to attain holiness in their married life' and in welcoming and educating their children.[2]

#317 What would happen if one or both spouses were not in a state of grace at the time of their marriage?

A mortal sin of sacrilege would be committed; however, the sacrament would have been performed, and the spouses would be truly married. Sanctifying grace would be restored as soon as the spouse or spouses made a good confession.

Preparation for Matrimony

#318 How should a Catholic prepare for marriage?

It is imperative to give suitable and timely instruction to young people, above all in the heart of their own families, about the dignity of married love, its role and its exercise, so that, having learned the value of chastity, they will be able at a suitable age to engage in honorable courtship and enter upon a marriage of their own.[3]

Once a Catholic has begun to date, he or she should pray for God's help in choosing a partner, consult his or her parents and confessor, live a virtuous and chaste life, receive the sacraments of Penance and the Holy Eucharist often, and attend the premarital courses set up by the local bishop once a partner has been chosen.

#319 What qualities should one look for in a marriage partner?

The most important criterion for choosing a spouse is that he or she will help us walk toward the cross and salvation. You should seek a spouse with reverence for God and the teachings of the Catholic Church, as well as a spirit of charity, industry, and thrift.

#320 What is meant by "impediments" to marriage?

Impediments are obstacles which can prevent a couple from marrying or can make a marriage unlawful. Some of these impediments are: lack of age, impotence, an existing valid marriage, a close blood relationship, or affinity.

#321 If a couple marries without being aware of a serious impediment, is the marriage valid?

No, the marriage is invalid. A priest should be consulted, because in some cases a dispensation can be obtained from the bishop for the impediment. Then the marriage can be rectified, or blessed by the Church. In other cases, the marriage is simply void—non-existent.

#322 If a marriage is found to be null, are the children illegitimate?

No. The children produced in such a marriage are *legitimate* children of a *putative* marriage. In other words, they are of the legitimate children of a marriage that was thought to be valid.

#323 What is a mixed marriage?

Strictly speaking, a mixed marriage is a marriage

between a Catholic and a baptized non-Catholic. A marriage between a Catholic and a non-baptized person is called "disparity of cult."

#324 Why does the Church discourage mixed marriages?

Married people are called to perfect union of mind and communion of life, and this union can be broken or weakened when differences of opinion or disagreements touch on matters of religious truths and convictions.

#325 May a dispensation be obtained for a mixed marriage?

Yes. It is normally sought from the bishop through a priest.

#326 What must the Catholic party express when asking for this dispensation?

The Catholic spouse must declare that he or she is prepared to remove all dangers to his or her faith. He or she also has the grave obligation to promise to have each of the children baptized and raised Catholic.

#327 What is the non-Catholic's role in this regard?

Prior to the marriage, the non-Catholic party must be informed of the Catholic party's promises and obligations. He or she is to be well instructed in the duties, responsibilities, and character of Matrimony.

#328 Is separation ever permitted by the Church?

The Church permits a couple to separate for serious reasons, with the bishop's permission, but without the right to remarry.

#329 Is civil divorce permitted?

Civil divorce with the right to remarry is never permit-

ted, because it is against God's law; however, a civil divorce
for legal reasons is sometimes permitted by the bishop, but
neither partner may remarry while the other partner is still
living.

Children

#330 Can one validly enter into marriage with the intention of not having children?

One cannot validly enter into a marriage with the intention of not having children, because procreation is one of
the primary purposes of marriage, as given by God.

#331 Are Catholic couples obligated to have as many children as possible?

Catholic couples are not obliged to have as many children as possible, but rather to act in a responsible manner in
bringing children into the world and rearing them well.
Included in this responsibility is the recognition that the
procreation of children is one of the fundamental purposes
of marriage. This means that abortion and artificial birth
control are forbidden by God and the Church.

#332 Is marriage rendered invalid by child-lessness?

No. If a couple married with the intention of accepting
the children that God would send them, childlessness does
not render the marriage invalid.

Duties of the Married

#333 What are the chief duties of spouses to one another?

The chief duties are fidelity, cohabitation, and mutual

assistance. Fidelity is the obligation of each partner to refrain from any activity that is proper only to marriage with anyone other than the spouse. Cohabitation means that a husband and wife are to live together. Mutual assistance means friendship and mutual love, and all that they imply.

#334 What are the special duties of a husband?

A husband's special duties are to exercise his God-given authority with love, kindness, and respect toward his wife (Ephesians 5: 25) and toward his children (Colossians 3:21). Contrary to the orthodoxy of radical feminism, a man must exercise proper spiritual and temporal authority over his family. Failure to exercise this authority is an abomination before Almighty God.

#335 What are the special duties of a wife?

A wife's special duties are to agree with her husband in everything that is not sinful, and to be loving, devoted, and generously dedicated to her children and the care of the home.

#336 How can couples accomplish their duties and persevere in love until the end of their lives?

By asking God daily for the assistance of His grace. This is absolutely necessary for couples to fulfill their roles as spouses and parents.

TWENTY-FOUR
SACRAMENTALS

I will focus on the rosary and Brown Scapular in this chapter, in an attempt to motivate the student to develop a devotion to these two sacramentals. You can replace these with sacramentals you're especially devoted to if you want, but I focus on these because they encompass the Gospel and I'm never without them.

Sacred Signs

#337 What is a sacramental?

Sacramentals...

are sacred signs which bear a resemblance to the sacraments. They signify effects, particularly of a spiritual nature, which are obtained through the intercession of the Church.[1]

#338 How does a sacramental obtain blessings from God?

These blessings are obtained from the prayers that the Church offers for those using the sacramental, and because of the devotion that the object, action or word inspires.

#339 What blessings are obtained through sacramentals?

Some of the blessings obtained through sacramentals are actual graces, the forgiveness of venial sins, the removal of temporal punishment deserved by our sins, health and other material blessings, and defense against the devil.

#340 How do sacramentals differ from the sacraments?

Sacramentals are instituted by the Church, but the sacraments were instituted by Jesus Himself. Sacramentals obtain grace by the prayers of the Church, but the sacraments operate by the direct action of Christ. Finally, sacramentals are partly dependent upon the faith and dispositions of the person using them, while the sacraments depend solely on the direct power of Christ.

#341 Why did the Church institute sacramentals?

Sacramentals were instituted by the Church to add more dignity to the ritual of the sacraments, to help us receive the sacraments with better dispositions, and to inspire us to strive for holiness.

#342 What are two principal sacramentals?

Two principal sacramentals are the liturgical year and the Liturgy of the Hours, called the breviary. However, among all sacramentals, blessings come first.

#343 What is the liturgical year?

The liturgical year is a sacred time embracing the entire year, from the first Sunday of Advent to the last Sunday of Ordinary Time. It is a sacramental because it has been established by the Church to help us reflect on the mystery of our salvation and thus be inspired to live our life in conformity with the life of our Redeemer.

#344 How is the liturgical year divided?

The liturgical year is divided into five seasons:

1. Advent: we prepare for the coming of Christ at Christmas and at the end of the world;[2]
2. Christmas Season: we adore Christ in His birth, infancy and hidden life;
3. Lent: we commemorate Jesus' passion and death for our sins;
4. Easter Season: we celebrate the greatest event in human history, the resurrection of Jesus from the dead, His ascension into heaven, and Pentecost;
5. Ordinary Time: we reflect on the teachings of Christ during the 33 to 34 weeks of this season.

#345 What is the Liturgy of the Hours?

I strongly recommend to all lay evangelists that you make this a part of your daily prayer regimen.

The Liturgy of the Hours is the public prayer of the Church, and it is obligatory for men of holy orders and most men and women religious, according to the rule of their communities. It is highly recommended for the laity. It's...

celebration, faithful to the apostolic exhortations to "pray constantly" , is "so devised that the whole course of the day and night is made holy by the praise of God."[3]

The Liturgy of the Hours consists of seven prayers spaced throughout the waking hours: morning prayer, three daytime prayers, office of the readings, evening prayer, and night prayer. Not at all inconvenient, the Liturgy of the Hours, if properly prayed, takes less than a total of one and a half hours—the longest office takes twenty minutes, the shortest requires five minutes—so it is ideal for the laity, especially for those who cannot attend daily Mass.

#346 What are the sacramentals most used by Catholics?

The sacramentals most used by Catholics are holy water, crucifixes, rosaries, medals, statues, scapulars, candles, blessed ashes and blessed palms.

The Rosary

#347 What is the rosary?

I always go into detail about what we mean by meditation while showing the student my own rosary. (Get into the habit of carrying yours with you. Better yet, get into the habit of praying it every day.) I also always make sure I have a rosary and rosary leaflet to offer the student. You do the same. It's been my experience that if I can convince a student to wear the Brown Scapular for a week and pray the rosary 4-6 times over a two-week period, Our Lady always gets them and claims them for her own; they also make the best Catholic converts! Don't be forceful or too forward about your offer. Not only should you respect the student's desire

here; you need to recall the rosary is not a necessary
part of our faith.

The rosary is a prayer in honor of the Blessed Virgin Mary consisting of one hundred-fifty *Hail Marys* and fifteen *Our Fathers* accompanied by meditation on the life, passion, and glory of Christ.

#348 How did the rosary originate?

In the first centuries of Christianity there were many hermits who could not read the one hundred-fifty psalms, their daily prayer devotion. So they would substitute one *Our Father* and one *Hail Mary* for each psalm, and they would use stones or seeds strung on a cord to keep track of the number.

St. Dominic was the first to make generally accepted the practice of substituting one hundred-fifty *Hail Marys* for the psalms. In the 13th century, heresy ravaged southern France and northern Italy, and the pope appointed St. Dominic to preach against the heretical doctrines. Dominic had little success, so he prayed to the Blessed Virgin Mary for the conversion of the heretics through the rosary that she herself had given him. God blessed Dominic's devotion, and he was then successful in converting the heretics.

#349 Has God given His approval to the rosary through miracles?

The greatest miracle is always the conversion of a sinner to repentance through Christ's Church. The rosary is a powerful prayer to obtain grace from God through the intercession of the Blessed Virgin Mary. The conversions that have their beginning in the devotion of the rosary are quite literally innumerable! Hundreds of millions of Catholics

The rosary has also been responsible for miracles in

times of danger and calamity. Such was the case with the defeat of the Turks in the Battle of Lepanto on October 7, 1571. It was in thanksgiving for this victory over the Moslems, who were trying to wipe Christianity from the face of the earth, that Pope St. Pius V Instituted the Feast of the Holy Rosary on the anniversary of that battle. September 11, 1683 is the anniversary of the Battle of Vienna, when the Polish king defeated the Moslems in their last effort to destroy Christendom.

#350 Is the rosary simple to pray?

The very simplicity of the rosary makes it an ideal prayer for children, as it is easily memorized and begins children in the good habit of the daily meditation. However, the contemplative aspects of the Rosary also make it satisfying to the soul and intellect of adults.

#351 How is the rosary prayed?

One fourth of the rosary is ordinarily prayed: fifty *Hail Marys* and five *Our Fathers* prayed on a string of beads slipped through the fingers. The rosary combines vocal and mental prayer. It is a summary of the most important parts of the Gospels. Catholic should not fail to pray at least five decades of the rosary every day.

Ordinarily, we begin the rosary with a *Sign of the Cross* and by reciting the Apostles' Creed. Then we pray one *Our Father*, three *Hail Marys*, and one *Glory Be to the Father* for an increase in the virtues of faith, hope, and charity.

We pray the *Our Father* on the beads between each decade, and the *Hail Mary* on each of the ten consecutive beads. One *Our Father* and ten *Hail Marys* are referred to as a decade. It is customary to close each decade with a *Glory Be to the Father*.

While we pray each decade, we should meditate upon one mystery of our faith. The rosary is divided into four sets of mysteries: the joyful, the luminous, the sorrowful, and the glorious, each honoring respectively five aspects of the life, passion and death, and glorification of Jesus Christ.

The rosary is typically ended by praying the *Hail Holy Queen* and the *Sign of the Cross*.

The Brown Scapular

#352 What is the Brown Scapular?

The full name of the scapular is the Brown Scapular of Our Lady of Mount Carmel. It is two small pieces of brown cloth, usually wool, attached by two cords. It is worn by placing it over their shoulders so that one piece of the cloth rests on the wearer's chest, the other on the back between the shoulder blades. The scapular is usually worn beneath the person's clothing.

#353 What is the origin of the Brown Scapular?

Our Lady of Mount Carmel goes all the way back to the 8th century BC. Elijah the prophet ascended Mount Carmel in Palestine to begin a long tradition of contemplation and prayer. Based on God's promise in Genesis 3:15 that the Savior would enter the world through a woman, Elias began a devotion to the Mother of God 800 years before she was even born. Elias and his followers dedicated themselves to this most chosen woman among all women to become the Mother of the Savior.

On the Jewish feast of Pentecost, the day the Holy Spirit awakened the Church, the spiritual descendants of Elijah and his followers came down from Mount Carmel to attend the ancient feast at Jerusalem.

At Peter's public preaching at the feast, the good

hermits realized the lady to whom they were devoted had to come and given birth to the Savior, and that He had completed the work of redemption. Consequently, they were baptized by the apostles. When the hermits were presented to Our Lady, they were overcome with a sense of majesty and sanctity which they never forgot. Upon their return to Mount Carmel, they erected the first chapel ever built in honor of the Blessed Virgin Mary. From that time to the present, devotion to the Mother of God has been handed down by the hermits of Mount Carmel.

In 1241, Baron de Gray of England returned from the Crusades, bringing with him a group of Carmelites from the holy mountain. He generously gave the hermits a manor house in Aylesford for the religious order to live in and grow.

Ten years later, at the donated manor house, St. Simon Stock was praying to Our Lady for help when she appeared to him. As Mary handed St. Simon the Brown Scapular she said, "This shall be the privilege for you and all Carmelites, that anyone dying in this habit shall be saved."

#354 Why do we wear the Brown Scapular?

When Our Lady gave the Brown Scapular to St. Simon Stock, she made the following promise: "Take this scapular. Whosoever dies wearing it shall not suffer eternal fire. It shall be a sign of salvation, a protection in danger, and a pledge to peace." On the very day that Our Lady gave the scapular to Saint Simon, Lord Peter of Lenton urgently called the saint: "Come quickly, Father, my brother is dying in despair!" St. Simon went immediately to the dying man, asking Our Lady to keep her promise. When draped with St. Simon's scapular, the man immediately repented, made a good confession, and died in the state of grace. That night the dead man appeared to his brother and said, "I have been saved through the most powerful Queen and the habit of that man as a shield."

#355 Has God given approval to the Brown Scapular through other miracles?

Yes! There are far too many miracles to mention here, so we shall treat only one.

In the late summer of 1845, the English ship *King of the Ocean* found itself in a terrible hurricane. A Protestant minister, together with his wife and children and other passengers, struggled to deck to pray for mercy and forgiveness, as the ship was about to sink and all aboard perish.

Among the crew was a young Irishman, John McAuliffe. Realizing the situation was hopeless, the young man opened his shirt, took off his Scapular, made this Sign of the Cross with it over the angry waves, and tossed it into the ocean.

At that moment, the sea became calm. Only one more wave washed over the deck, tossing young John's Scapular at his feet. He put it back on, and went about his business. Mr. Fisher, the minister, had observed all of McAuliffe's actions. When the minister questioned the young man, he told him and his family about the Holy Virgin and her Scapular. The Fishers were so impressed that they became Catholics as soon as possible, thus enjoying the Virgin's patronage.

#356 May a non-Catholic wear the Brown Scapular?

Yes! In doing so, a non-Catholic will receive many graces and blessings with this special sign of devotion to the Mother of God.

TWENTY-FIVE

CHRISTIAN MORALITY—A PRIMER

Conscience

#357 What is conscience?

Conscience is a judgment of reason whereby the human person recognizes the moral quality of a concrete act that he is going to perform, is a process of performing, or has already completed.[1]

#358 Must we follow our conscience?

After diligent reflection, when we are certain something is the right thing to do, we must follow our conscience.

#359 But isn't conscience merely a formation of thought from a person's culture or religious belief system?

No, conscience is not of human origin. Each human person "has in his heart a law inscribed by God."[2] The conscience is the most secret inner core of man, and it is part of the soul's faculty of intellect. We are not aware of our conscience from the brain, a mere human organ, but from a movement of the soul. No neurologist or scientist can tell us what part of the brain governs the conscience, because the brain is incapable, as an organ, of judging the difference between good and evil.

I learned much later in my career that millennials actually do grasp moral code and responsibility when you take the time to explain natural law. Although I have no formal questions and answers about this in my normal presentation of the catechism, I do supplementally explain natural law in a way they can understand. My presentation follows.

There are basically three types of law: human law, natural law, and divine law. Human law is largely based on natural law. In fact, our constitution in America is completely based on natural law. So that leads us to defining what natural law is.

Let's take God completely out of the picture and assume He doesn't exist. We can still know the difference between right and wrong through natural law. Natural law is what we can observe of nature. Natural law is our intuitive knowledge of right and wrong. For example, we intuitively know it is wrong to steal, murder, or tell a lie. But let's get specific with an example.

When we look at all animal life—from squirrels to humans—we can see that all species of animal life are male and female. From our observation we can reason that the existence of male and female is to propagate and perpetuate the species; in other words, to be fruitful and multiply. Therefore, since our reason tells us that natural law dictates the generation of life, we can deduce that any sexual activity that blocks the possibility of generating new life is a violation of natural law. Anything—absolutely anything—that violates natural law is a perversion of nature, which is where we get the term pervert.

Violating the natural law has its consequences. If our sexual activity cannot result in the possibility of human life, we do not produce enough children to support previous generations. Such is the case today in the western world; we are not producing enough children. Indeed, we are only producing half as many children as we need to support society.

Now let's bring God back into the picture. God has taken many aspects of natural law (which He authored) and elevated them to the level of divine law. Just as there are consequences for violating natural law, there are also consequences for violating divine law. The difference is, when we violate natural law there are natural consequences, but when we violate divine law there are both natural and supernatural consequences. This makes violation of some natural laws more consequential and greater perversions.

You will need to come up with your own way of explaining natural law and divine law in a way your particular student will understand.

#360 Are we truly responsible for our actions?

Yes, we are responsible for all of our actions, because God gave us an intellect and free will. We must use them to fulfill the purpose for which we were created, which is to know, love, and serve God in this life so we can be forever happy with Him in the next. To use the intellect and free will for anything contrary to God's law is an abuse of those gifts.

#361 What is a right conscience?

A right conscience is one in conformity with natural law, divine law, and the Church's moral teachings.

#362 How can a right conscience be formed?

We form a right conscience by studying God's moral code, as authoritatively taught by the Church. By learning and understanding Christian morality, and with the aid we ask from the Holy Spirit, we can form a conscience that will lead us to sanctity and salvation.

#363 What is a doubtful conscience?

A doubtful conscience is one that cannot decide for or against the morality of an act. One must either refrain from acting or resolve the doubt. We may never act upon a doubtful conscience, as it is a sin to do so.

#364 What is a scrupulous conscience?

A scrupulous conscience is one that is constantly in doubt. It is in dread of sin where none exists, or in dread of mortal sin when the sin is only venial. The ordinary cure for a scrupulous conscience is obedience to good and wise confessor. Absent such obedience, a person with a scrupulous conscience my eventually have to seek medical help from a competent mental health professional.

#365 What is a lax conscience?

A lax conscience is one that judges more by convenience than by God's law.

This is the case when a man "takes a little trouble to find out what is true and good, or when conscience is by degrees almost blinded through the habit of committing sin." In such cases, the person is culpable for the evil he commits.[3]

#366 Is everything that is legal morally right?

Not necessarily. Until the middle of the twentieth century, all the laws of our Occidental society could almost always be counted on to follow the moral norms of natural law. This is not so any longer, as the example of legalized abortion demonstrates. We are obligated only to obey laws that comport to God's law, even under the threat of imprisonment or death (Acts 5:29).

#367 Does a good end ever justify the use of evil means?

We may never commit evil that good may come from it. Indeed, we must be willing to make whatever sacrifices are necessary to keep God's law.

Let's say a police officer is called to testify in a criminal trial. The defense attorney has cornered the officer on a technicality during cross-examination. The defendant's guilt is not in dispute, but he could be freed on the basis of this minor legal technicality. All the officer has to do to avoid having the case dismissed and having the felon released is to tell a small lie. Can the officer tell this white lie? Absolutely not! He must be willing to see the case dismissed, the felon freed, and himself disgraced rather than to lie. So, despite Supreme Court rulings to the contrary, police officers cannot lie to suspects in order to gain information or a confession.

#368 If a person errs because of invincible ignorance, does this person sin?

No, a person cannot sin because he is invincibly ignorant (unavoidably unknowledgeable) of a moral situation. However, invincible ignorance

remains no less an evil, a privation, a disorder. One must therefore work to correct the errors of moral conscience.[4]

TWENTY-SIX

THE TEN COMMANDMENTS

An Overview

#369 What are the two great commandments?

The first is that

'You shall love the Lord your God with all your heart, and with all your soul, and with all your mind, and with all your strength.' The second is this, 'You shall love your neighbor as yourself.' There is no other commandment greater than these.[1]

#370 How can we practice the two great commandments?

Simply by fulfilling the ten commandments, which are encompassed by the two great commandments. The first three of the ten commandments deal with man's relationship to God. The fourth commandment is a sort of transitional commandment, in that it deals with both man's relationship to God and man's relationship to man. The last six commandments deal with man's relationship to man.

#371 Where did the ten commandments

come from?

They were written 'with the finger of God', unlike the other commandments written by Moses.[2]

They set forth the natural law.

#372 What are the ten commandments?

The ten commandments are:

1. I am the Lord your God. You shall have no other gods besides me.
2. You shall not take the name of the Lord, your God, in vain.
3. Remember to keep holy the Lord's day.
4. Honor your father and your mother.
5. You shall not commit murder.
6. You shall not commit adultery.
7. You shall not steal.
8. You shall not bear false witness against your neighbor.
9. You shall not covet your neighbor's wife.
10. You shall not covet anything that belongs to your neighbor.[3]

#373 Can we always keep the ten Commandments?

Yes. No matter how great the temptation, we can always keep God's commandments because He will always give us the necessary actual graces to do so.[4]

#374 Is it enough to merely keep the ten commandments?

No, keeping the ten commandments alone is not enough. We must always be willing to do the will of God in order glorify Him.

TWENTY-SEVEN

THE FIRST COMMANDMENT

I, the Lord, am your God. You shall have no other gods besides me.

Divine Worship

#375 What are we obligated to do by the first commandment?

The first commandment obligates us to love God above all things, and to worship and adore only Him.

#376 How do we show God our love?

We show God we love Him by believing in Him and His teachings, thanking Him, trusting Him, asking His forgiveness for failing him in sin, asking for his help, doing penance for our sins, and obeying His laws.

#377 Are we to pray to God privately or with others?

Since we are both individuals and social creatures, we should pray to God in private and with others.

#378 Is there any particularly important way to worship God?

Participating well in the Holy Sacrifice of the Mass is the most important way to worship God.

#379 What does the first commandment forbid?

The first commandment forbids superstition, idolatry, spiritism, sacrilege, atheism, and participating in certain acts of non-Catholic worship.

#380 What is superstition?

Superstition is attributing to a creature a power that belongs only to God. Examples would be to use lucky charms or to be ruled by dreams.

#381 What is idolatry?

Idolatry consists in divinizing what is not God. Man commits idolatry when he honors and revers a creature in place of God, whether this be gods or demons (for example, Satanism), power, pleasure, race, ancestors, the state, money, etc.[1]

#382 What is spiritism?

Spiritism often implies divination [conjuring the dead for having recourse to demonic powers] or magical practices.[2]

#383 What is sacrilege?

Sacrilege is an act of irreligion. It is the mistreatment of sacred persons, places, or things. An example would be to receive Communion in a state of mortal sin, since this would be an abuse of the Eucharist.

#384 What is atheism?

Atheism is the denial of God's existence. It is called *practical atheism* when a person lives a lifestyle that completely ignores God and His laws.

#385 Why is it wrong for Catholics to participate in certain acts of non-Catholic worship?

Although we should promote ecumenism[3] as often as possible, there are still certain acts of non-Catholic worship that are wrong, because such activity would imply that a Catholic believes that other religions that lack the fullness of truth are on an equal par with Catholicism. For example, Catholics may never participate in Protestant communion services, often called the "Lord's Supper" by them, because Christ is only truly present in the Holy Eucharist on Catholic altars. Another example is that normally Catholics are not permitted to attend the wedding of a Catholic who is being married outside the Church, because this implies that the sacrament of Matrimony, which is a form of worship because it is a sacrament, is not necessary to be married. When in doubt, consult your pastor.

Honoring the Blessed Virgin and the Saints

#386 Does the first commandment allow us to honor and pray to the Blessed Virgin Mary and the saints?

Not only does the first commandment permit us to honor the Blessed Virgin Mary and the saints, but Sacred Scripture encourages us to do so. In speaking of that is just who have passed on from this mortal life, Sirach writes:

Their bodies were buried in peace, and their names live to all generations. Peoples will declare their wisdom, and the congregation proclaims their praise.[4]

In her Magnificat, Mary makes this prophetic statement:

For behold, Henceforth all generations will call me blessed.[5]

#387 What do we call the honor given to Mary and the saints?

There are three types of honor that can be given: *latria, dulia,* and *hyperdulia.* Latria is adoration and must be given to God alone. Dulia is the honor we give to the saints on all three planes: in the Church Suffering, in the Church Victorious, and in the Church Militant. In other words, this is the honor due to all Christians in this life and next, but it is commonly thought of as the honor (also called veneration) given to the saints in heaven. Finally, there is hyperdulia, that veneration which is reserved for the Blessed Virgin Mary alone.

Hyperdulia is reserved for Mary because she is the most special saint of human history. The Catholic Church has always paid special honor to the Blessed Virgin, because God honored her above all creatures by granting her the highest dignity He could confer—the divine maternity.

#388 How does the Church honor the Mother of God?

The Church honors the Mother of God in the liturgy and various devotions. She encourages the faithful to know, imitate, love, and pray to the Blessed Virgin in a special way. After all, from the beginning of her Son's public ministry until today she has been His chief evangelist, as she proved when she first spoke the words:

Do whatever he tells you.[6]

#389 Why does the Church honor the angels?

The Church honors the angels for several reasons. Firstly, in the order of nature the angels hold a superior position to all of creation. Secondly, they perpetually adore the Blessed Trinity. Finally, God has made them His special messengers to help us obtain our salvation.

#390 Why do we honor and pray to the saints?

We honor and pray to the saints because they are His special friends who, through His grace, lived holy lives and reflected His virtues to a heroic degree. By honoring the saints we honor God Himself.

This should not seem unusual to non-Catholics, as honoring people has always been a common practice. We call ministers Reverend, judges Your Honor, and refer to politicians as The Honorable. Furthermore, God Himself commands us to "honor your father and your mother"; and in compliance with God's law, traditional wedding vows call upon the wife to "love, honor, and obey" her husband.

Karl Keating says that

If there can be nothing wrong with honoring the living, who still have an opportunity to ruin their lives through sin, or the uncanonized dead, about whose state of spiritual health we can only guess, certainly there can be no argument against giving honor to saints whose lives are done and ended them in sanctity. If merit deserves to be honored wherever it is found, it surely should be honored among God's special friends.[7]

#391 How do we honor the saints?

We honor the saints by learning about their lives so we can imitate their virtues, praying to them for their intercession, and respecting their relics and images.

#392 Why do we honor the bodies and relics of the saints?

By honoring the bodies and relics of saints we are not only venerating the bodies and objects connected with them (relics), but we are actually venerating the person whose relic it is. An excellent biblical example is found in Acts 19:11-12.

God Himself has given a great honor to the bodies of many of his special friends by not permitting them to know decay after death. These bodies, none of which were embalmed or mummified, have been left perfectly preserved as God's stamp of approval on the lives of the saints.

I always recommend the definitive book on this topic. It is called The Incorruptibles *by Joan Carroll Cruz. Over 100 saints are featured, and there are photographs of many of them and their incorrupt state.*

Images

#393 Does the first commandment allow us to make use of statues and images?

Yes, provided they do not become objects of false worship. God forbade the Jews to make graven images because they lived among pagans, and that influence made them inclined to worship images.

Those who would accuse Catholics of violating the first commandment because of our use of statues and holy cards do not properly interpret this commandment. We know that the Jews did not interpret this commandment as an absolute prohibition against images. There are many examples in the Bible to prove this. God forbade images in the first commandment, yet he ordered the brazen serpent (Numbers 29:8-9), and the golden cherubim atop the Ark of the Covenant (Exodus 25:18-20). Then there were also the carved garlands of flowers, fruit and trees (Numbers 8:4), and the carved lions that supported the king's throne (I Kings 7:27-37).

To criticize Catholics for the use of images is not honest. In order for these critics to be honest they would have to forbid themselves the personal use of coinage, currency, photographs, sculptures, paintings, and even television.

#394 How should images and statues of Christ and the saints be treated?

Such images and statues should be treated with the same respect we would treat pictures of our loved ones.

#395 Do Catholics pray to images, crucifixes and statues?

Absolutely not! When Catholics pray before such images they are praying to the persons those images represent. Many of us carry photographs of our spouse or children, but we never mistake the photograph for the child himself.

TWENTY-EIGHT

THE SECOND COMMANDMENT

You shall not take the name of the Lord, your God, in vain.

Reverence in Speech

#396 What are we obligated to do by the second commandment?

The second commandment obligates us to always speak of God, the Blessed Virgin Mary, and the saints and sacred persons, places and things with reverence. It also obligates us to take oaths truthfully, and to be faithful in fulfilling promissory oaths and vows.

#397 Why are we obligated to speak respectfully of sacred persons, places and things?

We are so obligated because sacred persons, places and things are consecrated to God.

#398 What does the second commandment forbid?

At this point, you're likely to get questions that are actually requests to define these words, but merely tell the student you're going to define each one.

The second commandment forbids profanity, blasphemy, cursing, and carelessness or deceit in taking oaths and making vows.

#399 What is profanity?

Profanity is

the abuse of God's name, i.e., every improper use of them names of God, Jesus Christ, but also of the Virgin Mary and all the saints.[1]

We violate this—usually in a venial way—when, for example, we use these holy names when expressing anger or surprise.

Blasphemy and Cursing

#400 What is blasphemy?

Blasphemy

consists in uttering against God—inwardly or outwardly —words of hatred, reproach, or defiance; in speaking ill of God, in failing in respect toward him in one's speech; in misusing God's name... The prohibition of blasphemy extends to language against Christ's Church, the saints, and sacred things... Blasphemy is contrary to the respect due God and his holy name. It is in itself a grave sin.[2]

#401 What is cursing?

Oddly, this is really a big point with many people... particularly millennials. As tasteless and tacky as this may seem, they really want to have it affirmed that it's morally okay to use vulgar language —"cussin". This is beyond a doubt the most foul-mouthed generation in history, often times using language that would have made me turn red when I was a young soldier. However, you owe your students every legitimate liberty they have. So don't hesitate to tell them vulgar language is morally neutral, except under certain conditions, if they display a penchant for foul language. But always set the example yourself... and keep your opinions to yourself, unless you're asked.

Many mistakenly believe that cursing is the use of vulgar language. This could not be further from the truth. While the use of vulgar language can be sinful if used in mixed company, or in the presence of children, in and of itself, vulgar language is not inherently evil. The equation of vulgar language with cursing is the result of Protestant fundamentalist influences that have crept into Catholicism.

Cursing is actually what the term implies: the invoking of evil upon a person, place or thing. It is sinful to curse animals chiefly because of the uncontrolled anger or impatience involved. It is sinful to curse a human being because that person is made in the image and likeness of God.

Oaths and Vows

#402 What is an oath?

An oath is calling upon God to witness the truthfulness of what we say.

#403 Under what conditions may we use an oath?

We may use an oath if:

- we have a good reason for taking it
- we are sure we are speaking the truth
- we do not have a sinful intention

#404 What constitutes a good reason for taking an oath?

The glory of God, the good of our neighbor, or our own personal good are valid reasons for taking an oath.

#405 What is perjury?

Perjury is deliberately asking God to witness a lie. The abuse of an oath is a mortal sin.

#406 Are we obligated to keep a promissory oath?

Such oaths are

promises made to others in God's name [to] engage the divine honor, fidelity, truthfulness, and authority. They must be respected in justice. To be unfaithful to them is to misuse God's name and in some way to make God out to be a liar.[3]

#407 What is a vow?

A vow is a free and deliberate promises made to God, by which a person binds himself under pain of sin to do something especially pleasing to God. The most common are the marriage vows and those of poverty, chastity, and obedience, taken by members of religious orders. These and other vows may be made by private individuals but they are cautioned to do so only after having consulted their confessor.

#408 What must one remember before taking a vow?

One must remember that one is obligated to fulfill any vow made.

TWENTY-NINE

THE THIRD COMMANDMENT

Remember to keep holy the Lord's day.

Participation in the Mass

#409 What are we obligated to do by the third commandment?

The precept of the Church specifies the law of the Lord more precisely: "On Sundays and other holy days of obligation the faithful are bound to participate in the Mass." "The precept of participating in the Mass is satisfied by assistance at a Mass which is celebrated anywhere in the Catholic rite either on the holy day or on the evening of the preceding day." [1]

This commandment also obligates us to avoid any activities which hinder the renewal of the body and soul.

#410 Why are we obligated to participate in the Mass rather than simply worship God in our hearts?

The Mass is the highest form of worship of God there is,

as it is the perpetuation of Christ's redeeming sacrifice on the cross. As St. John Chrysostom wrote:

You cannot pray at home as at church, where there is a great multitude, where exclamations are cried out to God as from one great heart, and where there is something more: the Union of minds, the accord of souls, the bond of charity, the prayers of the priests.[2]

#411 Is it necessary to be physically present at Mass?

Yes, we must be physically present at the Mass in order to fulfill our obligation. Televised Masses, although a consolation to the homebound who are unable to attend Mass, are not acceptable as a means of fulfilling our Sunday obligation. Furthermore, to miss a notable part of the Mass—that is, to arrive late or leave early—could be a sin and not meet the Sunday obligation.

#412 At what age does the obligation to participate in Mass begin?

The obligation to participate in the Mass begins at the age of the use of reason; that is, at about seven years of age.

#413 How grave is the obligation to participate in the Mass on Sundays and holy days of obligation?

Unless one is excused because of a very good reason, one commits a mortal sin if one fails to participate in the Mass on Sundays and holy days.

#414 Why was Sunday set aside as the Lord's Day in place of the Sabbath of the Old Testament?

It obviously took some time for the apostles to alter the Lord's day from the Sabbath to Sunday, as we see them continuing to attend the temple services on the Sabbath, followed by Mass on Sunday. From the apostolic tradition of celebrating the Mass on Sunday we have come to know that as the Lord's day (Acts 20:7).

A Day of Rest

#415 What does the third commandment tell us to avoid?

We are to refrain from unnecessary servile works; that is,

work or activities that hinder the worship owed to God, the joy proper to the Lord's Day, the performance of the works of mercy, and the appropriate relaxation of mind and body.[3]

#416 How else may we sanctify Sundays and the holy days?

Christians will also sanctify Sunday by devoting time and care to their families and relatives, often difficult to do on other days of the week.[4]

THIRTY

THE FOURTH COMMANDMENT

Honor your father and your mother.

Children and Parents

---

*In our modern culture, fatherhood is thought of as
the ability to sire a child and nothing more. This
attitude is not in keeping with common sense,
natural law, or divine law. I am a very strong
advocate of the proper role of a father in Christian
fatherhood. Unless I am working in small groups, I
work only with men. Therefore, I supplement this
section by focusing on the duties and
responsibilities of a father. I stress that if a father
doesn't discipline his children now, a criminal
judge will only be too happy to discipline the child
in the future. If I feel the student has the necessary
intellectual prowess and inclination to do so, I
always recommend he read* Be a Man *by Father*

Larry Richards and Into the Breach *by Bishop Thomas Olmstead,*[1] *an apostolic exhortation.*

#417 What are we obliged to do by the fourth commandment?

The fourth commandment obliges us to respect our parents, obey them in all that is not sinful, and help them in their needs.

#418 What is the source and basis of parental authority?

The divine fatherhood is the source of human fatherhood; this is the foundation and the honor owed parents. The respect of children, whether minors or adults, for their father and mother is nourished by the natural affection born of the bond uniting them. It is required by God's commandment.[2]

#419 How do children show love and respect for their parents?

Children show their love and respect by speaking and acting with gratitude, trying to please their parents, readily accepting corrections, seeking parental advice in important decisions, and praying for their parents.

#420 Do grown children still have obligations to their parents?

Yes. Children are obligated to continue in the respect of their parents, and are to give both material and moral support when their parents are in need.

#421 What are the duties of parents toward children?

Parents are to provide for the spiritual and physical needs of their children.[3]

The role of parents in education is of such importance

that it is almost impossible to provide an adequate substitute.[4]

#422 What does the fourth commandment forbid?

The fourth commandment forbids disobedience toward our parents and every form of disrespect, unkindness, stubbornness, spitefulness, wishing them evil, and violence.

All Lawful Authority

#423 Does the fourth commandment also obligate us to obey all lawful authority?

God's fourth commandment also enjoins us to honor all who for our good have received authority in society from God. It clarifies the duties of those who exercise authority as well as those who benefit from it.[5]

#424 Whom does the term "lawful authority" include?

Lawful authority includes teachers, employers, public officials, and Church leaders.

Workers and Employers

#425 What are the duties of workers toward their employer?

Workers are to respect their employer, and to serve him faithfully according to their agreement.

#426 How should employers treat their workers?

Employers are to treat their workers with respect and fairness, bearing in mind that the authority God has given them is limited.

Citizens and Public Officials

#427 What must a citizen do for his nation?

A citizen must love and be in the service of his country, obey just laws, respect the legitimate authority, pay his taxes, exercise his right to vote, and defend his country.[6]

#428 Is it a sin to vote for an enemy of religion or of the common good?

If, after responsibly informing ourselves of the political issues and candidates, we discover that a candidate is an enemy of religion or of the common good, it could be a sin to vote for that candidate. Such a vote could equate to voluntary participation in that candidate's evil. A common example in the modern political scene would be to vote for a candidate who favors legalized abortion over a candidate who is pro-life.

#429 What are the most important duties of public officials?

Political authorities are obliged to respect the fundamental rights of the human person... dispense justice humanely...[7] and work for the common good.

THIRTY-ONE

THE FIFTH COMMANDMENT

You shall not commit murder.

Sins Against Life

#430 What does the fifth commandment forbid?

The fifth commandment forbids intentional homicide, abortion, euthanasia, child abuse, sterilization, suicide, and all that can lead to physical or spiritual harm to oneself or others, such as anger, fighting, revenge, drunkenness, drug abuse, torments inflicted on mind or body, hatred, and bad example.

#431 What is intentional homicide?

Intentional homicide is the unjust taking of an innocent human life.

#432 What is abortion?

Abortion is the intentional killing of a pre-born child at any time after conception. The God-given authority of a parent **does not** extend to the taking of the life of a pre-born child. Abortion, in any form, is always a mortal sin.

The Church has taught from her inception that abortion is morally evil.

#433 Does rape or incest justify abortion?

Abortion is never justified, no matter what the cause of the child's conception. It is easy to understand how a mother would be inclined to not want a child conceived in the case of rape or incest, but the child still has as much right to life as the mother. The Church is very sympathetic to such involuntary mothers, and many organizations and agencies within the Church are set up to provide for counseling, temporal and medical assistance, and adoption as a moral alternative to abortion.

#434 Does the Church impose any penalty upon a person who procures an abortion?

Yes, the Church automatically imposes the penalty of excommunication upon any person who procures an abortion.[1] This penalty extends to anyone who aids in its procurement or otherwise participates in any way with an abortion. This automatic excommunication could extend to Catholic politicians who are pro-choice.

#435 What is excommunication?

Excommunication is

A penalty or censure by which a baptized Roman Catholic is excluded from the communion of the faithful, for committing and remaining obstinate in certain serious offenses specified in Canon Law; e.g. heresy, schism, apostasy, abortion... by excommunication [the Catholic] is deprived of [Church membership and its spiritual goods] until he repents and receives absolution.[2]

#436 What is "indirect abortion"?

Here is where I mention that indirect abortion falls under the moral theological principle of double effect. The principle of double effect says the moral event produces a secondary, unintended effect. The primary effect of an action is the intended result, but the secondary act is an unfortunate result of the primary act.

Indirect abortion is not really abortion at all. Indirect abortion occurs when a surgical procedure is performed on the mother for a serious pathological condition in which the intention is to save the mother's life. In such a case, the death of the fetus is then an incidental and secondary result, which would have been avoided if possible. The fetus should still be baptized.

#437 Why is euthanasia immoral?

Euthanasia is immoral because life is taken with the excuse of avoiding pain, shortening suffering, or eliminating someone who is supposedly useless to society because of old age, defect, or illness. Only God can decide when life should end.

Christ sanctified suffering on the cross. For those who suffer and are not Catholic, the Holy Spirit can use that suffering in the process of the suffering person's conversion. A person who is already a Catholic can unite his suffering with the crucified Christ, thereby making his prayers very powerful and honorable in the sight of Christ.

#438 Is it ever lawful to take the life of another?

It can be lawful to take the life of another person when

there is no other means to defend one's own life or the life of another.

The act of self defense can have a double effect: the preservation of one's own life; and the killing of the aggressor... The one is intended, the other is not.[3]

Legitimate defense can be not only a right but a grave duty for one who is responsible for the lives of others. The defense of the common good requires that an unjust aggressor be rendered unable to cause harm.[4]

It can also be lawful to take the life of another person in a just war.

#439 Does lawful public authority have the right to put a criminal to death?

Like abortion, capital punishment has become a political issue rather than the moral issue that it is. Capital punishment is a hotly debated topic, but the Roman Catholic Church has remained constant in her teachings.

The Church tells us that she

does not exclude recourse to the death penalty, if this is the only possible way of effectively defending human lives against the unjust aggressor.[5]

However, she continues to say that

[i]f... non-lethal means are sufficient to defend and protect people's safety from the aggressor, authority will limit itself to such means...[6]

Due to the advanced state of penology, this essentially rules out the use of capital punishment in Occidental society, but it still does not make it immoral.

#440 Why is direct suicide sinful?

Direct suicide is a mortal sin because God alone has the right over life and death. When a person commits suicide he attempts to displace God and His rightful authority. Of course, the victim of suicide who suffers from elements that restrict his free will may not be responsible for his act in the sight of God.[7]

#441 Is sterilization ever permitted?

When done with the intention of preventing conception, sterilization is always sinful. Direct sterilization removes for selfish reasons the procreative power given for the generation of human life. Indirect sterilization is not sinful, as it is done to correct a serious pathological condition.

#442 Is abuse of alcohol and drugs sinful?

Any access is sinful, and the abuse of drugs and alcohol is always excessive. Furthermore, the abuse of alcohol and drugs not only does harm to mind and body, but it places the abuser in a position where his own excesses can be harmful to others.

#443 What is scandal?

Scandal is giving a another person the occasion of committing sin through one's words, actions, or omissions.

Preserving Life

#444 To what does the fifth commandment obligate us regarding physical life and health?

We are all obligated to take the ordinary means to preserve our own life and health and that of our neighbor so far as we are able.

#445 Are we obligated to take extraordinary means to preserve our life?

We are not obligated to take extraordinary means which involve extreme difficulty in order to preserve our life. However, extraordinary means are to be taken when the person is very necessary to his family, the Church, or society.

I follow this up by trying to explain what extraordinary means are. I tell them I remember when the first open-heart surgery was performed. Bypass surgery was considered extraordinary means when it first began to be used, but with the advancements in medical technology, bypass surgery has become commonplace. It is no longer considered extraordinary means but rather ordinary.

#446 May a person ever risk his own life or health?

A person may risk his life for health if there is a proportionately serious reason. A good example would be to sacrifice your own life to save another. This is, after all, what Jesus did for us all on the cross.

#447 Is the transplantation of vital organs ever permitted?

The Church does permit the transplantation of vital organs, provided the donor is already truly dead, or if he can lead a normal life without the organ. Donating a kidney is an example.

THIRTY-TWO

THE SIXTH AND NINTH COMMANDMENTS

You shall not commit adultery.
You shall not covet your neighbor's wife.

The Commandments of Purity

#448 Why are the sixth and ninth commandments treated together?

These two commandments are treated together because they both deal with sexual purity. The six commandment deals with exterior sexual purity, and the ninth commandment deals with interior sexual purity.

#449 What is the sixth commandment?

"You shall not commit adultery" (Exodus 20:14).

#450 What are we obligated to do by the sixth commandment?

The sixth commandment obliges us to be pure and modest in behavior when both alone and with others.

#451 What does the sixth commandment forbid?

The sixth commandment forbids impurity and immodest behavior, and everything that leads to impurity.

#452 What are some of the common sins committed against sixth commandment?

Some of the common sins committed against sixth commandment are adultery, fornication, contraception, homosexual activity, prostitution, premarital sex, masturbation, and pornography.

Fornication and Adultery

#453 What is fornication?

Fornication is sexual intercourse between an unmarried man and an unmarried woman.

#454 What is adultery?

Adultery is sexual intercourse between two persons, at least one of whom is married (cf. Matthew 5:27-28).

Contraception

#455 Why is contraception seriously sinful?

Contraception is seriously sinful because it rejects chaste married love and defies God by wanting to increase pleasure while avoiding the God-given responsibility of appropriating children. Furthermore, the irresponsible use of sex by way of contraception leads to a lack of respect for sex, the marriage partner as a person, and life.

#456 What about the Pill?

The Pill is evil morally, ethically, and medically. It condemns women to a premature death, impedes the conception of children and destroys life in the womb. Furthermore, use of the Pill leads people into other immoral sexual activities that lead to eternal punishment in hell.

(*I always recommend that married students, as well as those who may consider marriage, read the following two papal encyclicals:* Humanae Vitae, *written by Pope Paul VI in 1968; and* Evangelium Vitae, *from St. John Paul II in 1995.*)

Overcoming Sterility and Natural Family Planning

#457 Are fertility drugs morally acceptable?

Yes. In fact, the Church teaches that

[r]*esearch aimed at reducing human sterility is to be encouraged...*[1]

#458 What about in vitro fertilization (test tube babies)?

This is a moral evil because it

dissociate[s] the sexual act from the procreative act.[2]

#459 What about the use of sperm or an ovum from a third-party?

Techniques that entail the dissociation of husband and wife, by the intrusion of a third person other than the couple (donation of sperm or an ovum, surrogate uterus), are gravely immoral.[3]

#460 How should married persons who are sterile view their situation?

The Gospel shows that physical sterility is not an absolute evil. Spouses who still suffer from infertility after exhausting legitimate medical procedures should unite themselves with the Lord's Cross, the source of all spiritual fecundity. They can give expression to their generosity by adopting abandoned children or performing demanding services for others.[4]

#461 Are there methods of birth control that do not offend God?

Yes, there are natural methods of birth control that do not offend God if used for right reasons.

#462 What is natural family planning (NFP)?

Natural Family Planning refers to several methods which are in conformity to the biological harmonies God has impressed upon the human nature. These methods use no chemicals nor gadgets. They are based on sound scientific knowledge; and they are completely harmless, reliable, and healthy.

It is here that I always recommend two resources. The first is Natural Family Planning International, founded by John and Sheila Kippley, the two foremost experts in natural family planning techniques in the United States. Their website is: http://www.nfpandmore.org/. They offer a free natural family planning guide utilizing all the current research in this type of family planning.

The second is the Creighton Model Fertility Care System, which is a form of natural family planning that involves identifying the fertile period during a woman's menstrual cycle. The Creighton Model was developed by Dr Thomas Hilgers, the founder and director of the Pope Paul VI Institute. This model, like the Billings ovulation method, is based on observations of cervical mucus to track fertility. Creighton can be used for both avoiding pregnancy and achieving pregnancy. The website is: https://www.creightonmodel.com/index.html.

#463 Is natural family planning morally and religiously acceptable?

Rightly used, natural family planning is morally and religiously acceptable.

#464 What do we mean by "rightly used"?

By "rightly used" we mean that natural family planning requires the use of intelligence and self-control, and that it should only be used when married people have serious motives for spacing out births.

#465 What might create serious reasons for spacing out births?

Serious reasons for spacing out births may come from physical or psychological conditions of the husband or wife, or from external conditions. However, selfishness is a sinful motive.

Homosexual Activity, Premarital Sex, Masturbation

#466 What is homosexual activity?

Homosexual activity is sexual relations between people of the same sex. Homosexuality is a gravely disordered condition, and homosexual activity is always mortally sinful.

#467 Why is homosexual activity immoral?

Basing itself on Sacred Scripture, which presents homosexual acts as acts of grave depravity, tradition has always declared that "homosexual acts are intrinsically disordered." They are contrary to the natural law. They close the sexual act to the gift of life. They do not proceed from a genuine affective and sexual complementarity. Under no circumstances can they be approved.[5]

We must remember, though, that it is homosexual activity that is immoral, not the homosexual person. Although being homosexual is disordered, as long as the homosexual lives a chaste life, it is no more immoral to be a homosexual than to be a heterosexual.

#468 What is premarital sex?

Premarital sex is sexual intercourse before marriage, founded on the error that in it consists the total commitment of the future spouses. Such sexual relations are mortally sinful, because sex is reserved for the bond of Matrimony.

#469 What is masturbation?

Masturbation is

the deliberate stimulation of the genital organs in order to derive sexual pleasure. "Both the Magisterium of the Church, in the course of a constant tradition and moral sense of the faithful have been in no doubt and have firmly maintained that masturbation is an intrinsically and gravely disordered action."[6]

The Ninth Commandment

#470 What is the ninth commandment?

"You shall not covet your neighbor's wife" (Exodus 20:17).

#471 What are we obligated to do by the ninth commandment?

The ninth commandment obligates us to be pure in all our thoughts and desires.

#472 What does the ninth commandment forbid?

The ninth commandment forbids all deliberate impure thoughts, intentions, imaginings, desires, and feelings deliberately aroused or indulged in.

#473 Are all impure temptations sinful?

Impure temptations are not sinful in themselves, but become sinful if they are deliberately aroused, indulged in, or consented to. They must be rejected at once.

THE PRESERVATION of Chastity

#474 What are the main dangers to chastity?

The main dangers to chastity are laziness, unbridled curiosity, bad company, excessive drinking and drug abuse, immodest dress, pornography, suggestive music, and obscene talk.

#475 How can chastity be preserved?

Chastity may be protected by avoiding the dangers to chastity whenever possible, praying for God's grace and help, going to confession and receiving communion often, and cultivating a tender devotion to the Blessed Virgin Mary.

While dating, it is extremely important to be on guard against dangers to chastity. Couples should avoid excessive petting, spending too much time in seclusion, and what is called "French kissing."

THIRTY-THREE

THE SEVENTH AND TENTH COMMANDMENTS

You shall not steal.
  You shall not covet your neighbor's goods.

Respect for Property

#476 Why are the seventh and tenth commandments treated together?

The seventh and tenth commandments are treated together because they both deal with respect for the property of others.

#477 What is the seventh commandment?

"You shall not steal" (Exodus 20:15).

#478 Does everyone have a right to private ownership?

Yes, God has given everyone the right to private ownership so that we can enjoy the fruits of our labors, live with the dignity due our humanity, and maintain a certain independence.

#479 To what does the seventh commandment obligate us?

The seventh commandment obligates us to respect the property of others, to keep our business agreements, and to pay our debts.

#480 What does the seventh commandment forbid?

The seventh commandment forbids stealing, robbery, cheating, contracting debts beyond our means, unjustly damaging the property of others, accepting bribes, and knowingly buying or receiving stolen goods.

Stealing, Damaging, Cheating

#481 How serious a sin is theft?

Stealing is a serious sin if the thing stolen is of considerable value. Stealing something of small value from a poor person can be mortally sinful. Stealing in small amounts over a period of time could eventually become mortal sin if the accumulated total becomes sufficiently large.

Let's say the cashier at the supermarket gives you a dollar too much in change, and you decide to keep it. This would be a venial sin. If that same dollar was stolen from, say, a blind beggar on a street corner, that could be mortally sinful.

If a bank teller manages to steal five dollars from his till, that is a venial sin. If he were to do this every week for an extended period of time he would commit a mortal sin.

Students often ask what the dollar amount or value is that determines the difference between mortal and venial sin. I give the same answer every time. Moral theologians tell us that, as a rule, the difference between mortal and venial can be best determined by going by your state law on the amount that designates the difference between larceny and grand larceny. I never get more specific than that, as the answer is usually more pastoral than fitting within a strict guideline. It has been my experience that students usually ask this question because they have something weighing on the conscience. I always tell them to consult a priest.

#482 Must a thief return stolen goods?

We are obligated to restore to the owner stolen goods, or their value, whenever we are able (Exodus 22:1). If the rightful owner is dead, the property must be restored to his heirs. If there are no heirs, it must be given to the poor or for some other charitable purpose.

If a thief can't restore all he is stolen, he must restore all he can. If he has used what has been stolen, he must repair the damage done by restoring the equivalent. If he cannot restore anything, he must at least pray for the person he has wronged.

If poverty or some other circumstance prevents the thief from making restitution immediately, he must resolve to do so as soon as possible, and must make an effort to fulfill his resolution.

Restitution may be made secretly, without letting the owner know that restitution is being made. For instance, a money order may be sent with an alias; or the priest, who is pledged to secrecy, may be entrusted with the property to be restored.

#483 If we know or find out we have purchased stolen goods, may we keep them?

No. We must restore such goods to their rightful owner, unless we have no way of locating him. It is also wrong for us to ask the owner to reimburse us for our monetary loss. The only person from whom we can ask reimbursement is the person who sold us the goods.

#484 May we keep what we find?

If we find an article of value, we must strive to discover the owner in order to restore the article. The more valuable it is, the greater our obligation to return the article. If, after all our earnest efforts, we are unable to find the owner, we may keep the article.

#485 Is it wrong to keep what we have borrowed?

Yes, it is wrong to keep we have borrowed beyond the length of time established or agreed upon with the owner. If no time has been established or agreed upon, we may not keep the borrowed item beyond what common sense and our conscience tells us is reasonable.

#486 Must we repair damage we have unjustly done to someone else's property?

We are obligated to repair damage unjustly done to the property of others, or to pay the amount of the damage, as far as we are able (Exodus 22:4).

#487 What are some forms of cheating?

Some forms of cheating are: negligence in working, tax evasion, false advertisement, fraudulent contracts, false insurance claims, and copying in an examination.

Specific Obligations

#488 What are the duties of workers by the seventh commandment?

Workers must conscientiously provide the quantitative and qualitative work that they are being paid to perform, as well as guarding against damage to their employer's property.

#489 May workers strike?

Strikes are justifiable when: rights are violated or ignored; lawful contracts are broken; other difficulties of a serious nature exist. A striking worker may not use violence to achieve his objective.

#490 What are the duties of employers by the seventh commandment?

Sacred Scripture tells us the duties of employers. The prophet tells us that

To take away a neighbor's living is to murder him; to deprive an employee of his wages is to shed blood. (Sirach 34:22)

And the apostle James states that

The wages of the laborers who mowed your fields, which you kept back by fraud, cry out; and the cries of the harvesters have reached the ears of the Lord of hosts. (James 5:4)

These passages tell us that employers must see to it that their workers are paid just wages, without undue delays. They must also see to it that working conditions are in accord with human dignity and are reasonably safe.

#491 What are the obligations of public officials?

Public officials or not to accept bribes or advance themselves by other dishonest means. They have a serious obligation to discharge their positions with honor, justice, and diligence.

#492 What is usury?

Usury is the charging of excessive interest on money. A usurer takes unjust advantage of the need of another in order to make excessive profits.

I always note here that payday loan and title loan businesses fit this definition of usury. These businesses are merely loansharking facilities, and they are highly immoral even if legal.

#493 Can someone who has broken the seventh commandment receive absolution if he does not intend to make restitution?

No, someone may not receive absolution after breaking the seventh commandment if he does not intend to make restitution.

Irresponsible Use of Money and Goods

#494 In the name of justice, may the wealthy leave the poor destitute?

Even if a wealthy person has a just claim on the possessions of a poor person, he may not exercise that claim if it would leave the poor person destitute.

#495 Is it wrong to live beyond one's means?

Yes, to contract debts beyond one's means is an injustice to both one's creditors and dependents.

#496 What is gambling?

Gambling is the staking of money or valuables on a future event or game of chance, the results of which are unknown to the participants.

#497 Is gambling a sin?

Opponents to gambling—particularly Protestant fundamentalists—claim gambling is wrong because it is irresponsible, wasteful, and the gambler has the desire to gain something for nothing. Such reasoning is flawed and intellectually dishonest.

Irresponsible and wasteful? The stock market is nothing more than gambling, according to the above definition. Our global economy would collapse without the stock markets, yet none of the gambling opponents are crying out for their abolition. Indeed, most people have their retirement funds heavily invested in the stock market.

Gambling opponents suggest that gambling is wasteful because the gambler, if he loses, has nothing to show for his money. But consider this.

If a couple hires a babysitter to watch the kids, goes out to dinner, then to a movie, what have they got to show for the usually hefty sum of money spent? Nothing, except a good time. Legitimate pleasure is what the couple paid for, and that is all gambling is—a legitimate pleasure.

Something for nothing? We have intellectual dishonesty here, too. Ask a gambling opponent if he would turned down a prize awarded by a merchant because he patronized the merchant's business. Of course not! And what is this but getting something for nothing? Indeed, merchants regularly practice such marketing methods, simply to get customers to come back.

Gambling is not sinful if done with moderation. It can become sinful—even a mortal sin—if it leads to dishonesty or risks the welfare of one's family. In other words, gambling should be fair and done only with money that has been budgeted for recreation.

#498 What is the tenth commandment?

You shall not covet anything which belongs to your neighbor (*Exodus* 20:17).

#499 What does "covet" mean?

Covet means to unlawfully desire something that belongs to another.

#500 What does the tenth commandment forbid?

The tenth commandment forbids the desire to take or keep what belongs to another. It also forbids envy of the good fortune or success of others.

#501 Is it ever permissible to desire what belongs to another?

Certainly it is morally permissible to desire what belongs to another if he is willing to make the possession a gift or to sell it. The prohibition of the tenth commandment applies only to dishonest desires. If this were not so, one could never purchase a car. The car belongs to the dealer, but he's certainly willing to sell it. Therefore, it's morally acceptable for you to desire it, provided you're willing to pay for it.

THIRTY-FOUR

THE EIGHTH COMMANDMENT

You shall not bear false witness against your neighbor.

When you and your student reflect on the teachings of the eighth commandment, you will come to realize that this is perhaps the most difficult commandment to obey. Not only is it difficult to obey, but most of the sins against this commandment can be mortally sinful. In fact, this is perhaps the most violated commandment and the least confessed one of the ten. Consequently, I always put tremendous emphasis on the teachings regarding this commandment.

Reputation

#502 *What does the eighth commandment obligate us to do?*

The eighth commandment obligates us to always be

truthful, especially when it concerns someone's good name and reputation. We are also obligated to interpret the actions of our neighbor in the best way possible.

#503 What does the eighth commandment forbid?

The eighth commandment forbids false witnessing, lying, rash judging, rash suspicions, flattery, tale bearing, detractions, calumny, contumely, libel, and the telling of secrets we are obliged to keep.

#504 What is a lie?

A lie is anything we know or suspect to be untrue, usually for the purpose of deceiving others.

#505 Can lying be excused if done for a good reason?

Man tends by nature toward the truth.[1]

It is a perversion of man's nature to tell a lie, because God made man to know and tell the truth. Therefore, no excuse can make the telling of a lie good, since lying in itself is an evil.

I'm very quick to point out there is no such thing as a "white lie." A lie is a lie, and it is always evil.

#506 What is a jocose lie?

A jocose lie is a story made up in order to amuse or instruct others. It is sinful if the storyteller fails to make it clear in some way that the story is not to be taken literally.

The parables Jesus told would fit into this definition.

#507 Are there lies in actions as well as in words?

Yes. Lies in actions are called hypocrisy (Sirach 1:29-30).

I always take the time to read any citation of Sirach, especially when dealing with the eighth, seventh and tenth commandments. This prophet's words are usually impactful, as he doesn't mince words.

#508 What is rash judging?

Rash judging is believing something harmful about someone's character without sufficient reason.

#509 Why is rash judging wrong?

Rash judging is wrong because such disrespect for someone's reputation equates to disrespect for the person being rashly judged, and everyone deserves our respect.

Uncharitable Telling of the Truth

#510 What is tale bearing?

Tale bearing is telling someone the unkind things others have said about him or her. It is sinful because it provokes a person to anger, revenge, and other sins.

#511 What is detraction?

Detraction is acting without objectively valid reason to tell

another's faults and failings to persons who did not know them.[2]

Detraction is wrong because our neighbor has a right to his good name and reputation, whether or not we subjectively believe he deserves it.

#512 Is anyone ever allowed to tell the faults of another?

We may tell the faults of another to the proper authority —teachers, parents, police, etc.—if we believe the wrongdoer can be helped or stopped from his wrongdoing, or to keep the wrongs from becoming worse. It is important to stress, though, that we should be more concerned with seeing a sinner break with sin then to see the sinner punished.

Calumny, Contumely, Libel

#513 What is calumny?

Calumny is the making of

remarks contrary the truth, [which harm] the reputation of others and give occasion [of] false judgment concerning them.[3]

#514 What is contumely?

Contumely is showing contempt for a person by unjustly dishonoring him. It is committed by ignoring the person, refusing to show the proper signs of respect, detraction, or ridicule.

#515 What is libel?

Libel is any false or malicious written or printed statement or any sign, picture, or effigy intending to injure a person's reputation in any way.

Secrets

#516 Must we keep secrets?

We must keep secrets if we have promised to do so, if our office requires it, or if the good of others demands it.

#517 Does the seal of confession obligate anyone other than the priest?

The secret of the sacrament of reconciliation *is sacred, and cannot be violated under any pretext.*[4]

Therefore, one who somehow gains knowledge of matter from confession must never reveal that knowledge.

If the person I am teaching appears to me to have a tendency to gossip, I explain that this even extends to learning of matter for a potential confession. In other words, when we see or hear of the sin of someone else that is matter for confession, so we are forbidden to tell others about it.

#518 Is one ever permitted to read the letters or private writings of others?

We may never read the letters or private writings of others without their permission, unless the motive is to prevent grave harm to one's self, another, or society.

Reparation

#519 *What must we do if we sin against the eighth commandment?*

Every offense committed against justice and truth entails the duty of reparation, even if its author has been forgiven. When it is impossible publicly to make preparation for a wrong, it must be made secretly. If someone who has suffered harm cannot be directly compensated, he must be given moral satisfaction in the name of charity. The duty of reparation also concerns offenses against another's reputation. This reparation, moral and sometimes material, must be evaluated in terms of the extent of the damage inflicted. It obliges in conscience.[5]

THIRTY-FIVE

THE PRECEPTS OF THE CHURCH

Specific Duties of Catholics

#520 Does the Catholic Church have the authority to make laws and precepts?

Yes, the Catholic Church has the authority to make laws and precepts, an authority granted by Christ Himself. Jesus gave this authority when He told the apostles

"He who hears you hears me, and he who rejects you rejects me, and he who rejects me rejects him who sent me."[1]

To Peter, the Catholic Church's first pope, Jesus said,

"I will give you the keys of the kingdom of heaven, and whatever you bind on earth shall be bound in heaven, and whatever you loose on earth shall be loosed in heaven."[2]

This power was given to the pope in a special way, as is evident by the presentation of the keys. Finally, the bishops, by way of their predecessors, the apostles, were given this same power in a lesser way when Jesus said

"Truly, I say to you, whatever you bind on earth shall be bound in heaven, and whatever you loose on earth shall be loosed in heaven."[3]

The reason the Church makes laws and precepts is

... to guarantee to the faithful the very necessary minimum of prayer and moral effort, [and] in the growth in love of God and neighbor...[4]

#521 Are we obligated to keep the Church's precepts?

All Catholics are obligated to keep the Church's precepts.

#522 What are some of the chief duties of today's Catholics?

Some of the chief duties of Catholics are (those traditionally called the precepts of the Church are in italics):

1. *You shall attend Mass on Sundays and holy days of obligation.* This precept requires us to make holy the Lord's day, to observe special holy days that are meant to recall us to the Gospel message, and to avoid those activities that hinder the renewal of soul and body.

2. *You shall confess your serious sins at least once a year.* This precept "ensures preparation for the Eucharist by the reception of the sacrament of re-conciliation."[5]

3. *You shall humbly receive your Creator in Holy Communion at least during the Easter season.* We must receive Holy Communion, under pain of mortal sin, between the first Friday of Lent and Trinity Sunday in the United States. The universal Church ends Easter season on Pentecost Sunday, but the Holy See granted permission to the U.S. bishops to extend it the

extra week to Trinity Sunday for the benefit of U.S. Catholics.

4. *You shall observe the days of fasting and abstinence established by the Church.* There are only two fast days in the United States: Ash Wednesday and Good Friday. All Fridays of the year are days of penance, but only the Fridays of Lent (beginning with the Friday after Ash Wednesday) are obligatory days of abstinence under pain of sin. On those Fridays outside of Lent we should perform some act of penance at least as sacrificial as abstinence, or abstain.[6]

5. "'You shall help provide for the needs of the Church' means that the faithful are obliged to assist with the material needs of the Church, each according to his own ability."[7]

6. The faithful are to study Catholic teaching in preparation for the sacrament of Confirmation, be confirmed, and then continue study and advance the cause of Christ.

7. The faithful are to observe the marriage laws of the Church and give religious training to their children.

8. The faithful are to join in the missionary spirit and apostolate of the Church.

Sundays and Holy Days

#523 Is it a grave obligation to attend Mass on Sundays and holy days of obligation?

Yes, this precept is binding under pain of mortal sin.

#524 Is there any other day on which this obligation can be fulfilled?

Yes, this obligation may be fulfilled by participating at an anticipated Mass on the evening before.

#525 What does it mean to confess our sins once a year?

Making an annual confession means preparing to receive the Eucharist by making a good confession, usually prior to the Easter season. This is the bare minimum. The Church recommends confession at least once a month, but teaches that weekly confession is much better.

#526 Why does the Church require us to receive Holy Communion once a year, during the Easter time?

The Church requires the annual communion as a minimum because of what Christ taught us in John 6:51:

"I am the living bread which came down from heaven; if anyone eats of the bread, he will live forever; and the bread which I shall give for the life of the world is my flesh."

Although the Church only requires annual reception of the Eucharist, it is to be understood that this is the minimum. The Church recommends weekly Communion, but teaches that daily reception is better.

#527 What is a day of fast?

A day of fast (Ash Wednesday and Good Friday) is a day on which we eat one full meal and two other meals that together do not equal one full meal. Eating between meals is forbidden; however, we are permitted liquids, including milk and fruit juice.

#528 Who is obliged to fast?

All Catholics from the age of eighteen through the age of fifty-nine are obliged to fast.

#529 What is a day of abstinence?

A day of abstinence (Ash Wednesday and all the Fridays of Lent) is a day on which we do not eat meat. (Seafood is permitted.)

#530 Who is obliged to abstain?

All Catholics fourteen years of age and over are obliged to abstain.

THIRTY-SIX

THE LIFE OF VIRTUE

The Virtues

#531 What is a virtue?

A virtue is the habit of doing good.

It allows the person not only to perform good acts, but to give the best of himself.[1]

#532 How many kinds of virtues are there?

There are two kinds of virtues: supernatural virtues, which are infused into the soul by God; and natural virtues, acquired by repeating naturally good acts.

#533 What are the most important virtues?

The most important virtues are those called the theological virtues.

The Theological Virtues

#534 What does "theological virtues" mean?

[T]he theological virtues relate directly to God. They dispose Christians to live in a relationship with the Holy

Trinity. They have the One and Triune and God for their origin, motive, and object.[2]

#535 What are the theological virtues?

The theological virtues are faith, hope, and charity.

#536 What is faith?

Faith is the theological virtue by which we believe in God and believe all that he has said and revealed to us, and that holy Church proposes for our belief, because he is truth itself.[3]

#537 Can we be saved by faith alone?

No, we cannot be saved by faith alone. This is a heresy that was begun by Martin Luther in 1517. It was condemned by the Council of Trent (1545-1563) because it clearly contradicted the Bible. St. James tells us that

... faith apart from works is dead.[4]

Luther's idea of faith meant a man's confidence that his sins had been forgiven by God for Christ's sake, but Christ and his apostles always taught that faith implied the acceptance of all God's revelation on His word. Without faith, justification is impossible. But other dispositions are required, as faith necessarily leads to action. We must not only believe, but we must hope, repent, and love.

We are saved by hope.[5]

Repent and be baptized every one of you in the name of Jesus Christ for the forgiveness of your sins...[6]

[I]f I have all faith, so as to move mountains, but have not love, I am nothing.[7]

#538 How do we live by faith?

We live by faith by studying the Church and Her teachings, reading the Bible, believing God's revelation, and openly professing our faith, even at the risk of death.

#539 How can a Catholic sin against faith?

A Catholic sins against faith by joining a non-Catholic church, denying a truth of faith, being indifferent toward the Catholic religion, and, in many cases, by taking an active part in non-Catholic worship. We must protect our faith by praying for an increase in faith, studying the truths of Catholicism, living by God's holy will, choosing friends and associates wisely, and avoiding all that is contrary to the teachings of the Church.

#540 What is hope?

Hope is the theological virtue by which we desire the kingdom of heaven and eternal life as our happiness, placing our trust in Christ's promises and relying not on our own strength, but on the help of the grace of the Holy Spirit.[8]

#541 How do we live by hope?

We live by hope by trusting in God to give us the graces necessary for salvation.

#542 How can we sin against hope?

We can sin against hope by presumption and despair.

#543 What is presumption?

Presumption is thinking that God will save us without any effort on our part, or of thinking that we do not need God's help to reach heaven. Presumption is a mortal sin.

#544 What is despair?

A direct opposite of presumption, despair is deliberately refusing to believe that God will always give the necessary help for salvation to all who ask for it. This, too, is a mortal sin.

#545 What is charity?

Charity is the theological virtue by which we love God above all things for his own sake, and our neighbor as ourselves for the love of God.[9]

#546 How do we live by charity?

We live by charity by obeying the two great commandments (cf. questions 368-369). In practice this means obeying the commandments of God and His Church, and performing the works of mercy.

#547 How can we sin against charity?

There are many ways to sin against charity: hating God, hating our neighbor, envy, sloth, scandal, *et cetera*.

The Moral Virtues

#548 What is meant by "moral virtues"?

A moral virtue is a virtue that disposes us to treat others and ourselves in a way that is morally right.

#549 What are the most important moral virtues?

The most important moral virtues are religion, which helps us to worship God, and the cardinal virtues: prudence, justice, fortitude, and temperance.

#550 What is prudence?

Prudence is the virtue that disposes practical reason to discern our true good in every circumstance and to choose the right means of achieving it... Prudence is "right reason in action"... It is not to be confused with timidity or fear, nor with duplicity or dissemination... it guides the other virtues by setting rule and measure. It is prudence that immediately guides the judgment of conscience... With the help of this virtue we apply moral principles to particular cases without error and overcome doubts about the good to achieve and the evil to avoid.[10]

#551 What is justice?

Justice is the moral virtue that consists in the constant and firm will to give their due to God and neighbor... The just man, often mentioned in the Sacred Scriptures is distinguished by habitual right thinking and the uprightness of his conduct toward his neighbor.[11]

#552 What is fortitude?

Fortitude is the moral virtue that assures firmness in difficulties and constancy in the pursuit of the good. It strengthens the resolve to resist temptations and to overcome obstacles in the moral life. The virtue of fortitude enables one to conquer fear, even fear of death, and to face trials and persecutions. It disposes one even to renounce and sacrifice his life in defense of a just cause.[12]

#553 What is temperance?

Temperance is the moral virtue that moderates the attraction of pleasures and provides a balance in the use of created goods. It ensures the will's mastery over instincts and keeps desires within the levels of what is honorable. The temperate person directs the sensitive appetites toward what it is good and maintains a healthy discretion... Temperance is often praised in the Old Testament... In the New Testament it is called "moderation" or "sobriety".[13]

#554 What are some of the moral virtues?

Some of the moral virtues are:

- *Filial piety* and *patriotism*, which help us to love, honor, and respect our nation
- *Obedience*, which helps us to obey any legitimate authority, which represents God
- *Truthfulness*, which helps us to always tell the truth
- *Liberality*, which helps us to use created things wisely

- *Patience*, which helps us take the trials and difficulties God permits to help make us holy
- *Humility*, which helps us to know ourselves and to recognize that whatever is good in us comes from God
- *Chastity*, which helps us to be pure in mind, heart, and body

There are many other virtues in addition to these.

The Beatitudes

#555 What are the beatitudes?

The beatitudes are qualities that Jesus asks His followers to live by that will pave their road to heaven.

#556 What are the eight beatitudes?

The eight beatitudes are:

1. Blessed are the poor in spirit, for theirs is the kingdom of heaven. (Matthew 5:3)
2. Blessed are those who mourn, for they shall be comforted. (Matthew 5:4)
3. Blessed are the meek, for they shall inherit the earth. (Matthew 5:5)
4. Blessed are those who hunger and thirst for righteousness, for they shall be satisfied. (Matthew 5:6)
5. Blessed are the merciful, for they shall obtain mercy. (Matthew 5:7)
6. Blessed are the pure in heart, for they shall see God. (Matthew 5:8)
7. Blessed are the peacemakers, for they shall be called sons of God. (Matthew 5:9)

8. Blessed are those who are persecuted for
    righteousness' sake, for theirs is the kingdom of
    heaven. (Matthew 5:10)

#557 Why does Jesus apply the term "blessed" to those in the beatitudes?

Jesus calls such persons blessed because those who practice the beatitudes live with peace of mind and a clear conscience, and will reap great rewards in heaven.

The Works of Mercy

#558 Are there any particular acts of virtue that Jesus recommended to everyone?

Jesus is recommended to His followers, by way of word and example, the works of mercy. There are the corporal works of mercy, which allow us to serve God in our neighbor, and the spiritual works of mercy, which are directed toward perfection of soul.

#559 What are the corporal works of mercy?

The corporal works of mercy are found in Matthew 25 by direct instruction from Jesus, and then Tobit 1:16 by example (burying the dead).

The corporal works of mercy consist especially in feeding the hungry, sheltering the homeless, clothing the naked, visiting the sick and the imprisoned, and burying the dead.[14]

#560 What are the spiritual works of mercy?

The spiritual works of mercy are to admonish the sinner, instruct the ignorant, counsel the doubtful, comfort the sorrowful, bear wrongs patiently, forgive of all injuries, and pray for the living and the dead.[15]

#561 Are we all to perform works of mercy?

All of us are obligated to perform works of mercy, so far as we are able and in accord with our neighbors' need.

It is here when I usually tell my students that they can fulfill most of the corporal works of mercy every day and in little ways. For example, they can help to clothe the naked by donating their old clothes to the St. Vincent de Paul Society. Another way would be to help support, in some way, a prison apostolate or homeless shelter. I also drive home the fact that we are all required by Jesus to perform the corporal works of mercy. Indeed, our salvation depends on it, according to Jesus' final judgment narrative in Matthew 25.

Vices

#562 What is the opposite of virtue?

The opposite of virtue is vice, which is the habit of doing evil.

#563 What are the principal vices?

The principal vices are the capital sins, of which there are seven: pride, covetousness, lust, gluttony, anger, envy, and sloth.

#564 How can we overcome these principal vices?

We can overcome these principal vices by prayer and practicing their opposite virtues:

- Pride—humility

- Covetousness—justice and liberality
- Lust—chastity
- Gluttony—temperance
- Anger—meekness
- Envy—love of neighbor
- Sloth—love of God and diligence in his service

THIRTY-SEVEN

THE LIFE OF PRAYER

Prayer

#565 What is prayer?

Prayer is raising our hearts and minds to God in loving conversation with Him so we may ask for His good in our lives.

#566 Why should we pray?

We should pray to God to adore Him, thank Him for his blessings, ask His forgiveness, and beg Him for the graces we need.

#567 How should we pray?

As Jesus Himself taught us through word and example, we should pray with an awareness of God's presence, humility, confidence, and perseverance.

#568 For whom should we pray?

We should pray for ourselves, our friends and loved ones, the poor souls in purgatory, and all those in authority, religious, priests, bishops, the laity, and especially the pope.

#569 Does God always hear our prayers?

God always hears our prayers if we pray well (John 15:16).

#570 Will God always give us what we pray for?

Just as a parent knows what is best for his or her child, so too, does God know what is best for us. We often ask for things that God knows are not for our benefit, so His answer is sometimes either "no" or "yes, but later."

I may or may not get a comment or question at this point, but I've been through this so many times that I can almost guarantee what the student is thinking. Most of them don't really believe God answers prayer. So I spend a few minutes talking about Matthew's version of the Sermon on the Mount. I begin near the end of the sermon in Matthew 7:7-11. This is where Jesus makes a profound promise to give us whatever we ask for in prayer. When people read this passage, they hone in on the promise made, but they don't stop to think of it in context.

Matthew's version of that sermon takes all of chapters five, six and seven. It's the longest example of Christ's preaching in the Gospels. Everyone isolates the promises, but fails to pay attention to the rest. In the Sermon on the Mount, Jesus tells us a lot of other things besides His promises. He gives us the beatitudes, tells us to make our faith shine to others, preaches of the evil of anger, demands we be chaste in mind and body, condemns divorce and remarriage, warns us about the taking of oaths, insists we love our enemies, teaches us how to pray and insists we do so with earnest, tells us to fast and do penance for our sins, tells us to trust in God for even the smallest of things, demands that we not judge others, and tells us to treat everyone else how we want to be treated.

Whew!

Yes, He made a great promise about getting anything we ask in prayer, but He also gave us all these conditions that must be met as well. I tell them, "God doesn't run some sort of heavenly lottery. He doesn't just hand out whatever we want the way a parent spoils a child. Would you slap your parent in the face then ask for a favor? Of course not, and if you did you'd be a fool to expect that parent to grant the favor, but that is exactly what we do if we haphazardly live our faith or remain in invincible ignorance of it. Jesus so hates our complacency in faith that He said, 'I know your works: you are neither cold nor hot. Would that you were cold or hot! So because you are lukewarm, and neither cold nor hot, I will spew you out of my mouth' (Revelation 3:15-16). (Some versions of Scripture replace the word spew with the word vomit—and that's an eye-opener.)

"He places conditions on getting what we ask for. God demands that we live wholly and unreservedly the faith established by Jesus Christ— which is the faith taught and jealously guarded by His Holy Catholic Church—if we are to expect Him to fulfill the promises made to us."

This usually causes the student to gain a whole new perspective on the promise of answered prayer.

#571 What is mental prayer?

Mental prayer is made from within our mind, uniting our thoughts and hearts to God.

#572 What is vocal prayer?

Vocal prayer is praying with words, but we are to unite the words with our heart and mind.

#573 What is an aspiration?

An aspiration, also call an ejaculatory prayer, is a short prayer. An example would be a prayer like: "My Jesus mercy."

#574 Which prayers should Catholics memorize?

The minimum prayers that every Catholic should memorize are the: Our Father, Hail Mary, Glory Be, Apostles' Creed, act of faith, act of hope, act of love, act of contrition, and the rosary.

#575 Are distractions in prayer sins?

Distractions in prayer can be a venial sin if they are deliberate. If distractions are not deliberate, and if we refuse to dwell on them, our prayers become even more pleasing to God.

#576 Is it good to use our own words in prayer?

Formulated prayers are good, because they are well-thought-out and cover all the bases, so to speak. However, prayers that are impromptu are especially pleasing to God, because such prayers are how we develop an intimate relationship with Him.

The Our Father

#577 Why is the Our Father a perfect prayer?

The Our Father is a perfect prayer because Jesus, who is Himself perfect, taught it to us. It is perfect because we ask first for God's glory and then for everything we need, both spiritually and materially, for ourselves and for all men.

The Lord's Prayer is truly the summary of the whole Gospel. It is at the center of the Scriptures.[1]

#578 When we say "Our Father," what do we mean?

When we say "our" Father, we recognize first that all his promises of love announced by the prophets are fulfilled in the new and eternal covenant in Christ: we have become "his" people and he is henceforth "our" God.[2]

#579 What does "Our Father who art in heaven" mean?

"Our Father who art in heaven" means that God is truly our loving Father, who cares for us and made us his adopted children through sanctifying grace and who wants us with Him in heaven forever.

This biblical expression does not mean a place ("space"), but a way of being; it does not mean that God is distant, but majestic... The symbol of the heavens refers us back to the mystery of the covenant we are living when we pray to our Father. He is in heaven, his dwelling place; the Father's house is our homeland.[3]

#580 What does "hallowed be Thy name" mean?

This phrase means that we pray that everyone may know, respect and love God's holy name.

#581 What does "Thy kingdom come" mean?

When we pray "Thy kingdom come," we are praying that God's kingdom of love, mercy, and justice is spread all over the world so that we may share His kingdom of heaven together.

#582 What does "Thy will be done on earth as it is in heaven" mean?

This phrase means we are praying for ourselves and others to be as quickly obedient to the will of God as are his Holy angels.

#583 What does "give us this day our daily bread" mean?

"Give us": The trust of children who look to their Father for everything is beautiful... Jesus teaches us this petition, because it glorifies our Father by acknowledging how good he is, beyond all goodness. "Give us" also expresses the covenant.[4]

"Our bread": The Father who gives us life cannot but give us the nourishment of life requires—all appropriate goods and blessings, both material and spiritual.[5]

#584 What does "And forgive us our trespasses as we forgive those who trespass against us" mean?

This petition is astonishing. If it consisted only of the first phrase, "And forgive us our trespasses," it might have been included, implicitly, in the first three petitions of the Lord's Prayer, since Christ's sacrifice is "that sins may be forgiven." But, according to the second phrase, our petition will not be heard unless we have first met a strict requirement. Our petition looks to the future, but our response must come first, for the two parts are joined by the single word "as."[6]

#585 What does "lead us not into temptation" mean?

This petition goes to the root of the preceding one, for our sins result from our consenting to temptation; we therefore ask our Father not to "lead" us into temptation... We ask him not to allow us to take the way that leads to sin. We are engaged in the battle "between flesh and spirit"; this petition implores the Spirit of discernment and strength.[7]

#586 What does "deliver us from evil" mean?

The last petition to our Father is also included in Jesus' prayer: "I am not asking you to take them out of the world, but I ask you to protect them from the evil one." It touches each of us personally, but it is always "we" who pray, in communion with the whole Church, for the deliverance of the whole human family.[8]

#587 What does "Amen" mean?

"Amen" means "so be it." By this closing statement we are expressing our agreement with and belief in everything contained in the prayer.

The Spiritual Life and the Bible

#588 What are the main enemies of our spiritual life?

The main enemies of our spiritual life are the world, the flesh, and the devil.

#589 How is the devil an enemy of our spiritual life?

Scripture witnesses to the disastrous influence of the one Jesus calls "a murderer from the beginning," who would even try to divert Jesus from the mission received from his Father.[9]

The power of Satan is, nonetheless, not infinite. He is only a creature, powerful from the fact that he is pure spirit, but still a creature... It is a great mystery that providence should permit diabolical activity, but "we know that in everything God works for the good of those who love him." [10]

#590 How is the world an enemy of our spiritual life?

The world, which is to say its man-made pleasures, entices us to embrace a love of wealth, pleasure, and power. When these things become more important than God in our lives, the spiritual life is destroyed by our new gods.

#591 How is the flesh an enemy of our spiritual life?

The flesh is an enemy of our spiritual life because of our weak and fallen nature, which makes us inclined to follow our passions. Our Lady of Fatima told Jacinta that more souls go to hell because of sins of the flesh than for any other reason. That was in 1917. Imagine how much more dangerous this is for us today.

#592 How can we overcome these enemies?

These main enemies can be overcome by reliance on God's grace, prayer, constant and careful vigilance, frequent reception of the sacraments, and penance.

#593 What does it mean to take up our daily cross?

Taking up our daily cross means to unite all of our activities to the crucified Christ, especially our sufferings. Many people believe Jesus promised us a bed of roses, when he actually promised us only thorns. Those thorns, or sufferings, are the consequence of our fallen, sinful nature. Suffering is evil in itself, but through His sacrifice on the cross, Jesus made a way to sanctify those sufferings, making them holy by giving to our suffering a supernatural value.

Jesus told us that "he who does not take up his cross and following me *is not worthy of me.*" Our Lord's words are very strong, but they were even stronger to the audience listening to him for the first time. To the Jew, there was no more humiliating way to die than on the cross. To the Roman, the cross was the most excruciatingly painful mode of death imaginable. In effect, Jesus is telling us we must die daily for Him, to Him, and with Him. He tells us we must die to ourselves to follow him, and to accept our sufferings so they can be offered back to the Father—through Jesus—in reparation for our sins and the sins of the whole world.

#594 What is meditation?

Meditation is above all a quest. The mind seeks to understand the why and how of the Christian life, in order to adhere and respond to what the Lord is asking. The required attentiveness is difficult to sustain. We are usually helped by books...[11]

To meditate on what we read helps us to make it our own by confronting it with ourselves. Here, another book is opened: the book of life. We pass from thoughts to reality. To the extent we are humble and faithful, we discover in meditation the movements that stir the heart and we are able to discern them. It is a question in acting truthfully in order to come into the light: "Lord, what do you want me to do?"[12]

#595 Should we meditate daily?

Absolutely! Meditation, like anything else worth doing on a regular basis, must become a habit by daily discipline and perseverance. It is recommended that the best way to begin in meditation is to start by meditating on one of the events in the passion and death of Christ.

The ideal period for daily meditation is an hour, nobody

starts at such length. Begin with just five minutes daily, and gradually build it from there over a period of weeks or months.

The best time of day for meditation is early in the morning, before beginning the hustle and bustle of the day's work and activities. Ideally, the place for your daily meditation is before Our Lord in His tabernacle, but any quiet place will do. Many people who cannot go to meditate before the tabernacle in their parish church find the appropriate setting to be outdoors, where nature helps them commune with God.

Although it is difficult to build a habit of meditating, this is a very simple form of prayer. Its benefits cannot be captured by mere words.

#596 Is spiritual reading helpful in the spiritual life?

Yes, the reading of spiritual books is most helpful in the spiritual life. This reading helps inspire us to greater sanctity, and gives us material for daily meditation. It also helps us to be stronger in resisting temptation.

It is recommended to read the Bible for at least 15 minutes a day. Then it is always good to begin reading the lives of the saints. As we grow in knowledge and piety, deeper theological works will become important.

#597 What is the Bible?

The Bible is the book that contains God's inspired word. It was written by men inspired by the Holy Spirit so they would write only what he wanted written. God speaks to us through the Bible, and His Church, which alone has the authority to interpret Scripture, helps us understand best what he is saying to us.

#598 How do we know the Bible is inspired?[13]

The Council of Trent in 1546 declared that all the books of the Old and New Testaments contained in the Catholic Bible were inspired and canonical. While non-Catholic Christians are dependent upon the fallible witness of critical arguments for their canon, Catholics depend upon the divine witness of an infallible teaching Church.

The canon solemnly defined by the Council of Trent is identical to the lists of the books promulgated by the Councils of Florence (1441), Carthage (397), Hippo (393), Laodicea (363), and by Popes Innocent (401), Hormisdas (514-523), Gelasius (492-496) and Pope Damasus (366-384).

#599 How is the Bible divided?

The Bible is divided into two parts: the Old Testament, with forty-six books, and the New Testament, with twenty-seven books.

#600 What is the Old Testament?

The Old Testament was written before the birth of Christ. It tells us the history of God's people and His covenant with them. It shows us how God prepared His people for the coming of Christ.

#601 What is the New Testament?

The New Testament was written after Jesus returned to the Father in heaven. It tells us about the birth, life, teachings, passion, death, resurrection, and ascension of Jesus. It also tells us about life in the early Church. Finally, working with Sacred Tradition, the New Testament—indeed, the whole Bible!—tells us how to apply Christ's teaching to our own lives.

#602 Why do Catholics include the apocrypha on their list of biblical books?

The deuterocanonical books, call the apocrypha by

Protestants, were included in the above-mentioned lists. They are Tobit, Judith, Wisdom, Sirach, Baruch, and the two books of Maccabees, together with fragments of Esther and Daniel. These books were contained in the Alexandrian Canon, in Asia Minor, Greece and Italy. The Palestinian Canon, used by the Semitic-speaking Jews of Palestine, Syria, and Mesopotamia, omitted these books in the first centuries after Christ, although probably it originally contained them.

Christ Himself never expressly cited the deuterocanonical books, but, of the 350 quotations from the Old Testament, 300 are taken directly from the Greek Septuagint. The Christians of early Rome must have known them, because the frescoes of the catacombs picture Susanna and the elders, as well as Moses and Jonah. The writers of the first three centuries in both East and West often quote or allude to them: St. Clement of Rome, the Shepherd of Hermas, St. Irenaeus, St. Hippolytus, Tertullian, Cyprian, Polycarp, Athenagoras, Clement of Alexandria, Origen, and Dionysius of Alexandria.

While many of the Fathers of the fourth and fifth centuries, influenced greatly by St. Jerome, denied the canonicity of the deuterocanonical books, in practice they quoted them for both instruction in doctrine and for guidance in conduct. The Bible they used was the Greek Bible, which had been handed down to them by their predecessors, and which contained all the books we have today. The popes of the day—Damasus, Innocent, and Gelasius—taught the same canon as the Fathers of the Council of Trent.

The term apocrypha means writings falsely attributed to the prophets of the Old Law or the apostles of the New, whose claim to inspiration was rejected, or at least ignored by the Church. Examples would be the Book of Enoch, the Assumption of Moses, the proto-Evangel of St. James, the Acts of St. Peter and St. Paul, the letter of Christ Abgar, *et cetera*.

#603 How should we read the Bible?

We should read the Bible prayerfully in order to get the greatest good God would have us gain, and humbly in order to avoid personal interpretation that leads to false interpretation. Being humble in order to avoid personal interpretation means always accepting the Church's interpretation when their is an official one, because the Catholic Church is "the pillar and bulwark of the truth" (I Timothy 3:15).

APPENDIX

Daily Prayers

Apostles' Creed

I believe in God, the Father Almighty, Creator of heaven and earth, and in Jesus Christ, His only Son, our Lord, who was conceived by the Holy Spirit, born of the Virgin Mary, suffered under Pontius Pilate, was crucified, died and was buried; He descended into hell; on the third day He rose again from the dead; He ascended into heaven, and is seated at the right hand of God the Father Almighty; from there He will come to judge the living and the dead.

I believe in the Holy Spirit, the Holy Catholic Church, the communion of Saints, the forgiveness of sins, the resurrection of the body, and life everlasting.

Amen.

Our Father

Our Father, Who art in Heaven, hallowed be Thy name; Thy Kingdom come, Thy will be done on earth as it is in Heaven. Give us this day our daily bread; and forgive us our trespasses as we forgive those who trespass against us;

and lead us not into temptation, but deliver us from evil. Amen.

Hail Mary

Hail Mary full of Grace, the Lord is with thee. Blessed are thou among women and blessed is the fruit of thy womb, Jesus.

Holy Mary Mother of God, pray for us sinners now and at the hour of our death.

Amen.

Glory Be

Glory be to the Father and to the Son and to the Holy Spirit. As it was in the beginning is now, and ever shall be, world without end. Amen.

Fatima Prayer—after each decade of the rosary

O my Jesus, forgive us our sins, save us from the fires of hell. Lead all souls to heaven, especially those who are most in need of Thy mercy.

Hail, Holy Queen

Hail, holy Queen, Mother of mercy, hail, our life, our sweetness and our hope. To thee do we cry, poor banished children of Eve: to thee do we send up our sighs, mourning and weeping in this vale of tears. Turn then, most gracious Advocate, thine eyes of mercy toward us, and after this our exile, show unto us the blessed fruit of thy womb, Jesus, O merciful, O loving, O sweet Virgin Mary! Amen.

Act of Faith

O my God, I firmly believe that you are one God in three divine Persons, Father, Son, and Holy Spirit. I believe that your divine son became man, died for our sins, and that He will come to judge the living and the dead. I believe these and all the truths which the holy Catholic Church teaches, because you who have revealed them, who can neither deceive nor be deceived. Amen.

Act of Hope

O my God, relying on Your almighty power and infinite mercy and promises, I hope to obtain pardon of my sins, the help of Your grace and life everlasting, through the merits of Jesus Christ, my Lord and Redeemer. Amen.

Act of Charity

O my God, I love you above all things with my whole heart and soul because You are all good and worthy of all my love. I love my neighbor as myself for the love of You. I forgive all who have injured me and ask pardon of all whom I have injured. Amen.

Act of Contrition

O my God, I am heartily sorry for having offended Thee, and I detest all my sins because of Thy just punishments, but most of all because they offend Thee, my God, Who art all-good and deserving of all my love. I firmly resolve, with the help of Thy grace, to sin no more and to avoid the near occasions of sin.

OR

My God, I am sorry for my sins with all my heart. In choosing to do wrong and failing to do good, I have sinned against You whom I should love above all things. I firmly intend, with Your help, to do penance, to sin no more, and to avoid whatever leads me to sin. Our Savior Jesus Christ suffered and died for us. In His name, my God, have mercy.

OR

O my God, I am sorry for my sins because I have offended You. I know I should love You above all things.

Help me to do penance, to do better, and to avoid anything that might lead me to sin. Amen.

St. Michael Prayer

St. Michael, the Archangel, defend us in battle. Be thou our protection against the wickedness and snares of the devil. May God rebuke him, we humbly pray; and do thou, O Prince of the heavenly host, by the power of God cast into hell Satan and all the evil spirits who roam throughout the world seeking the ruin of souls.

Amen.

Rosary Mysteries

Used with there kind permission of Catholic Online www.catholic.org.

Joyful Mysteries of the Rosary—Monday and Saturday

The Annunciation of the Lord to Mary

1st Joyful Mystery

I was in prayer: it was evening. I was praying toward Jerusalem because my people prayed three times a day, morning, noon, and evening facing Jerusalem. I was praying for the Liberation of my people. I was praying that soon the Messiah would come to take away all hatred: to take away all sins from my people. As I was praying, there suddenly appeared an angel. At first I was afraid because it was the first time an angel had ever come to me. When I heard him say "Hail, full of grace, the Lord is with you," I was very confused at this greeting and yet I was very humbled that an angel would call me full of grace: that I had gained favor from God: that I was called to bear His Son. I asked the angel how this could happen. I am a virgin: I had intended to be a virgin the rest of my life even though I agreed to live with Joseph. The angel assured me, "The Holy Spirit will come upon you: the shadow of the Most High will enwrap you and the child to be born of you will be called Son of God." At that instance, I remembered the prophesy of Isaiah. The prophesy of the Messiah. The prophesy that He would be a suffering servant. A servant rejected by His own people and yet raised by God. Knowing that, I said, "Behold the handmaid, the servant of the Lord: be it done to me according to Your word."

My children, be always open to seek the will of God in your life no matter what it is. Never be afraid of God's will. God's will always does contain suffering but God's will also brings peace. God's will contains Joy. Pray to the Heavenly Father: pray that He will give you the grace through my prayers to accept His will in all things. Place yourself at God's disposal and He will do great things for you and with you.

The Visitation of Mary to Elizabeth
2nd Joyful Mystery

As soon as I realized by Gabriel's message that Elizabeth, my cousin, who had been barren for a long time and who was yet now old, had nonetheless conceived, I was prompted by God's grace to go to help her in her need. She was in her sixth month: I went from Nazareth to Judea. I was only pondering the message that the angel had given me. It all seemed so wonderful that God would use me for His kingdom; for His glory. As I arrived at Zechariah's house, I greeted Elizabeth. I had heard that Zechariah had become mute: he had doubted the Lord: he doubted that God could work a miracle in his life. As I entered and greeted Elizabeth, Elizabeth shouted for joy and said,

"Blessed are you among all women and blessed is the fruit of your womb. Who am I that the Mother of my Lord should come to me." Out of Elizabeth's mouth came the confirmation of Gabriel's message: that I had conceived the Son of God and later all ages were to proclaim me as blessed as the Mother of their Lord; the Mother of God. I began to sing the hymn of praise that came from my heart. I was so filled with God's Love that I had to share my Joy with Elizabeth and her household.

My children, never doubt that God can work a miracle in your Life even if things seem humanly impossible: all things are possible with God. Trust Him, trust Him my children. As I visited Elizabeth out of love, I wish to visit you out of love. I wish to come into your situation whatever it may be: to be present with you and to pray with you and for you. God will manifest His power if we believe. Elizabeth told me, "Blessed are you who have believed that the Lord's words would be fulfilled in you." Trust in the Lord. I am with you to pray with you. Offer this mystery to the Heavenly Father that He will also work a miracle of grace in your life: ask the Heavenly Father for the gift of faith and absolute trust in His work. I am praying with you and for you.

The Nativity of our Lord Jesus Christ
3rd Joyful Mystery

Joseph and I came to Bethlehem because there was a decree that all should go to their ancestral town to be registered. In obedience, Joseph and I went. God even used the oppression of the Roman government to bring about your salvation: because in this time of oppression, my Son, your Savior, was born. We looked for a place but there was no room in the inn: the town was so full. What was offered us was a stable not too far from where the shepherds were guarding their flock. It was soon that my Son was born: that the King of Kings would be born a pauper. It was soon that the very Word would be made flesh. Joseph left me in the stable and went outside for a while thinking that he was not worthy to be present at such a great miracle. While he was thinking, the moment came when my Son was introduced to the world. Because of the immensity of Love that the Lord had filled me with, I felt no pain at His birth. There was pure joy at the coming of my Son. I held Him in my arms: He was the very Savior of the world. A while later, Joseph came in, he saw me with the Child and he was also filled with wondrous joy. As some time past, the shepherds that were near the stable also came. They knew about the birth of my Son: the angels had told them. Heaven was rejoicing at the birth of my Son.

My children, look upon the greatness of your Lord Who has loved you so much as to come down to show the immensity of His Love for you. Show your immensity of love for Him: be humble, be grateful for what you have, be it little or great, and whatever you do have, use it in a way that will give pleasure to my Son. See the face of my Son in those in need, those in want, and respond in love to Him. Pray to the Heavenly Father in this mystery for the gift of simplicity and for the woes of the poor and I will pray with you. I will ask the Father to give you the grace to be generous with those less fortunate.

The Presentation of our Lord

4th Joyful Mystery

In obedience to the Law of Moses, forty days after my Son was born, Joseph and I went to Jerusalem to present my Son before the Lord and to redeem Him with two turtle doves. I was presenting to God, the Father, your Redeemer in anticipation of the sacrifice He would make on Calvary for your salvation. When we entered the temple, there was a holy priest by the name of Simeon. Simeon took the Child into his arms and said, "Now Lord You can release your servant according to Your word in peace, for my eyes have seen the salvation which You have raised for all peoples to see: a light of revelation to the nations and the glory of Your people Israel." Then Simeon turned to me and said "Blessed are you, woman: but behold this Child will be the fall and the rise of many in Israel, a sign to be opposed and your own heart will be pierced so that the hearts of many will be exposed." Simeon was talking about my destiny: a destiny that would be so intimate with my Son.

My greatest pain, my children, is that people reject my Son: people reject His message of love and peace. People reject His message of repentance and holiness. My children, ask the Heavenly Father that He will make you holy in all things. Take away from your life whatever is displeasing to God so that your worship at Mass and your worshiping prayer will be acceptable to God the Father. I will pray for you in your time of worship. I will pray for you so that your prayer may reach the Father.

Finding Jesus in the Temple

5th Joyful Mystery

Jesus was twelve years old and Joseph and I, as custom dictates, wished to take Him to Jerusalem for the Passover. We went and we were filled with joy to worship God with His people. After the days of Passover were done, Joseph and I went back to Nazareth in the caravan of family members and friends that we came in. Joseph went with the men and I with the women. The children were either with their fathers or mothers. Both of us thought that Jesus was with the other. When evening came, Joseph and I came together and we did not find Jesus neither among our relatives nor among our friends. So we decided to go back to

Jerusalem to look for Him. My heart was torn in two: the sufferings predicted by Simeon were already starting. "What happened to my Son?" I questioned. It took us two days to go back to Jerusalem and on the third day we found my Son in the temple. He was among a group of elders, rabbis, and He was reading the Law with them. They were discussing the Law of Moses: He astonished the elders who marveled at His insight to the Law. As I was hearing Him, there was an amount of joy: joy to hear my Son teaching. God was giving me a taste of what my Son would be doing during His earthly ministry. I ran up to Him and said, "My Son, why did You do such a thing? Your father and I with so much sorrow have been looking for You." Jesus looked at me with Love and yet with conviction and He said to me, "But why were you looking for Me? Did you not know I should be about My Father's business?"

My children, do not cling to anyone that you love. Everyone has a mission, especially your children that God has given to you. Pray for religious vocations. Pray for vocations to the priesthood. Pray that Christian families will be obedient to the Father. Pray for the unity and the strengthening of all Christian families that they will truly bring the Kingdom of the Father to this earth.

Sorrowful Mystery of the Rosary—Tuesday & Friday

The Agony of Jesus in the Garden
1st Sorrowful Mystery

My Son came with His apostles to the mount of Olives. There was a garden there that He frequently went to pray: He felt a sadness; a deep, deep sadness. He felt lonely: my Son in His humanity felt a deeper sadness than anyone could ever feel because He was pure of heart: He was sinless. He took His closest friends, Peter whom He was to give charge of the Church, James, and John. John was the one who was going to take care of me after Jesus had risen from the dead. Jesus said to them: "My heart is sorrowful to the point of death: stay here and pray and keep watch while I go and pray by Myself." Jesus went over further to pray: He wanted to pray by Himself. He wanted to pour out His heart to His Father as I often have seen Him do with His prayer. My Son always prayed continuously to His Father: He always looked to the Father for His consolation. During the time He prayed, He saw all the agony He was going to suffer: and the agony was not so much the pain of the crucifixion as the pains of the sins of the world. Every sin, every injustice, every infidelity He saw and felt at that very moment, caused Him to sweat blood. His agony, His sorrow, and so much sinfulness caused the blood to burst from His forehead. It was just another anticipation of when His Precious Blood would be shed on the cross. That Blood that was sweat on Gethsemane blessed that very spot into Jesus' sacred place of prayer.

My children, never seek your comfort in anyone but God. In your times of loneliness, in your times of depression, in your times of doubt, have recourse to prayer. When you go to the Father, offer this mystery for those who are in doubt: those who do not know where to turn to: those who are depressed: the mentally ill: the emotionally ill. Pray that as the Father sent an angel to comfort my Son, the Lord in His mercy will comfort them and enlighten them.

The Scourging at the Pillar
2nd Sorrowful Mystery

My Son was sent to Pilate after being judged by the Jewish authorities, I was there in spirit: I heard Pontius Pilate as he came out to talk to the crowd. He said: "I find no fault in this Man worthy of death: so I will have Him scourged: then I will set Him free." Pilate said this to placate the crowd because he knew my Son was innocent of all the accusations that they were throwing at Him. Pilate sent my Son to be scourged: He was whipped. The normal procedure was to be whipped thirty-nine times. My Son was whipped furiously: the demons took possession of the soldiers. All the anger of hell was vented out on my Son. At that moment, I asked the Father to spare my Son from dying at the scourging and the Father answered my prayer: and still the soldiers that scourged my Son were filled with the very hatred of hell itself. That was the reaction they had to the purity of my Son. When Jesus received all this scourging for the love of you, it was because He loved you that He took all this pain: because He wanted you to be healed of your sins: of all the diseases of the soul, mind, and body that Jesus took all this punishment. Jesus did not take all this punishment to condemn you: He took it all to save you. Behold the love of my Son for you and yet behold His meekness as the Lamb that is brought to the slaughter: my Son was scourged without even opening His mouth.

My children, my Son wishes to heal you by His stripes. By the scourging He received, He wants to set you free of all types of oppression, of all types of bondage. By the stripes of my Son you are healed and set free. My children, pray to the Father that He will heal the wounds of your heart so that you can pray with love. Ask the Father to teach you how to love the way my Son loves. Pray for those who are possessed by hatred: pray for those who have an insatiable need to seek revenge. Pray that they too will be liberated and healed by the stripes of my Son.

Jesus is Crowned with Thorns
3rd Sorrowful Mystery

After the scourging, my Son was led to the praetorium where the soldiers wanted to further amuse themselves. They took some twine filled with thorns and made a skull-like cap. They placed the cap on the head of Jesus and pressed, causing the thorns to penetrate His scalp until He began to bleed. Then they put a reed in His hand and they knelt before Him and they mocked Him and said to Him, "All Hail, King of the Jews," and they spit in His face, they hit His head with the reed, they slapped His face, and plucked His beard. Jesus continued to say nothing. He received it all.

My children, Jesus still receives a crown of thorns from many. It is normal for Jesus to be mocked by His enemies but it is more painful when Jesus is mocked by His own people. Even today, my children, Christians mock Him by living in mortal sin, by receiving Communion in mortal sin, by not believing the truth contained in the scriptures which is the word of God. My children, Christians mock Jesus and crown Him with thorns when they invent their own doctrines at their convenience: when they use the Gospel of my Son, they use it to justify their own teachings, their own doctrine. My children, I call you to make reparation to my Son. Follow Him by leaving all sin behind: by loving Him and revering Him in the Blessed Sacrament. When you receive Him in Holy Communion, tell Him that you love Him for those who will not love Him. Offer this mystery to the Father in reparation for all the blasphemes that were ever said against my Son. Pray for those who take the name of God in vain: pray for those who will not keep Sunday holy. Promise the Father that you will keep Sunday holy by going to Mass and receiving Holy Communion and avoiding all unnecessary work in order to give yourself to prayer and doing the will of God. I am praying for you, my children and I will guide you in loving Jesus for those who will not love Him.

Jesus Carried the Cross
4th Sorrowful Mystery

That Friday, that first Good Friday, Jesus, my Son, after He was scourged and was crowned with thorns, was given a cross to carry through the streets of Jerusalem all the way to Mount Calvary where they had crucified others. He carried the cross through the same streets which He had come triumphantly the Sunday before. The people who cried "Hosanna" now cried "Crucify Him." I was there along the way and I met my Son: His face all beaten, all covered with blood from His bleeding head, tired and dirty, and yet our eyes met. Our eyes filled with love for each other. Both of us knew that it was totally unavoidable that He should go through this agony for the salvation of the world. The weight of the cross on Jesus' body was not as heavy as the weight of the sins of the world on His soul. Out of obedience to His Father, Jesus continued the journey until He reached Calvary. He met a group of women who were weeping and He said to them: "Daughters of Jerusalem, weep not for Me, but for yourselves and your children."

My children, pray for the gift of tears, that through that gift the Lord will cleanse your souls of sin and the effects of sin. My children, pray for the gift of obedience: that each one of you will be obedient to the call that the Father has given to you. Pray for those who have burdens on their hearts and the weight of their trials seems more than they can bear, pray to the Father that these people will have the strength to carry their crosses following Jesus. Finally, ask the Father for the gift of being true disciples of Jesus: ask the Father that you will always say yes to Jesus and to His way even though it may mean suffering and sorrow. Pray to the

Father that you will have the grace to take all out of love for Him.

The Crucifixion of our Lord

5th Sorrowful Mystery

When we had finally reached Mount Calvary, my Son was thrown on the cross after being stripped naked in front of the crowd. They drove spikes through His hands and feet and yet the Lord gave me the strength to withstand the sight of my Son being nailed on the cross and literally butchered by the soldiers. They lifted the cross to its place, and then my Son hung there for three hours. I heard my Son say, "Father, forgive them, for they do not know what they're doing." Jesus prayed for His enemies and pleaded for their ignorance: He also pleaded for your ignorance. There were two thieves crucified with Jesus, one on His right and the other on His left, and to the repentant thief He promised paradise. Finally He looked at me and at John: He told me, "Woman, behold your Son" and to John, "Behold your mother." My spiritual motherhood is Jesus' gift to you: Jesus gave me to His disciples and to the whole Church to be mother and intercessor for everyone who calls himself a Christian. When the third hour came, the sky became dark and Jesus cried out, "Father, into Your hands I commend My Spirit."

My Son bowed His head, the symbol of obedience to the Father, and then the earth began to quake. There was a great storm in heaven, the whole of creation was reacting at man's crime, the killing of their God, the killing of their Savior. After it was calm, Nicodemus, Joseph of Arimethea, and John took my Son down and then placed Him in my arms. I remembered while I was holding Him the prophecy of Simeon, "The sword of sorrow will pierce your soul." That prophecy was coming true: but just as I was holding my Son in my arms, I remembered His words that He would rise, again. All that I needed to do was to wait until that prophecy was fulfilled.

My children, ask the Father to extend His salvation and forgiveness to your enemies. Pray for those who abuse you: pray for those who hurt you in any form. Ask the Father that they will also be cleansed by the blood of Jesus shed on the cross. Come, my children, to the foot of the cross and there I will pray with you and for you that your sins will be blotted out: that you will experience the redeeming power of my Son. Pray before the crucifix and I will pray with you. Ask the Father that you will constantly remember the death of my Son and be ever grateful for the salvation He has obtained for you.

Glorious Mystery of the Rosary—Wednesday & Sunday

The Resurrection of Jesus Christ

1st Glorious Mystery

At dawn of the first day of the week, I was with John and Peter. I was in my room alone: John and Peter were in the next room. I woke up. There was a light: it was all over the room. There was my Son: He came forward, He said to me, "Come, for you are the one worthy to be the first to see My risen body." The Lord permitted me to kiss His hand and to be embraced. The Lord in His glorified body in which He had the scars of the nail prints in His hands and feet and the scar of the lance in His side, was no longer the bleeding Son I saw on the way to Calvary: His body was full of light, a light that was emanating from His body. Jesus then said to me , "Do not, My mother, tell My disciples until I have sent Mary Magdalene because it is all in the plan of the Father. They will come to faith by seeing and touching. I have come to you because you have faith. Pray that My disciples will accept Me risen from the dead." Then He went away to appear to Mary Magdalene, to the women, and then to His disciples.

My children, the most precious gift you have is your faith. Your faith must not be hidden: your faith must be your main motivation in your life. Cast away all doubt by prayer: give yourselves totally to Jesus Who will illuminate your mind and heart through the power of the resurrection.

The Ascension of Jesus to Heaven
2nd Glorious Mystery

After forty days when Jesus appeared to His disciples, Jesus led us to the outskirts of Bethany to the mount of Olives: that mount where He was transfigured in the sight of Peter, James and John. Jesus took us to the mount of Olives and He lifted up His arms and He blessed His apostles and He blessed His disciples. He blessed the holy women and He blessed me, His mother. He said to His apostles, "Go to the whole world and preach the good news to every creature. Teach all that I have commanded you. Baptize them in the name of the Father, and of the Son, and of the Holy Spirit. I am with you always even to the end of time." Then He said to them, "Go to Jerusalem and stay there until My Father has sent you the promise: then when the Holy Spirit comes upon you, you will have power to be My witnesses: you will be My witnesses in Jerusalem, in Judea, and even to the ends of the earth." As Jesus was saying this, He was lifted up before our eyes. I longed to go with Him but Jesus said to me. "Woman, these are your children. It is not time for you to go now: stay, I will call you when it is the proper time. Stay and pray with My disciples." He went up into heaven when finally a cloud came and took Him from our sight and we saw Him no more.

Then I saw two men dressed in white. They were angels and said to the apostles, "Men of Galilee, why are you standing there looking up into the heavens. This Jesus who you saw go up into heaven will come again as He went." Then we went to Jerusalem to the upper room where Jesus had changed bread and wine into His Body and Blood. There we stayed to pray.

My children, learn from this mystery: learn that Jesus is Lord of Heaven and earth and all authority belongs to Him. There is no authority permitted without my Son's consent. Pray for those in authority: for government leaders that they be submissive to the authority of Jesus. Pray for missionaries: that they will be faithful in teaching the Gospel of Jesus and will teach people the means of salvation. Pray for holy patience: pray that you will wait upon the Lord and wait till He tells you what to do and when to do it. Be disposed to listen to the voice of God and to obey the voice of God. My children, finally be alert in prayer and be united in prayer: prayer is the means that God wishes to use to bring the Church together. I am among you even now in prayer asking the Lord to bless you.

The Descent of the Holy Ghost

3rd Glorious Mystery

It was the day of Pentecost: the city of Jerusalem was crowded. Every people from every known nation of the world who were of the Jewish faith came to Jerusalem to celebrate the feast of Booths. The disciples and the relatives of my Son and I were still in the upper room, when suddenly we heard a rushing wind: In the room we could feel wind on our faces and then we saw fire right in the midst of us: a fire that was not of this world but a fire that came upon our heads and as it touched us we were filled with the immense power of God. We felt joy and peace: we felt love. All our fear was gone: we no longer had a fear of who came to the door. The disciple John came to me and said, "Mother we are free! We are free!" Peter came to me, "My Lady, look, the promise of your Son is here." I said to Peter, "This must not be kept to yourself: go and tell everyone about Jesus." The apostle Peter took the lead and opened the door of the upper room and the apostles and the disciples went out. There were people from every nation, from every language, and yet everyone was understanding Peter's sermon. Everyone was understanding the message of salvation. Peter said, "We are not drunk. This is the fulfillment of what was said by the prophet Joel: the Spirit of the Lord will come down on all flesh. Save yourselves," he said, "Repent of your sins and be baptized in the name of the Lord Jesus and you too will receive the Holy Ghost." On that day three thousand entered the Church of my Son. I was still in the room listening to Peter and seeing the apostles baptizing those who came forward. Jesus again fulfilled His words: the power of the Spirit was upon His disciples who bore witness to Him.

My children, pray to the Heavenly Father in this mystery for the power of the Holy Ghost to fill you with love and with boldness. Pray to the Father that the fire of the Spirit will purify you from all trace of sin. My children, if you are in sin, go and seek forgiveness in the sacrament of reconciliation and then pray to my Son that the Holy Ghost will fill your soul with every grace necessary for your salvation and for the salvation of others. Also, my children, share the good news that Jesus is the Savior of the world and there is no other Savior but Jesus. I will pray that the Lord will use you in power and by the grace of the Holy Ghost you will be transformed into witnesses for Jesus.

The Assumption of Mary into Heaven

4th Glorious Mystery

I knew that my last days were to come. After Pentecost, John and I went to Ephesus and we lived there for thirty years. I told John, "My days on earth are coming to an end. I wish to go back to Jerusalem and to be with all the apostles and to say farewell." John complied and we went to Jerusalem. I asked once we arrived in Jerusalem to send for the apostles. This was before James was executed by Herod. They all met with me except Thomas. I told the apostles, "It is time for me to leave you, my sons. I must go to be with Jesus but I am not leaving you orphans like my Son did not leave you orphans. Now that I am going to be with Jesus I will pray for you and I will be concerned with your welfare." Peter came to me and said, "Mother, when you see Him, tell Him I love Him." I told Peter, "He knows that you love Him, by you feeding His sheep." I laid back and I fell asleep. With great sorrow, my sons, the apostles, laid me in a tomb. No sooner that they closed the door of the tomb I heard my Son's voice, "Come, My beloved mother. Awake, I have come for you." My eyes opened and Jesus in all glory came for me and angels were attending Him. "Come, My beloved Mother," He said, "Come, and inherit the Kingdom prepared for you by My Father." The angels lifted me up in their hands and I went and followed my Son into heaven. I heard the choirs of angels and the choirs of the Just as they sang a hymn of praise to the most Holy Trinity. They said, "Blessed are you, oh God of host: You in Your greatness have exulted Your handmaid. For the one who bore Your Son, the spotless Virgin Mary, has been made worthy to sit at His right hand. Welcome, oh daughter of God. Welcome oh Mother of the Savior. Oh welcome, bride of the Holy Spirit. Welcome, handmaid and Queen."

My children, in this mystery ask the Heavenly Father

for an intense desire to be with Jesus. My children, the things of this world are temporary. Nothing in this world will satisfy the longing of your hearts. Only Jesus, my Son will satisfy you. Only Jesus, my Son, can fill the void in your hearts and make you happy. Let your satisfaction be in Jesus. My children, I wish for you to do deeds of mercy and love for the honor of Jesus and when you pray, my children, pray that your hearts will be filled with only one thing: JESUS.

Mary is Crowned as Queen of Heaven and Earth

5th Glorious Mystery

When I arrived in heaven, the angels quickly put a robe of gold upon me. Then they put a mantle full of jewels and then I was led to the throne of the Trinity. God the Father said to me, "Oh My daughter you have been faithful as My instrument. You have brought up my Son in dignity and goodness. You have been faithful as My servant and as My daughter. You have kept your soul spotless by being faithful to My grace which I have given to you since you were conceived in your mother's womb. Welcome, My daughter into Our presence: come closer, you merit the crown of Our favor." I approached the throne of the Trinity and then God the Father, Jesus my Son, and the Holy Spirit Who is God, crowned me with a crown of gold and jewels. There was great rejoicing in heaven: the angels began to sing, "Glory to God! Glory to God! Glory to God!" and the saints began to sing "Blessed are You, oh God Most High, for You have exalted Your servant Mary to be Queen: to be honored above all creatures." And the angels also joined in the praises by saying, "Blessed are You, oh God of host, for You have thought it worthy to exalt and crown the lowly creature Mary as Queen of the universe." My Son took me by the hand and led me to the throne prepared for me. "Sit here, My Mother," He said, "This throne is yours. I have prepared it for you. It is here that you will rule with Me for all eternity: it is here that you will intercede for the world and I will hear whatever you say for I love you and I wish to honor you." I said, "Oh my Son, it is good for me to be here but I also pray that soon Your apostles, Your disciples, and all Your people will be here with us to praise You, to love You for all eternity." "Yes My Mother," He said to me, "I will give to you whatever your heart desires and from now on all men that acknowledge Me as their King must also acknowledge you as their Queen and Mother."

My children, I come to pray for you and to ask Jesus' blessing upon you. Give yourselves to me, my children. Entrust yourselves to my prayers. Jesus is always ready to respond to my prayers: give yourselves to me, my children, and your prayers will be answered by my Son. Children, come to me in prayer and I will whisper in your hearts. Obey me, your mother, and it will go well with you and I will intercede for you and you will gain favor from the Lord and yes my children pray for the grace to become totally holy in the eyes of God and I will be waiting for you my children until we are together to praise the Lord for all eternity.

Luminous Mystery of the Rosary—Thursday

The Baptism in the Jordan
1st Luminous Mystery

John was baptizing in the Jordan proclaiming a baptism of repentance.

"I am the voice of one crying in the desert, make straight the way of the Lord." "One mightier than I is coming after me." "I have baptized you with water, He will baptize you with the Holy Spirit." Seeing Jesus, John exclaimed: "Behold the Lamb of God." After Jesus' Baptism, a voice from heaven: "This is my beloved Son in whom I am well pleased." The Spirit descended upon Jesus in the form of a dove. In this heavenly manifestation was instituted the sacrament of Baptism. The divine Trinity was manifested: the voice of the Father was heard as the Spirit descended upon the Son. Filled with the Holy Spirit, Jesus was led by the Spirit into the desert for 40 days.

The Wedding at Cana

2nd Luminous Mystery

Jesus, His Mother and disciples were invited to a wedding in Cana. During the wedding feast the wine ran short. Mary turned to Jesus: "They have no wine." Jesus replied: "What would you have me do? My hour has not yet come." Mary said to the waiters: "Do whatever he tells you." There were six stone water jars, each holding fifteen to twenty gallons. Jesus bids the waiters to fill the jars with water, and then draw some out and take it to the chief steward. The chief steward said to the groom: "Every man serves the good wine first... but you have saved the good wine until now." At Mary's request, Jesus worked His first miracle. By His presence, Christian marriage was raised to the dignity of a Sacrament.

The Proclamation of the Kingdom

3rd Luminous Mystery

"Repent, for the kingdom of God is at hand."

"My kingdom is not of this world."

"Unless a man be born again of water and the Spirit, he cannot enter the kingdom of heaven."

"Whoever does not accept the kingdom of God as a little child will not enter into it."

"I have come to call sinners, not the just."

"Love your enemies, pray for those who persecute you."

"Blessed are the poor in spirit, for theirs is the kingdom of heaven."

"Blessed are they who hunger and thirst for justice, for they shall be satisfied."

"Blessed are they who suffer persecution for justice' sake, for theirs is the kingdom of heaven."

"You are Peter, and upon this rock I will build My Church... I will give you the keys of the kingdom of heaven."

The Transfiguration
4th Luminous Mystery

Jesus took Peter, James and John up a high mountain to pray. Jesus was transfigured before them. "His face became as dazzling as the sun, his clothes as radiant as light." This was to fortify their faith to withstand the coming tragedy of the Passion. Jesus foresaw the 'scandal of the cross,' and prepared them for it by this manifestation of His glory. Moses and Elias (representing the Law and the prophets of the Old Testament) were conversing with Jesus about His passion. "Do not think I have come to destroy the Law or the Prophets... but to fulfill them." From a cloud came a voice: "This is my beloved Son, listen to Him." Jesus admonished them not to tell the vision to anyone until the Son of Man rises from the dead. We too will behold the transfigured Jesus on the Last Day.

The Institution of the Eucharist
5th Luminous Mystery

I have eagerly desired to eat this Passover with you before I suffer. Jesus took bread, blessed it: "Take and eat, this is My Body." Taking the wine: "This cup is the new covenant in my Blood, shed for you." At that Eucharistic meal, Jesus celebrated the first Mass. At every Mass the sacrifice of Calvary is made present. At the Last Supper Jesus instituted the sacrament of Holy Orders to perpetuate this sacrifice. "Whoever eats my flesh and drinks my blood remains in me and I in him." The Eucharist is a sacrifice inasmuch as it is offered up, and a sacrament inasmuch as it is received. In the Mass we offer ourselves to God, and God gives Himself to us. The Mass will be fruitful in the measure of our surrender to the Father.

Thanksgiving After Communion

Thanksgiving After Communion #1

Lord, Father all-powerful, and ever-living God, I thank Thee, for even though I am a sinner, Thy unprofitable servant, not because of my worth, but in the kindness of Thy mercy, Thou hast fed me with the precious Body and Blood of Thy Son, our Lord Jesus Christ. I pray that this Holy Communion may not bring me condemnation and punishment but forgiveness and salvation. May it be a helmet of faith and a shield of good will. May it purify me from evil ways and put an end to my evil passions. May it bring me charity and patience, humility and obedience, and growth in power to do good. May it be my strong defense against all my enemies, visible and invisible, and the perfect calming of all my evil impulses, bodily and spiritual. May it unite me more closely to Thee, the one true God and lead me safely through death to everlasting happiness with Thee. And I pray that Thou willest lead me, a sinner to the banquet where Thou with Thy Son and Holy Spirit, art true and perfect light, total fulfillment, everlasting joy, gladness without end, and perfect happiness to Thy saints. Grant this through Christ our Lord. Amen.

Thanksgiving After Communion #2

We give Thee thanks, O most merciful Lord and Redeemer of our souls, for this day Thou hast made us worthy by means of these immortal and heavenly mysteries. Direct our way; keep us in fear of Thee; guard our lives; and make our steps firm through the prayers and intercessions of the glorious and holy Mother of God and ever-Virgin Mary. Be exalted above the heavens, O God, and above all the earth, Thy glory, now and forever and ever. Amen.

Thanksgiving After Communion #3

O Lord Jesus Christ, Son of the living God, who according to the will of the Father, with the cooperation of the Holy Spirit, hast by Thy death given life unto the world, deliver me by Thy most sacred Body, which, I, unworthy, have presumed to receive, from all my iniquities and from every evil, and make me ever to hold fast to Thy command-ments and suffer me never to be separated from Thee. Amen.

Thanksgiving After Communion #4—Anima Christi

Soul of Christ, sanctify me. Body of Christ, save me. Blood of Christ, inebriate me. Water from the side of Christ, wash me. Passion of Christ, strengthen me.

O good Jesus, hear me. Within Thy wounds, hide me. Separated from Thee let me never be. From the malignant enemy, defend me. At the hour of death, call me to come to Thee, that I may praise Thee in the company of Thy Saints, for all eternity. Amen.

Thanksgiving After Confession

Eternal Father! I thank Thee, I bless Thee, for Thy goodness and mercy. Thou hast had compassion on me, although in my folly I had wandered far away from Thee and offended Thee most grievously. With fatherly love Thou hast received me anew after so many relapses into sin and forgiven me my offenses through the holy sacrament of penance.

Blessed forever, O my God, be Thy loving-kindness, Thy infinite mercy! Never again will I grieve Thee by ingratitude, by disobedience to Thy holy will. All that I am, all that I have, all that I do shall be consecrated to Thy service and Thy glory.

Amen.

JOE SIXPACK APOSTOLATE

I hope you have enjoyed this book, and my earnest prayer is that it be an aid to you in your own efforts at Catholic evangelization. Remember, if you have any questions, need advice, or just want to learn a little bit more about our holy an ancient Faith, contact me anytime through the JoeSixpackAnswers.com website.

At the very least, you should go to my website right now and sign up on the form at the right side of the page to get my free email course and to begin getting invitations to my free weekly webinars.

At the very beginning of this book I stated that the primary purpose of this book is to teach you how to evangelize anybody. There is a secondary purpose to this book, though. Operating the apostolate at JoeSixpackAnswers.com costs money. I am expecting the royalties from this book to help me continue to finance the apostolate. Therefore, I greatly appreciate your purchase of *The Lay Evangelist's Handbook*. If you are interested in helping to support this apostolate, there are a couple of ways you can do it.

I have a store on the Etsy website called the Every Catholic Guy store. I have 150 products on the store—T-shirts and coffee mugs—with sayings from the saints and some famous Catholics, and a few spiffy sayings I came up with. When you purchase a T-shirt or coffee mug, 100% of the profit goes to help this apostolate.

Finally, another way you can help is to visit my website and become a Joe Sixpack Partner. Your help would be greatly appreciated!

The Sixpack System

The last thing I want to tell you about is something I hope you'll pass along to your parish priest. I call it the Sixpack System. It's intended to defeat parish catechetical illiteracy, increase collections, and fire up your parishioners!

The Sixpack System manages to involve the entire parish... without asking them to do a single thing! And the Sixpack System is so simple that it requires no effort on your part. It works in three phases.

Phase One

The Sixpack System begins with the weekly bulletin insert, *What We Believe... Why We Believe It*. Surveys show that 70% of all Catholics get 100% of their Catholic information from your parish Sunday bulletin. So your bulletin is the ideal place to begin with this new system.

What We Believe is intrusive, meaning it's read by parishioners because it's the first thing they see when they open the bulletin. It's been my experience that people eagerly embrace the fullness of Catholic truth when they know and understand it. Each issue of *What We Believe* is a

thumbnail lesson in the Catholic faith that's easy to understand and faithful to the Magisterium. The inserts are so
compelling that many priests report that some folks collect
each issue for future reference, and all subscribing pastors
report that their flock love and learn from them. Each issue
invites the reader into the second part of the system.

Phase Two

Each issue of the bulletin insert invites readers to a website
set   up   for   your   people   called
JoeSixpackAnswers.com. Parishioners will go to this website
to find answers to all their questions in complete
anonymity... questions they may be embarrassed to ask you.
If they can't find the answer on the site, there is a way to
address their questions directly to **Joe Sixpack–The
Every Catholic Guy**.

Most visitors to the website sign up for a free email
course, designed to get them into the third part of the
system.

When a visitor enters a first name and email, two things
begin to happen. And that leads us to the third phase of the
system!

Phase Three

About 53% of visitors to the website join the Joe
Sixpack mailing list. Then they'll automatically get a free
email course that teaches them the unvarnished truths of
the faith.

The other thing that happens is every week they'll
receive special invitations to attend a free live webinar

about a particular topic on the faith. Attendees can interact with me and ask any question pertaining to the subject matter. And boy, do they ask questions!

Here's What Pastors and Parishioners Are Saying...

This was the first full webinar the I've sat through. And I was amazed when you said it was time for questions. It just blew me away, as I didn't think an hour had gone by already. So I would've never guessed that an hour would've gone by. It was amazing! I was totally shocked. You have me sucked in! It was a great experience for me. Thank you for everything you do.

Randy M

I truly need to tell you that this simple instrument of What We Believe... Why We Believe It is a wonderful tool and a great way to catechize every Christian brethren in this age of Wi-Fi, all over the world. I am very sure that many would soon follow your pioneering footsteps in this unique apostolic venture. Please keep up this good work and more grease to your elbow. Remain blessed always.

Fr. Felix O

Please accept my sincere thanks for the extraordinary work you are doing to shed light on and share the truth of the Catholic faith. Your strength is the comprehensive and faithful exposition of the faith in language "Joe Sixpack" can appreciate and embrace. You are sharing an amazingly rich gift with others and I pray that your online audience continues to grow.

Fr. Willy Raymond, C.S.C. *President of Holy Cross Family Ministries*

The weekly catechetical webinars offered by Joe Sixpack are perfectly sound, accurate and engaging. They precisely address the questions troubling the three sadly un-catechized generations who make up most of today's Catholic laity.

I most warmly endorse the Sixpack System.
Donna Steichen *Best Selling Ignatius Press Author*

Our parish has had an installation of Joe Sixpack each week in our bulletin. Reading these inserts is the highlight of my week. I am a cradle Catholic, who left the Church for a while, but returned. I am now deeply in love with my Catholic faith and these writings reinforce the beauty of the Catholic faith, but also answer questions that I had not yet resolved. God has richly blessed Joe Sixpack with deep wisdom and the ability to express basic faith issues in ways that a common person can understand. Keep up the good work!!
JoAnne B

I wholeheartedly recommend the new weekly parish bulletin insert "What We Believe... Why We Believe It" written by my friend, Joe Sixpack...

"Joe Sixpack" is a veteran catechist with a God-given gift for explaining the truths of the Faith in terms that are clear, unambiguous, doctrinally correct and firmly rooted in Sacred Scripture, Sacred Tradition and Magisterial teaching. The name "Joe Sixpack" accentuates his remarkable ability to make the teaching of the Church easily understandable for the average guy and gal. His gift for story-telling and the use of concrete examples will help to provide his subscribers with both engaging and thought provoking reading each Sunday.

Pastors who wish to find new catechetical tools to help their parishioners develop a greater understanding and a deeper appreciation for the timeless truths of our Catholic faith will find "What We Believe and Why We Believe It" a valuable resource for instruction and a great little addition to their weekly bulletins.

Rev. William P. Casey, C.P.M. *EWTN Personality*

Tell your pastor to let **Joe Sixpack—The Every Catholic Guy** help you re-educate and re-evangelize your parishioners today.

They can subscribe FREE for the first three months! After that, it's merely $19.95/mo.

Subscription rates will never increase—**GUARAN-TEED!** That even applies to lay people, as we have a few who do indeed subscribe.

NOTES

1. Why This Book and How to Use It

1. *From his DuMont Television Network television show "Life is Worth Living" from 1951-1957.*

2. The souls I started with were virtually all non-Catholic. Sadly, today we have to focus on evangelizing our own Catholic people, and this book is ideally suited for just that kind of evangelization. This works with non-Catholics, too, but only if they are still interested after they hear the word "Catholic." Since the mere mention of our faith will produce a nearly audible "bang" as minds slam shut, I use what I call the Curiosity Approach to great effect, which may be yet another book.

3. These "lay evangelists" are largely ineffective at motivating the laity to get active into evangelization, as the people you lead will only do about 10% of what you do yourself. How do I know? About 85% of my adult godchildren (many of whom I haven't seen in years) are actively evangelizing in their respective locales.

4. If you're interested in checking out our webinars, visit *JoeSixpackAnswers.com*. Enter your name and email into the form on the right hand side of the page. You'll begin getting invitations to register for these *free* webinars... as well as a free email course.

5. Admittedly, I have gone much further in my efforts than any Catholic is required to do. Still, there is no excuse for almost any Catholic to not share the faith with others.

6. If you can't be excited about the faith, it's because you haven't thoroughly learned it yet. If you know the faith like the back of your hand and you still aren't excited, figure out some other way to serve Our Lord, because you can't evangelize at the funeral home.

7. The definition of a true man or a true woman is the same: **one who does always and only the holy will of God**.

8. I'll quote it here for your convenience: *"I know your works: you are neither cold nor hot. Would that you were cold or hot! So, because you are lukewarm, and neither cold nor hot,* **I will spew you out of my mouth**.*"* Some translations replace *I will spew you out of my mouth* with *I will vomit you out of my mouth.*

9. Even as these words are being written, I'm working on a book that leads readers down the path of my curiosity approach. Hopefully, even in retirement and death I can continue evangelizing!

10. Of course, you could attend the webinars I put on. To make sure you

get invitations to them every week, just go to JoeSixpackAnswers.com and register for the free email course in the form on the right hand side of the page. This automatically puts you on a list where invitations to the webinars will be sent out each week.

11. Fr. Hardon was a friend of mine. He was the greatest English-speaking theologian alive at the time, and one of only five people in the world who could go to the Vatican unannounced and have a private audience with St. Pope John Paul II.

12. Get a copy of Terry's magnificent book on evangelization, *How to Share Your Faith with Anyone: A Practical Manual of Catholic Evangelization*.

13. I operate under St. John Bosco's motto: "Give me souls; keep the rest!" You might want to begin adopting this same mindset.

14. St. Michael the Archangel, defend us in battle; be thou our defense against the wickedness and snares of the devil. May God rebuke him, we humbly pray. And do thou, O prince of the heavenly host, by the power of God drive into hell Satan and all the evil spirits who roam about the world seeking the ruin of souls. Amen.

15. It kind of helps sell them on Catholicism too, as I cover the angels in the first article of the Creed.

16. You *must* treat such revelations as though they were protected by the seal of confession. Best Practice: Hear them without hearing them, then forget them.

3. The First Article of the Creed

1. John 8:48-59.
2. Exodus 3:13-14.

11. Ninth Article of the Creed

1. Karl Keating, *Catholicism and Fundamentalism* (San Francisco: Ignatius Press, 1988).
2. Keating, *Catholicism and Fundamentalism*, 205-206.
3. This is the text of the *Revised Standard Version*. Most versions read "and the gates of hell" instead of "and the powers of death." Of course, the "powers of death" are "the gates of hell".
4. Keating, *Catholicism and Fundamentalism*, 208.
5. Keating, *Catholicism and Fundamentalism*, 208.
6. Bertrand L. Conway, C.S.P., *The Question Box* (New York: Paulist Press, 1929), 146-147.
7. *Lumen Gentium*, 18.
8. *Catechism of the Catholic Church*, 1547.

9. Ignatius of Antioch, *Ad Smyrnæans*, 8:2.
10. *Catechism of the Catholic Church*, 767.
11. *Dei Verbum*, 9.
12. St Irenaeus, *Adversus Haereses*, 3:3.
13. *Lumen Gentium*, 25.
14. Keating, *Catholicism and Fundamentalism*, 217 (emphasis added).
15. *Lumen Gentium*, 14.
16. *Lumen Gentium*, 16.
17. Freemasonry has a long 350 year history of antagonism toward the Catholic Church. In fact, Freemasonry's official stance is "the violent overthrow of church and state."
18. *Catechism of the Catholic Church*, 2255-2256.

13. Eleventh Article of the Creed

1. *Catechism of the Catholic Church*, 966.

14. Twelfth Article of the Creed

1. *Catechism of the Catholic Church*, 1030-1031.
2. Keating, *Catholicism and Fundamentalism*, 193.

16. The Sacraments in General

1. *Catechism of the Catholic Church*, 1084.

17. Baptism

1. *Catechism of the Catholic Church*, 1213.
2. St Irenaeus, *Adversus Hæreses*, 2:22.
3. Origen, *Commentarii in Romanos*, 5:9.

18. Confirmation

1. *Lumen Gentium*, 11.
2. This instruction is not left up to the parish DRE, but rather up to the parents. You can have your children attend ant PSR classes at the parish, but you are obligated to follow that up with the moral certitude the child has been properly instructed.

19. Holy Eucharist

1. Lorraine Boettner, *Roman Catholicism* (Philadelphia: Presbyterian and Reformed, 1962).
2. Karl Keating, *Catholicism and Fundamentalism*, 42-43.
3. *Catechism of the Catholic Church,* 1365.
4. *Council of Trent,* 1743.
5. I personally pray St. Thomas Aquinas' *Thanksgiving After Communion* and the *Anima Christi.* See the appendix on prayers.

20. Penance

1. Loraine Boettner*, Roman Catholicism*, 8.
2. Gregory the Great*, Homily* 26.
3. Caesarius of Arles, *Sermon* 253:1.
4. Caesarius of Arles, *Sermon* 211.
5. Leo the Great, *Epis.* 108.
6. Augustine, *De Agon. Christ,* 3: Ser. 295, 2.
7. Ambrose, *De Poen.,* 1:2.
8. Paulinus of Milan, *Vita Ambrosii,* 39.
9. Origen, *In Psalmos homiliae* 2, 6.
10. Keating, *Catholicism and Fundamentalism,* 189.
11. *Catechism of the Catholic Church,* 1461.
12. *Catechism of the Catholic Church,* 1449.
13. *Catechism of the Catholic Church,* 1468.
14. Daughters of St. Paul, *Queen of Apostles Prayerbook* (50 St. Paul's Avenue, Boston, Massachusetts 02130).
15. Fathers Belmonte and Socias, *Handbook of Prayers* (Scepter Publishers, Inc., 20 Nassau Street, Princeton, New Jersey 08542).
16. *Catechism of the Catholic Church,* 1451.
17. *Catechism of the Catholic Church,* 1452 (emphasis added).
18. *Catechism of the Catholic Church,* 1455.
19. *Catechism of the Catholic Church,* 1458.
20. Pope St. Paul VI, *Apostolic constitution, Indulgentiarum doctrina* (1967) Norm 1.

21. Anointing of the Sick

1. *Catechism of the Catholic Church,* 1520-1523.
2. *Catechism of the Catholic Church,* 1519.

22. Holy Orders

1. *Catechism of the Catholic Church*, 1536.
2. *Catechism of the Catholic Church*, 1577-1578.
3. Unless otherwise noted, we use the word priest here as a term that is inclusive of the office of bishop.
4. St. Thomas Aquinas, *Summa Theologiae*, III, 22, 4c.
5. *Catechism of the Catholic Church*, 1579.

23. Holy Matrimony

1. *Catechism of the Catholic Church*, 1640.
2. *Catechism of the Catholic Church*, 1641.
3. *Gaudium et spes*, 49.3.

24. Sacramentals

1. *Catechism of the Catholic Church*, 1667.
2. Advent and Lent are seasons of penance.
3. *Catechism of the Catholic Church*, 1174.

25. Christian Morality—A Primer

1. *Catechism of the Catholic Church*, 1778.
2. *Gaudium et spes*, 16.
3. *Catechism of the Catholic Church*, 1791.
4. *Catechism of the Catholic Church*, 1793.

26. The Ten Commandments

1. Mark 12:30-31.
2. *Catechism of the Catholic Church*, 2056.
3. Exodus 20:1-17.
4. Sirach 15:15.

27. The First Commandment

1. *Catechism of the Catholic Church*, 2113.
2. *Catechism of the Catholic Church*, 2117.
3. Ecumenism is the dialogue between Catholics and non-Catholics which leads to the leads to the reconciliation of all Christians in the unity of the one and only Church Of Christ.
4. Sirach 44:14-15.
5. Luke 1:48.
6. Luke 1:48.
7. Karl Keating, *Catholicism and Fundamentalism*, 260-261.

28. The Second Commandment

1. *Catechism of the Catholic Church*, 2146.
2. *Catechism of the Catholic Church*, 2148.
3. *Catechism of the Catholic Church*, 2147.

29. The Third Commandment

1. *Catechism of the Catholic Church*, 2180.
2. St. John Chrysostom, *De incomprehensibili* 3, 6:PG 48,725.
3. *Catechism of the Catholic Church*, 2185.
4. *Catechism of the Catholic Church*, 2186.

30. The Fourth Commandment

1. *https://intothebreach.org/wp-content/uploads/2015/10/INTO-THE-BREACH-ROMAN-CATHOLIC-DIOCESE-OF-PHOENIX.pdf*.
2. *Catechism of the Catholic Church*, 2214.
3. *Catechism of the Catholic Church*, 2221-2226.
4. The Second Vatican Council's Declaration on Christian Education, *Gravissimum educationis*, 3.
5. *Catechism of the Catholic Church*, 2234.
6. *Catechism of the Catholic Church*, cf. 2238-2240.
7. *Catechism of the Catholic Church*, 2237.

31. The Fifth Commandment

1. *Catechism of Catholic Church*, cf. 2272.
2. Felician A. Foy, ed., *1994 Catholic Almanac* (Huntington, Indiana: Our Sunday Visitor, 1993), 308.
3. St. Thomas Aquinas, *Summa Theologiae*, II-II, 64, 7, corp. art.
4. *Catechism of the Catholic Church*, 2265.
5. *Catechism of the Catholic Church*, 2267.
6. *Catechism of the Catholic Church*, 2267.
7. *Catechism of the Catholic Church*, cf. 2280-2283.

32. The Sixth and Ninth Commandments

1. *Catechism of the Catholic Church*, 2375.
2. *Catechism of the Catholic Church*, 2377.
3. *Catechism of the Catholic Church*, 2376.
4. *Catechism of the Catholic Church*, 2379.
5. *Catechism of the Catholic Church*, 2357.
6. *Catechism of the Catholic Church*, 2353. The quote is from the Congregation for the Doctrine of the Faith document *Persona humana*, 9.

34. The Eighth Commandment

1. *Catechism of the Catholic Church*, 2467.
2. *Catechism of the Catholic Church*, 2477.
3. *Catechism of the Catholic Church*, 2477.
4. *Catechism of the Catholic Church*, 2490.
5. *Catechism of the Catholic Church*, 2487.

35. The Precepts of the Church

1. Luke 10:16.
2. Matthew 16:19.
3. Matthew 18:18.
4. *Catechism of the Catholic Church*, 2041.
5. *Catechism of the Catholic Church*, 2042.
6. *Catechism of the Catholic Church*, 2043.
7. *Catechism of the Catholic Church*, 2043.

36. The Life of Virtue

1. *Catechism of the Catholic Church*, 1803.
2. *Catechism of the Catholic Church*, 1812.
3. *Catechism of the Catholic Church*, 1814.
4. James 2:26.
5. Romans 8:24.
6. Acts 2:38.
7. I Corinthians 13:2.
8. *Catechism of the Catholic Church*, 1817.
9. *Catechism of the Catholic Church*, 1822.
10. *Catechism of the Catholic Church*, 1806.
11. *Catechism of the Catholic Church*, 1807.
12. *Catechism of the Catholic Church*, 1808.
13. *Catechism of the Catholic Church*, 1809.
14. *Catechism of the Catholic Church*, 2447.
15. Ibid.

37. The Life of Prayer

1. *Catechism of the Catholic Church*, 2774.
2. *Catechism of the Catholic Church*, 2787.
3. *Catechism of the Catholic Church*, 2794-2795.
4. *Catechism of the Catholic Church*, 2828-2829.
5. *Catechism of the Catholic Church*, 2830.
6. *Catechism of the Catholic Church*, 2838.
7. *Catechism of the Catholic Church*, 2846.
8. *Catechism of the Catholic Church*, 2850.
9. *Catechism of the Catholic Church*, 394.
10. *Catechism of the Catholic Church*, 395.
11. *Catechism of the Catholic Church*, 2705.
12. *Catechism of the Catholic Church*, 2706.
13. For a very good and strong apologetic on this topic, I would refer you to Karl Keating, *Catholicism and Fundamentalism*, (San Francisco: Ignatius Press, 1988), 121-133.

WHO IS JOE SIXPACK?

Joe Sixpack—The Every Catholic Guy is obviously my *nom de plume*. My real name is Addledorf Clinkerdaggar Rostefuten. (Not really, but if you stay with me long enough you'll figure out my real name.) As a catechist, speaker and author, I'm beloved by millions of people the world over! Well, actually, my wife and mother love me. So does the house cat, but I think that's only because I feed him. And now that I think about it, I'm not a public speaker either.

Mrs. Sixpack (affectionately known to me as "The Warden") and I live in the best rural parish in the whole Archdiocese of St. Louis, Missouri in the United States. Beyond our love of attending the Holy Sacrifice of the Mass, we enjoy sitting on our back deck to watch the deer and other assorted wildlife, violating our diets about once a week, watching the paint peel when we're snowed in, and reaching out to share our holy and ancient Catholic faith with other people.

We used to live in the Deep South. Moving to the Ozark Mountains of Missouri a few years ago was a real eye-opener. Would you believe these Ozark folks are so sophisticated that they have the bathroom *in the house*? And if we want pork chops for dinner, I don't have to go out back and slaughter a pig anymore. I can actually go to the general store and buy pork already cut up! Except they don't call them general stores up here; they're called supermarkets. So we "came up" by moving to the North.

These Ozark Mountain people are real well educated, too. Most everyone I've met has a college degree. It's not like the thriving metropolis of Slapout, Alabama. Most people there only went clean through high school. Well, most of the time they were clean.

At the end of the day, we're as happy as a tornado in a trailer park to be living in our Ozark Mountain home. We have a great young priest, a lot of friends, devout fellow parishioners... and indoor plumbing. (I just can't get over having the toilet in the house!)

Prior to a devastating stroke, I was an architectural wood carver and furniture maker. I also carved gunstocks and tooled & fabricated leather products. I now make up for my inability to do those things by examining and studying the work of others, taking great pleasure in their talents and abilities. After the resurrection, and (dangerously) assuming I make it to heaven, I intend to ask God to give me a new, fully equipped shop to continue pursuing my passions as a craftsman. I sure hope He lets me, because I really miss carving wood, building furniture and making leather products.

Let me invite you to visit the famous (or infamous, depending on who you are) JoeSixpackAnswers.com website so you can sign up for a free email course that will teach you things about the Catholic faith you never knew. In fact, if you'll allow me, I'll teach you everything about Catholicism you could ever possibly want to know.

You will also begin receiving special invitations to attend the free webinars I host each week. All of the webinars, email courses and website are free! I do all this outreach for one purpose and one purpose alone: to help make heaven as crowded as possible! After all, everyone—Catholics and non-Catholics alike—needs to learn more about the one, true Church established by Jesus. The Church is how we all will get to heaven, you know.

Give me souls; keep the rest!

And always remember one thing: Comfort and Conviction don't live on the same block!

Made in the USA
Middletown, DE
24 March 2019